Paddling Michigan

Kevin Hillstrom
and
Laurie Collier Hillstrom

FALCONGUIDES®

GUILFORD, CONNECTICUT
HELENA, MONTANA

AN IMPRINT OF THE GLOBE PEQUOT PRESS

FALCON GUIDES

Cover photo: Index Stock Imagery
Text design: Amy Bransfield/Bransfield Design
Photo credits: Kevin Hillstrom and Laurie Collier Hillstrom unless otherwise noted.
Maps: Tony Moore/Moore Creative Designs © Morris Book Publishing, LLC

Library of Congress Cataloging-in-Publication Data
Hillstrom, Kevin 1963–
Paddling Michigan / by Kevin Hillstrom and Laurie Collier Hillstrom.
p. c.m.
ISBN 978-1-56044-838-9
    1. Canoes and canoeing—Michigan—Guidebooks. 2. Michigan—Guidebooks.
I. Hillstrom, Laurie Collier, 1965–

GV776.M5 H55 2001
917.7404'44—dc21

                                                                    00-051868

Manufactured in the United States of America
First Edition/Fourth Printing

To buy books in quantity for corporate use
or incentives, call **(800) 962–0973**
or e-mail **premiums@GlobePequot.com**.

The authors and The Globe Pequot Press assume no liability for accidents happening to, or injuries sustained by, readers who engage in the activities described in this book.

To our parents, Dwight and Edie Hillstrom and John and Martha Collier, for giving us love, support, and an appreciation for the outdoors.

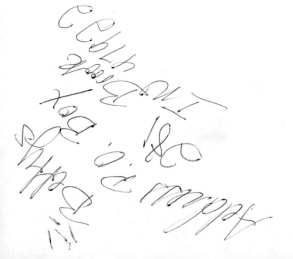

CONTENTS

The Paddling

Southern Lower Michigan

Upper Peninsula

Note: (k) designates sea kayaking destinations

Acknowledgments

The authors would like to thank Rah Trost, Stewart Joseph, and Sue Belanger of Great Northern Adventures for sharing their knowledge and impressions of many of the sea kayaking destinations included in this book. We also extend special thanks to Chris and Ione White of Arctic Divide Expeditions for an incredible trip through the Sturgeon River Gorge, as well as for their input on several Upper Peninsula rivers included in this book. We'd also like to thank Jim Patrick of Drummond Island's Woodmoor Resort and Roger Stevens of the Sports Connection in Jackson for their help, along with the many canoe livery operators and paddling outfitters around the state who provided information on access sites or assistance with car spotting.

We are indebted to a number of natural resource professionals throughout the state for answering our questions, providing maps and other information, and updating us on current conditions. We are particularly grateful to the following individuals for their assistance: Anne Okonek and Toby Rhue of Hiawatha National Forest; Smitty Parratt of Isle Royale National Park; Tracy Tophooven of Manistee National Forest; Linda Sybeldon of Ottawa National Forest; Gregg Bruff of Pictured Rocks National Lakeshore; Michael Tansy of Seney National Wildlife Refuge; Neal Bullington of Sleeping Bear Dunes National Lakeshore; Doug Barry of Craig Lake State Park; and Joyce Angel-Ling, Mark Buchinger, Duane Hoffman, John Krzycki, George Madison, and Jim Waybrant of the Michigan Department of Natural Resources.

Finally, we would like to thank the many friends and family members who accompanied us on our travels, took or posed for photos, and generally made working on this book a great deal of fun. The list includes Doug Bieske, Steve Brock, Jay Capozzoli, Johnny Collier, John Cremin, Jim Graham, Deb Hausler, Dwight Hillstrom, Heidi Hillstrom Van De Mark, Jeff McCormack, Katie Mooney, Tony Noxon, and Kristina and Nathan Wray.

Locator Map

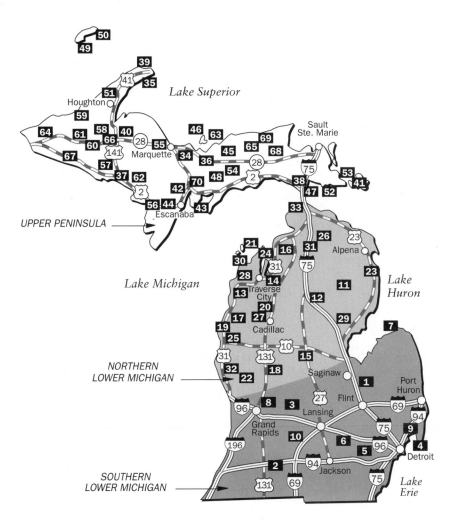

Map Legend

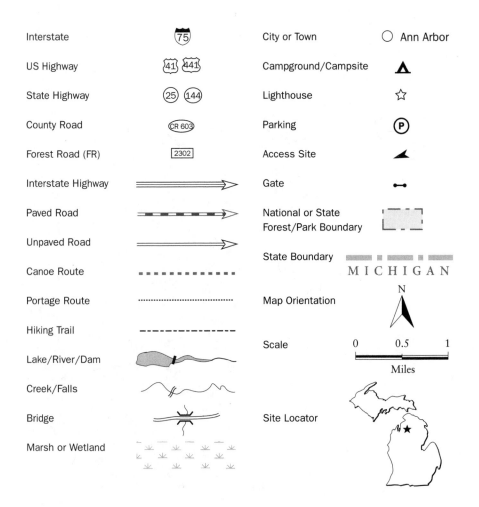

Interstate	75
US Highway	41 441
State Highway	25 144
County Road	CR 603
Forest Road (FR)	2302
Interstate Highway	⟹
Paved Road	⟹
Unpaved Road	⟹
Canoe Route	▪ ▪ ▪ ▪ ▪ ▪ ▪
Portage Route	··············
Hiking Trail	- - - - - - -
Lake/River/Dam	
Creek/Falls	
Bridge	
Marsh or Wetland	

City or Town	○ Ann Arbor
Campground/Campsite	▲
Lighthouse	☆
Parking	Ⓟ
Access Site	◤
Gate	•—•
National or State Forest/Park Boundary	
State Boundary	MICHIGAN
Map Orientation	N
Scale	0 0.5 1 Miles
Site Locator	

Introduction

A Land of Great Waters

When we first began working on this guidebook, we knew that it would be a great challenge to cover the numerous paddling destinations that lace Michigan's forested interior and rocky Great Lakes shorelines. After all, Michigan boasts dozens of scenic rivers, from placid streams suitable for novices to whitewater rivers that will challenge veteran canoeists and kayakers. In addition, it features several clusters of inland lakes that promise both solitude and natural beauty to visitors. And of course, Michigan's location in the heart of the Great Lakes—or the "Sweetwater Seas," as they are sometimes affectionately called around the state—makes it a premier destination for sea kayaking. But after three years of paddling through early spring showers, hazy summer sunshine, and falling autumn leaves, we think that we've put together a cross-section of the finest canoe and kayak excursions that this state has to offer, from easy afternoon paddles to extended trips deep into remote wilderness areas.

How to Use This Guide

Paddling Michigan is designed to help you sort through the abundant waterways of the Great Lakes State and choose a destination that is well suited to your tastes and skills. Each of the 70 chapters covers a single river, lake system, or stretch of coastline that has something special to offer paddlers. The chapters are organized to make it easy to select a destination based on location, level of difficulty, type of scenery, camping or fishing opportunities, or other factors.

We have included Michigan's most popular destinations for paddling (Au Sable River, Manistee River, Pere Marquette River, Pictured Rocks National Lakeshore, etc.) as well as a number of lesser-known gems that feature unique natural beauty, great wildlife viewing, lighthouse tours, urban escapes, multi-day wilderness trips, challenging whitewater runs, or opportunities for quiet reflection. The destinations in the book are divided into three geographical regions: Southern Lower Michigan; Northern Lower Michigan; and the Upper Peninsula.

Each chapter in *Paddling Michigan* begins with a summary of pertinent information under standardized headings. This format is designed to help you determine at a glance whether the destination is a good match for your interests and abilities. This information includes:

Character: A brief description of the river, lake, or coastline, including what makes it worth visiting.

Location: The region or county where the destination can be found.

Length/Size: Total length of the river—or size of the wilderness area or coastline—in miles.

Run: Approximate length of the trip described, in miles (included for river entries only).

Average run time: The estimated time it would take paddlers of average ability to complete the run at a steady but unhurried pace (included for river entries only).

Class: The difficulty level of the river, based on the International Scale of River Difficulty. The scale runs from class I to class VI, moving from easiest to most difficult. In general, rapids rated with a difficulty of class III or higher should only be attempted by experienced and highly skilled paddlers. Another factor to consider is the water level, as many rapids become more difficult to negotiate at higher water levels. Inland lakes and easy rivers with a light current and no rapids are designated as "flatwater."

Skill level: Divided into Beginner, Intermediate, and Advanced categories, based on the level of difficulty and potential hazards. Some destinations may include portions that are appropriate for different skill levels. For example, a river might be well within the comfort level of beginning paddlers with the exception of one or two short stretches of rapids, or a kayaking destination might include protected areas suitable for beginners as well as sections of exposed coastline more appropriate for experienced paddlers. In such cases, we have sometimes used a combined skill level, e.g., Beginner/Intermediate. On occasion, we have increased our estimation of the skill level required based on the remoteness of a particular destination. Our basic parameters for the various skill levels are as follows:

Beginner: Destinations appropriate for relatively inexperienced paddlers, including families. Beginning paddlers should be familiar with the basic strokes and capable of steering a boat around easily avoided obstacles in a light-to-moderate current or moderate winds. While we do not assume a great deal of paddling experience, we generally expect beginners to be able to keep a canoe or kayak upright and under control in riffles or light waves.

Intermediate: Destinations appropriate for paddlers with good skills and some experience. Intermediate paddlers should know the basic strokes and be able to use them effectively. River paddlers should be able to make sharp turns in a swift current, steer a boat through narrow passages to avoid strainers and other obstacles, and negotiate straightforward rapids with confidence. Intermediate paddlers should also be able to catch eddies or bring a boat quickly to shore in order to scout difficult runs. Sea kayakers at this level, meanwhile, should be able to paddle effectively for significant distances in windy or choppy (1- to 3-foot waves) conditions and be proficient in assisted- and self-rescue techniques. Finally, paddlers who tackle intermediate destinations should have basic outdoors skills, appropriate paddling equipment (helmets for whitewater and wetsuits or drysuits for paddling on Lake Superior, for example), and first-aid supplies.

Advanced: Destinations that are appropriate for highly experienced paddlers with strong skills and top-notch equipment. Advanced paddlers should possess a complete mastery of all strokes. Canoeists and kayakers on moving water should be proficient in reading the river and be able to negotiate complex and difficult rapids (class III and

Kayaker silhouetted in the setting sun off Harsens Island on Lake St. Clair. Photo by Deb Hausler.

above) with confidence. Advanced sea kayakers, meanwhile, should be able to paddle effectively in very rough seas and tackle 25 to 30 miles per day in good conditions. They should also have a mastery of various assisted- and self-rescue techniques, including the Eskimo roll. These destinations have the potential to be quite hazardous or even deadly to paddlers who do not possess the requisite skills, equipment, or knowledge, so you should assess your abilities and gear honestly before venturing on to them. Intermediate paddlers wishing to test or improve upon their skills on these waters should be sure that their party includes advanced paddlers or an experienced guide.

Optimal flow: The prime months for paddling a given river. Many of Michigan's rivers, particularly in the Lower Peninsula, have sufficient flow for good paddling from the first warm days of spring through the first snow flurries of winter. But some rivers, especially in the western Upper Peninsula, are highly seasonal and may only be runnable for a few weeks each year. River levels depend on annual precipitation and other unpredictable factors, of course, but the time periods listed under "optimal flow" should give you an idea about the best time to plan a trip on the river in question.

Average gradient: The steepness with which a river falls, calculated as vertical feet per mile. In general, rivers with higher average gradients will have a swifter current and greater potential for rapids than those with lower average gradients.

Hazards: Any risks associated with the trip described, such as dams, rapids, waterfalls, variable water levels, exposed coastline, or a lack of accessible landing spots.

Fishing: Included for rivers and inland lake systems, this provides an overview of the quality of the fishing, the types of species caught, and certain special regulations that may apply.

Maps: A list of the detailed topographical/nautical maps covering a particular waterway, available from the U.S. Geological Survey (800–USA–MAPS) or the National Oceanic and Atmospheric Administration—NOAA (301–436–8301 or 800–638–8972). The maps in this book are intended to give you a general idea of the water route and major access sites. They are meant to be used as an aid in trip planning rather than as navigational tools.

The paddling: A narrative description of what you would be likely to see and experience on a particular trip. This includes everything from the character of the river, lake, or coastline to access sites and camping opportunities.

Access: Provides directions from the nearest town to public canoe landings or boat launches on the waterway. In the case of rivers, many of the access sites are located at roadway bridges. We have tried to include directions only to those bridges that offer good access and a reasonably safe place to park a vehicle.

MA & G grid: The page numbers and map coordinates where the waterway can be located in the *Michigan Atlas and Gazetteer*. The atlas is available from Delorme Publishing, P. O. Box 298, Yarmouth, ME 04096; (800) 452–5931.

The Pere Marquette River is one of the state's most popular paddling destinations.

Camping: A listing of public campsites along the river or shoreline, as well as information about nearby public campgrounds. Private camping is also available in many areas, but we generally have not included this information due to the difficulty of locating and evaluating private sites.

Food, gas, and lodging: A listing of nearby cities and towns where paddlers can find these basic amenities.

For more information: Provides the names of offices or agencies that can provide greater detail on the destination in question. Complete addresses and phone numbers for these agencies can be found in the appendix.

Canoe liveries/Rentals and guided trips: Gives the names of liveries and/or outfitters that offer services on a particular waterway, including rental equipment, shuttles, car-spotting, and guided trips. Complete addresses and phone numbers for these companies can be found in the appendix.

Safe Paddling

One of the most important aspects of safe paddling in Michigan—whether you are canoeing through a chaos of Upper Peninsula whitewater or kayaking around Lake Michigan's Manitou Islands—is to have respect for the water and the weather systems that can quickly transform paddling conditions, both inland and on the big lakes. Most of Michigan's rivers

Little boats stay out of the way of big boats on Lake Huron.

are relatively small in size, but many still feature powerful currents that can be very hazardous, especially when combined with fallen trees, rocky rapids, and deep water. In addition, many rivers become considerably more dangerous at higher water levels, such as during early snowmelt and after heavy rains.

Kayakers venturing out onto the Great Lakes, meanwhile, should check—and heed—marine forecasts when planning their itineraries. Storms can move in quickly on these lakes, transforming paddling conditions from sublime to downright frightening in relatively short order. Paddlers should exercise particular caution when attempting routes that include open-water crossings.

Another important factor in paddling safety is to be candid about your abilities, both with yourself and others. Many paddlers (especially recent converts to paddling who are both enthusiastic and impatient to improve their skills) get in trouble by attempting river runs or sea kayaking trips that are beyond their capabilities. When this happens, they may put the safety of other members of the paddling party in jeopardy as well (e.g., they are forced to attempt a difficult rescue in frothing rapids or slow their pace to stay by the struggling paddler's side during a long open-water crossing in weather that is quickly turning sour). Instead, you should assess your abilities honestly and, if necessary, paddle elsewhere until you have developed the necessary skills to tackle that whitewater river or exposed section of coastline. Don't worry, the water will be waiting for you when you're ready.

You should also make sure that you have appropriate equipment and that you know how to use it. For example, kayakers have no business being out on Lake Superior's icy waters without a wetsuit or drysuit because of the risk of hypothermia in the event of a capsize. Similarly, paddling parties running whitewater should be equipped with whitewater helmets, personal flotation devices (PFDs), boat flotation, rescue ropes, and other essential gear. Other handy items for paddling parties include a complete first-aid kit, compass, emergency whistle, waterproof matches or lighter, extra food and clothing, and (for sea kayakers) bilge pump and paddle float. If you are an avid paddler, all of these items will prove handy at one time or another, and they can assume extra importance if problems (bad weather, injury or illness, etc.) develop when your party is traveling through relatively remote and undeveloped areas.

Finally, you should be aware that the potential for mishap is much greater if you decide to paddle alone, especially on challenging water. Instead, enlist paddling companions with whom you can share the experience. If you can't find a fellow canoeist or kayaker from among your circle of family and friends, consider joining one of the several paddling clubs that have sprung up around the state in recent years.

International Scale of River Difficulty

(Based on the definitions provided by the American Whitewater Association)

Class I: Easy. Moving water with riffles or small waves. Few obstructions, all of which are obvious and easily avoided. Self-rescue is easy and the risk to swimmers is small.

Class II: Moderate. Straightforward rapids with wide, clear channels that are apparent without scouting. Some maneuvering may be required around rocks and medium-sized waves, but it should not pose a problem for paddlers with some experience. Self-rescue is possible and swimmers are rarely injured.

Class III: Difficult. Fast current and rapids with high, irregular waves that can swamp an open canoe. The route is no longer obvious, and numerous obstacles may require complex maneuvering in narrow passages. Large waves, strainers, holes, and strong current may be present, making scouting or portaging advisable for less experienced paddlers. Self-rescue is usually possible, though swimmers may require group assistance. Generally considered the limit of navigability for open canoes.

Class IV: Very Difficult. Intense, powerful, but predictable rapids requiring precise maneuvering and expert boat control. Dangerous obstacles may be present, including large, unavoidable waves or holes and constricted passages. Failure to make certain "must" moves above hazards can result in injury. Self-rescue is difficult and risk to swimmers is moderate to high. Paddlers should be accomplished at fast eddy turns and Eskimo rolls before attempting a run. Advanced scouting from shore is highly recommended.

Class V: Expert. Extremely long, obstructed, powerful, and demanding rapids which expose a paddler to significant risk and must be scouted from shore. Drops may contain very large, unavoidable waves and holes or steep, congested chutes with complex routes. Rapids may continue for a long distance between pools, requiring a high level of fitness. Eddies may be infrequent, turbulent, or difficult to reach. Swimming is very dangerous, and rescue is often difficult. A foolproof Eskimo roll, extensive experience, and practiced rescue skills are imperative.

Class VI: Limit of Navigability. Extremely dangerous, difficult, and unpredictable rapids. The consequences of errors include serious injury or death, and rescue may be difficult or even impossible. Should only be attempted by teams of experts at favorable water levels after taking all precautions.

The rugged, rocky coastline and offshore islands are characteristic of Isle Royale National Park, a beautiful and wild paddling paradise. Photo by Deb Hausler.

An Ethic of Stewardship

During our travels throughout this beautiful state, we have encountered numerous people who love the outdoors and treat our rivers and woodlands with the reverence and respect that they deserve. We're happy to say that, in our experience, canoeists and kayakers are among the folks who tread most lightly upon this state's natural wonders.

Unfortunately, we have also run across ingrates during our travels—and yes, some of them were paddling canoes or kayaks—who treat Michigan's rivers, trails, and shorelines thoughtlessly or with outright hostility. They foul our streams with trash, litter our campsites with broken glass, and then walk away with nary a backward glance, leaving our magnificent state a little more tarnished than it was before.

Don't be one of these people. Clean up after yourself (and others). Be considerate of other campers and river users. Respect the rights of private property owners whenever you're looking for an access, a campsite, or a rest stop. Protect Michigan's rivers, lakes, campsites, and other public recreation places for future generations to enjoy.

⬚ Cass River

Character: A surprisingly pretty and remote-feeling river near the industrial centers of Flint and Saginaw.

Location: Between Flint and Saginaw at the base of Lower Michigan's Thumb.

Length: Approximately 60 miles.

Run: 23 miles, from Chambers Road Bridge near Caro to Gera Road Bridge in Frankenmuth.

Average run time: 7–9 hours.

Class: Flatwater.

Skill level: Beginner/intermediate.

Optimal flow: May–June.

Average gradient: 2 feet per mile.

Hazards: 3-foot drop over an old dam in Vassar.

Fishing: Smallmouth bass, northern pike, and walleye.

Maps: USGS 1:25,000 - Caro-MI, Gilford-MI, Vassar-MI, Frankenmuth-MI; 1:100,000 - Bay City-MI, Flint-MI; 1:250,000 - Flint-MI.

The paddling: The Cass River maintains a wild, remote character despite its close proximity to the major industrial areas of Flint and Saginaw. The river flows southwest about 60 miles, from its headwaters near Cass City in eastern Tuscola County to its junction with the Saginaw River. It is nominally canoeable for much of its length, although the upper reaches tend to be shallow and rocky, while the lower section tends to be slow and marshy. In our view, the best option for paddling is the 23-mile stretch between Caro and Frankenmuth.

Beginning at the Chambers Road Bridge near Caro, the Cass flows between rolling hills covered with hardwood forest. The river generally ranges from 60 to 80 feet wide and 1 to 2 feet deep. The water, which is fairly clear, flows over a mostly gravel bottom punctuated by occasional large rocks. Since much of the land along the banks is part of the Tuscola or Vassar State Game Areas, paddlers will enjoy a secluded feeling with ample opportunities to view wildlife.

About 5 miles below the Chambers Road Bridge, there is good access at a roadside park along M–46. From here, it is another 7 miles to the small town of Vassar. As the community park appears on the right side, look out for a 3-foot drop over an old dam. All but the most confident paddlers should portage on the right through the park. The remaining concrete structure could create dangerous standing waves in high water or hang up a canoe in low water.

Cass River

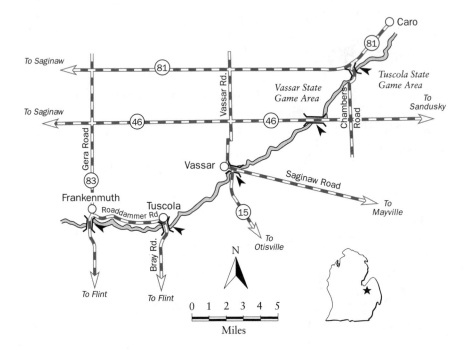

Below Vassar, paddlers will encounter occasional riffles and light rapids as the river cruises through rock gardens. By the time the Cass reaches Tuscola, about 5 miles downstream, it has increased in size to 100 feet wide and 2 to 3 feet deep with the addition of water from several feeder streams. It is another 6 miles to the tourist town of Frankenmuth, where you can take out at a park near the Gera Road Bridge. Over these last few miles, the Cass continues to slow and widen as it approaches a flood-control dam in Frankenmuth.

Access: To reach the **Chambers Road Bridge**, take M–81 southwest about 3 miles from Caro, then go south 0.5 mile on Chambers Road. The **M–46 roadside park** is located 7 miles northeast of Vassar. Take Vassar Road north 2.5 miles out of the city and then head east 4.5 miles on M–46. The **Vassar community park** is located on Saginaw Road (known as Huron Street in town). To reach the **Bray Road Bridge** in Tuscola, take Roadammer Road east 5 miles from Frankenmuth and go south 0.5 mile on Bray Road. The take-out in Frankenmuth is a park near the bridge on **South Gera Road** (M–83), 0.5 mile south of the city.

Additional Help

MA & G grid: 50, B4; 51, B5, and A6.

Camping: Limited campsites are available along the river in the Tuscola and Vassar State Game Areas. There is a large private campground on M–46 west of Chambers Road near Vassar, and another just south of Frankenmuth off M–83.

Food, gas, and lodging: Caro, Vassar, Frankenmuth.

For more information: Vassar State Game Area.

Canoe liveries: None.

Access Point	Float Distance To Next Access Point
Chambers Road Bridge	5 miles
M–46 Roadside Park	7 miles
Vassar Community Park	5 miles
Bray Road Bridge	6 miles
Gera Road Access	Take Out

Dowagiac River

Character: A moderately paced, family-friendly river that winds under a shady canopy of shoreline hardwoods for much of its length.

Location: Eastern Cass County and southern Berrien County.

Length: 25 miles.

Run: 13.5 miles, from Dowagiac (M–62 Bridge) to Niles (U.S. 31 Bridge).

Average run time: 5–7 hours.

Class: Flatwater.

Skill level: Beginner.

Optimal flow: May–September.

Average gradient: 4 feet per mile.

Hazards: Deep water at Niles Dam impoundment and scattered deep holes below Sink Road put-in.

Fishing: Brown trout, steelhead, walleye, smallmouth bass, and panfish.

Maps: USGS 1:25,000 - Niles West-MI, Niles East-MI, Summerville-MI, Dowagiac-MI; 1:100,000-South Bend-MI, Benton Harbor-MI; 1:250,000 - Chicago-MI, Racine-MI.

The paddling: The Dowagiac is an attractive tributary of the St. Joseph River. Shaded by overhanging hardwood trees (maples, oaks, beeches, poplars) for a good portion of its length, the narrow river flows at a generally relaxed pace. The stream is not a good choice for overnight trips, as much of the shoreline is privately owned. But the Dowagiac's generally undemanding nature makes it a good option for families looking to venture out for a few hours of paddling.

Some paddlers begin their journeys on the river at the M–62 Bridge just west of the town of Dowagiac, even though parking space is limited. The river joins with Dowagiac Creek about 0.25 mile downstream. From there to past the Sink Road Bridge, the river is about 25 to 30 feet wide and 2 to 6 feet deep. You may run into occasional fallen trees that will require portaging or carryovers, but this portion of the float is basically shady and peaceful in character. Much of the river bottom in this stretch is mucky or sandy.

Three miles below Sink Road Bridge is Dodd Park, which features plentiful parking and an attractive picnic area. From above Dodd Park to Kinzie Road Bridge, the Dowagiac widens somewhat, though the river maintains its moderate pace as it passes through fields and woodlands. Homes and cottages remain infrequent, but they do pop up from time to time.

Kinzie Road Bridge is the last take-out before Niles Dam. Paddling the backwaters of this dam was once an unpleasant chore, but run-of-river regulations have eliminated the mudflats that previously marred this stretch of the stream. To portage around the dam itself, take out on the right and cross Pucker Street to the small park that lies on the other side.

Dowagiac River

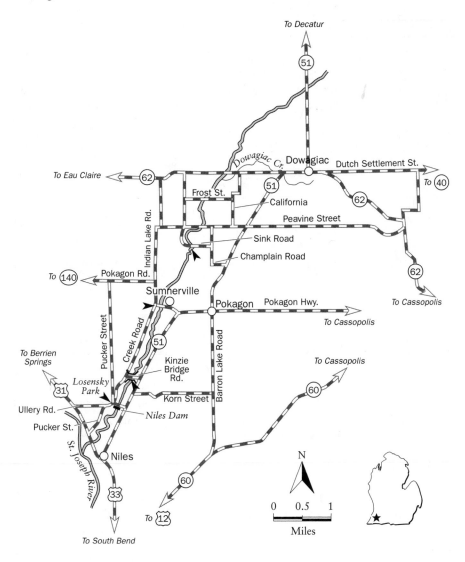

A spring float on the peaceful Dowagiac River.

The Dowagiac's current quickens immediately below the dam, creating the most challenging run on the river. For a half-hour or so, you'll encounter lively water and a steady diet of tree limbs, rocks, and other obstacles that require basic maneuvering skills to negotiate. The stream then slows again. In the last few miles above its juncture with the St. Joseph River, the Dowagiac resembles its upper reaches—narrow, shady, and shallow, with a bottom mix of sand and gravel. These last few miles offer pleasant paddling, but you should keep in mind that the stretch of river from the dam down to the St. Joseph attracts big crowds of tubers on summer weekends.

Access: The **M–62 Bridge** is located approximately 2 miles west of Dowagiac on M–62. To reach **Sink Road Bridge**, take M–62 west out of Dowagiac for 3 miles, then turn south on Sink Road and go 3 miles. **Dodd Park** can be reached from Dowagiac by going 5 miles west on M–62, then 5 miles south on Indian Lake Road. Or access the park from Niles by taking M–51 north out of town for 6 miles to Pokagon Road (also known as Crystal Springs Road). Turn left and cross over the river, then turn south for 1 mile on Indian Lake Road. **Kinzie Road Bridge** lies 3 miles north of Niles off M–51. **Losensky Park** lies on the southwest side of Niles Dam. To reach it, drive 2 miles north out of Niles on M–51, then turn west on Pucker Street, which passes over the river. The park is located on the western bank of the river off of Pucker Street. The **U.S. Highway 31 Bridge** is located in the center of Niles.

Additional Help

MA & G grid: 19, A5, and B5.

Camping: No public campgrounds exist along the route; a modern private campground lies off Business U.S. 31, just above where the Dowagiac joins the St. Joseph River.

Food, gas, and lodging: Dowagiac, Niles, Buchanan.

For more information: Contact area liveries.

Canoe liveries: Niles Canoe Rental, Doe-Wah-Jack's Canoe Rental.

Access Point	Float Distance To Next Access Point
M–62 Bridge	3 miles
Sink Road Bridge	3.5 miles
Dodd Park	3 miles
Kinzie Road Bridge	1.5 miles
Losensky Park	2.5 miles
U.S. 31	Take Out

Flat River

Character: A gentle but scenic river that is ideal for family excursions.

Location: Montcalm and Ionia Counties in the west-central section of the Lower Peninsula.

Length: 60 miles.

Run: 28 miles, from Greenville to Fallasburg Park.

Average run time: 7–10 hours.

Class: Flatwater.

Skill level: Beginner.

Optimal flow: April–June, September–October.

Average gradient: 3 feet per mile.

Hazards: Class I rapids at washed-out dam in Smyrna.

Fishing: Smallmouth bass and rock bass account for much of the fishing action, but anglers can nab northern pike and walleye as well.

Maps: USGS 1:25,000 - Trufant-MI, Langston-MI, Greenville West-MI, Greenville East-MI, Smyrna-MI, Belding-MI; 1:100,000 - Cedar Springs-MI, Grand Rapids-MI; 1:250,000 - Midland-MI.

The paddling: The peaceful Flat River is a particularly attractive destination for beginning paddlers or those looking to introduce youngsters to the pleasures of floating a Michigan stream. Mild-mannered and shallow for most of its length, the Flat threads its way through long stretches of public land that house a wide variety of wildlife. Best of all, the river sees relatively little recreational use, although area liveries get brisk business on summer Saturdays.

Most folks looking to float the Flat put in at Greenville, where the river is 30 to 40 feet wide and 1 to 2 feet deep. Good parking and access can be found at the town's community park, located next to the Greenville Dam, or at Jackson's Landing, just below the M–57 bridge. Large rocks pock the stream's sandy bottom here and farther downstream, but the Flat's mellow current takes the bite out of these and occasional other obstacles.

About 2 miles downstream, you'll cross into the Flat River State Game Area, a sure highlight of any trip on the river. This stretch features lots of wildlife, ranging from stately swans and gangly herons to swooping red-tailed hawks and sleepy turtles. The river widens to 50 to 70 feet through the game area and maintains a depth of 1 to 2 feet as it meanders past heavily wooded shorelines. During mid-summer and other low-water periods, however, you may run aground occasionally.

As you approach Belding Dam, the river deepens and slows. An easy portage around the dam can be found on the left, beyond the fence at a shoreline park. Immediately below the dam, the river returns to its shallow ways, albeit at a slightly livelier clip. As with certain stretches farther upstream, paddling pleasure through here is somewhat dependent on water level. During dry summers, you may feel like you're spending more time walking alongside your canoe than sitting in it. But during normal water levels, you can concentrate on watching for some of the area's abundant wildlife.

Flat River

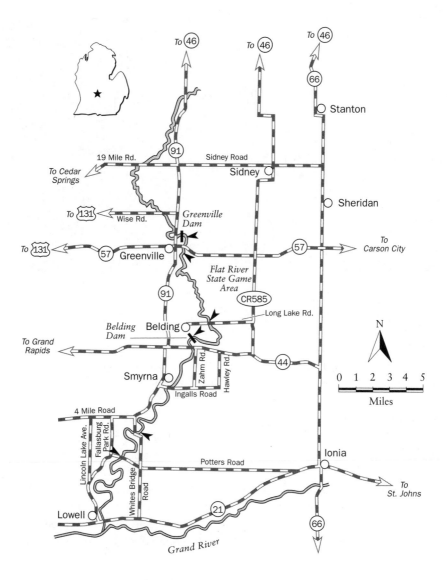

The aptly named Flat River is a great destination for families.

The Flat gradually widens to as much as 80 feet as it nears Smyrna. Immediately below Smyrna and above Ingalls Road Bridge is a blown-out dam that offers the only rapids of any note on the river. Experienced paddlers will have no difficulty with this short run (stick to the river center to avoid larger remnants of the dam), but beginners may want to portage on the left, especially during spring and other high-water periods.

Immediately below Smyrna, the Flat remains wide and shallow with a moderate flow and occasional rocky riffles. After about 2 miles, though, it flows into the backwaters of White's Bridge Dam, which can be portaged on the left. Below the dam is a nice float that takes paddlers through the wooded hills of the Lowell State Game Area and under White's Bridge, one of the state's original wooden covered bridges. Another historic bridge spanning the stream—Fallasburg Park Bridge—lies just below the recommended take-out at Fallasburg Park. Paddlers also have the option of pushing on past Fallasburg Park to Lowell.

Access: In Greenville, paddlers have two put-in options. The first is located in the center of town, at a community park off of Greenville Road (M–91), just below the **Greenville Dam**. A second option is **Jackson's Landing**, located just below the bridge at M–57. The **Long Lake Road Bridge** lies 2.5 miles east of Belding on Long Lake Road. To put in at **Belding Dam**, use the community park just west of Zahm Road. To reach **White's Bridge**, take M–21 east out of Lowell for 2 miles, then turn north on White's Bridge Road for 6 miles. To reach the put-in sites at **Fallasburg Park** and **McPherson Road Bridge**, take Lincoln Lake Avenue north out of Lowell for 2 miles, then proceed north on Fallasburg

Park Road for another 2 miles. The put-ins are located next to one another on the east side of the road.

Additional Help

MA & G grid: 47, 5C and 6C, 5D and 6D; 37, 5A.

Camping: You won't find any established public campgrounds along this stretch of the Flat, but streamside campsites can be found in the Flat River State Game Area. In addition, a private campground with primitive sites (the Double R Ranch) is located just downstream from Smyrna.

Food, gas, and lodging: Greenville, Belding, Lowell, Ionia.

For more information: Flat River State Game Area.

Canoe liveries: Double R Ranch Campground, Curler Canoe Rental.

Access Point	Float Distance To Next Access Point
Greenville Dam	0.25 mile
Jackson's Landing	9 miles
Long Lake Road Bridge	4 miles
Belding Dam	7.5 miles
White's Bridge	7 miles
McPherson Road Bridge	0.25 mile
Fallasburg Park	Take Out

Harsens Island

Character: A little-known watery paradise that offers a variety of pleasant day trips for Detroit-area kayakers.

Location: In the St. Clair Flats at the north end of Lake St. Clair.

Size: The island is 8 miles long and 3 miles wide.

Skill level: Beginner/intermediate.

Hazards: Cold water in spring and late fall; potential for high waves with winds out of the southwest; motorboat traffic, especially on weekends; potential for becoming lost in marshy areas.

Maps: USGS 1:25,000 - St. Clair Flats-MI, Algonac-MI; 1:100,000 - Lake St. Clair North-MI; 1:250,000 - Detroit-MI. NOAA chart 14850.

The paddling: Harsens Island is the centerpiece of the St. Clair Flats, a fan-shaped pattern of islands, marshes, and channels that has formed where the St. Clair River empties into Lake St. Clair. With an intricate network of canals and inlets that are more important means of transportation than the local roads during the summer months, Harsens Island is sometimes referred to as "the Venice of the Midwest." In many ways, the area is reminiscent of the fishing villages of the Eastern Seaboard or the bayous of the Mississippi Delta. Yet it is located less than an hour's drive from downtown Detroit, via a five-minute car-ferry ride from the city of Algonac.

Needless to say, Harsens Island offers a wide range of possibilities for exploration by kayak—from shallow, protected bays, to marshes full of aquatic plants and wildlife, to shores lined with docks and cottages. A good day trip begins at the end of South Channel Drive, a road that traces one of the two narrow tails of the island that enclose Muscamoot Bay. From the turnaround at the end of the road, it is a 1.5-mile paddle to the Old South Channel Lights. These two historic lighthouses became operational in 1859 and guided ships making their way across Lake St. Clair for the next half-century. Despite preservation efforts, the smaller front light has been leaning precariously for many years. You can follow the shoreline for the first half of the trip, but the second half is on open water that can become wavy from southwest winds or motorboat traffic.

About 0.75 mile east of the lighthouses is Gull Island, a spit of sand and trees that is a popular weekend gathering place and camping spot for boaters. During the week, however, it would make a nice picnic spot for kayakers. Gull Island offers a good view of the parade of freighters coming up Lake St. Clair, and on clear days you can see the silhouette of downtown Detroit on the horizon. Just 0.25 mile north of Gull Island—at the very tip of Harsens Island—is the Old Club, a private yacht club that features a golf course and pool, as well as a row of colorful cabanas perched on a boardwalk overlooking the South Channel. If you venture out into the channel, however, keep in mind that it is cold and deep, flows with a 7-knot current, and sees lots of motorboat traffic.

A longer day trip might begin at the public boat launch off Middle Channel Drive, which traces the western tail of Harsens Island. From here, paddle south 0.5 mile through

Harsens Island

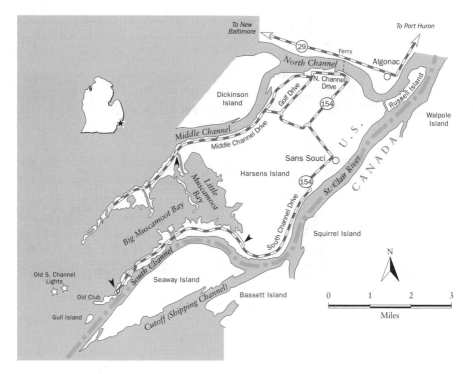

a narrow channel into Little Muscamoot Bay. You can either explore the shallow, sheltered waters of Little Muscamoot or continue paddling southeast 1.5 miles to the end of the point that separates the two parts of the bay. If you turn southwest, you can paddle about 4 miles across Big Muscamoot Bay to reach the Old South Channel Lights.

Another possible launching spot is a Department of Natural Resources (DNR) fishing access located about 6 miles from the ferry, just after M–154 turns into South Channel Drive (this is the third DNR fishing access you'll pass heading south from the ferry). From the launch, paddle north about 0.5 mile through a marshy channel to reach the southeast corner of Little Muscamoot Bay. Then follow the shoreline west and south about 5 miles through Big Muscamoot Bay to reach the lighthouses.

Access: To reach the put-in at the end of **South Channel Drive**, take the Harsens Island Ferry ($5.00 round-trip) across to the island and turn left on M–154 South. Follow 154 about 6 miles until it turns into South Channel Drive. Take South Channel Drive (which is paved but very bumpy) about 3 miles until it ends at a circular turnaround. The **DNR fishing access** is located 6 miles from the ferry, at the point where 154 turns into South Channel Drive. To reach the DNR boat launch on **Middle Channel Drive**, turn right from the ferry onto M–154 North, which becomes North Channel Drive. In about 1 mile

The St. Clair Flats area offers a number of marshy areas to explore by kayak. Photo by Deb Hausler.

turn left onto Golf Drive, and follow it 1.5 miles until it ends at Middle Channel Drive. Turn left onto Middle Channel Drive and proceed 3 miles to the boat launch.

Additional Help

MA & G grid: 43, D6.

Camping: Algonac State Park (220 modern sites on the St. Clair River and 76 modern sites inland), about 5 miles north of the Harsens Island Ferry dock on M–29; at-large camping is allowed on Gull Island near the mouth of Big Muscamoot Bay.

Food, gas, and lodging: San Souci, Algonac.

For more information: St. Clair Flats Wildlife Area office; Department of Natural Resources Mount Clemens office.

Rentals/guided trips: Great Lakes Docks and Decks.

Huron River

Character: A highly accessible river with a mellow temperament that makes it a favorite getaway for families throughout the Detroit metropolitan area.

Location: Oakland, Livingston, Washtenaw, and Wayne Counties in southeastern Lower Michigan.

Length: Over 100 miles, from Commerce Lake in Oakland County to Lake Erie.

Run: Upper Huron, 55 miles from Proud Lake Recreation Area to Ann Arbor; Lower Huron, 26 miles from Lower Huron Metropark to Pointe Mouillee State Game Area.

Average run time: Upper Huron 24–30 hours; Lower Huron 10–12 hours.

Class: Flatwater, except for a short stretch of class II at Delhi Rapids.

Skill level: Beginner/intermediate.

Optimal flow: May–October.

Average gradient: 3.5 feet per mile between Hudson Mills Metropark and Ann Arbor, 2 feet per mile for remainder of run.

Hazards: Deep water and possible windy conditions in lake areas; several dams requiring portages.

Fishing: Smallmouth bass, bluegill, perch; also northern pike and walleye on Kent Lake.

Maps: USGS 1:25,000 - Walled Lake-MI, Milford-MI, Kent Lake-MI, Brighton-MI, Pinckney-MI, Hamburg-MI, Dexter-MI, Ann Arbor West-MI, Ann Arbor East-MI, Ypsilanti West-MI, Ypsilanti East-MI, Belleville-MI, Flat Rock Northeast-MI, Flat Rock-MI, Rockwood-MI; 1:100,000 - Pontiac-MI, Detroit-MI; 1:250,000 - Detroit-MI.

The paddling: The Huron River is a constant and comforting presence in the Detroit metropolitan area. From the pricey lakeside developments of northwestern Oakland County, to the peaceful farm country around the growing villages of Hamburg and Dexter, to the leafy campus of the University of Michigan in Ann Arbor, to the busy industrial communities downriver from Detroit—the Huron is always there. Despite its proximity to numerous small towns and larger cities, the river still has a rural feel for much of its length due to the abundance of public land along its shores. State and local governments have worked together to create an extensive system of parks that make the Huron one of the most accessible rivers in the state. A moderate current, few obstacles or hazards, a variety of wildlife, and plentiful picnic and camping options add to its appeal as a quick getaway destination for families.

Proud Lake Recreation Area is the earliest practical put-in spot on the Upper Huron. Above here, access is limited by private property and the river tends to be too shallow for good paddling. A state motor vehicle permit is required for entry into Proud Lake and the other recreation areas along the Huron. From the boat launch on the north shore of marshy Proud Lake, paddlers should stay right to find the river's outlet. Within 2 miles you reach the first portage—a short path to the right of a bridge and control dam. About 1 mile later is a second potential launch site in Proud Lake Recreation Area, just off of Wixom Road. The river leaves the recreation area 2 miles later at Burns Road Bridge. For the next

Huron River

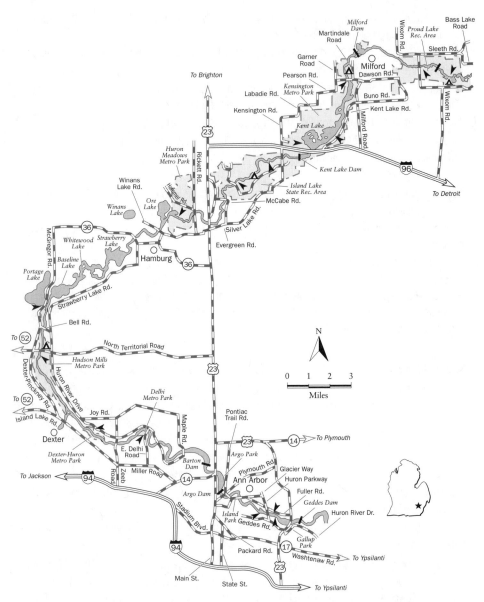

3 miles it flows through the city of Milford, with another portage to the right around Milford Dam.

A short distance below the dam, the Huron enters Kensington Metropark, one of a chain of parks developed by the Huron-Clinton Metropolitan Authority (HCMA) to provide area residents with access to and recreational opportunities on its namesake rivers. Another motor vehicle permit is required for entry into the metroparks. About a mile below the dam on the left bank is the first of four HCMA canoe camps along the Huron. Paddlers need to call ahead to obtain a camping permit for these sites. Over the next 5 miles, the river opens into the broad, island-dotted waters of Kent Lake. Traversing the lake can be difficult on windy days, so beginners or those not interested in lake paddling may want to take out at Dawson Road Bridge, less than a mile below the canoe camp. There are two boat launches along the shores of Kent Lake—which is a popular spot for both fishing and sailing—as well as several beaches and picnic areas. Those electing to paddle across can proceed to the southwest corner of the lake, cross under busy Interstate 96, and then portage to the left of the Kent Lake Dam.

At this point, the Huron enters Island Lake Recreation Area near Brighton. This is one of the most remote-feeling stretches of the river, and paddlers often see deer and waterfowl. Over the next 7 miles, the river is 30 to 40 feet wide and 1 to 3 feet deep, with a sandy bottom and almost no current. It passes through marshy lowlands at first, then the shoreline gradually becomes more wooded. The first access site in Island Lake is about 2 miles downstream from the dam. In another mile, paddlers will reach the tranquil Riverbend Picnic Area, which would make a nice spot for lunch. From there it is less than a mile to the Island Lake Canoe Camp, the second of the four HCMA camping areas along the river. The next access site, the Bridge Picnic Area, appears about 2 miles later. The river exits Island Lake in another mile. Then traffic sounds, houses on the banks, trash in the river, and other signs of civilization increase over the next 2 miles as you approach busy U.S. Highway 23. We also encountered a few logjams that required liftovers in this stretch.

About a mile past the U.S. 23 bridge, paddlers will cross under Rickett Road and enter Huron Meadows Metropark. The river becomes a bit wider between heavily wooded banks. There is an access site at the picnic area in the metropark about a mile downstream from Rickett Road. It is not possible to bring a car to the water's edge, however, so taking out here requires a 750-foot portage through the picnic area to the parking lot. This is the last public access site on the Huron for approximately 12 miles.

After exiting the metropark in another mile, the Huron enters about a 9-mile stretch of interconnected lakes with mostly private property along the shorelines. There is no public access at Winans Lake Road or M–36, both of which cross the river in the first 3 miles, or along the shores of Strawberry, Gallagher, Whitewood, and Baseline Lakes. However, there is a Department of Natural Resources boat launch in the southeast corner of Portage Lake that connects to the Huron via a short channel. Brisk winds can make paddling across the chain of lakes difficult, and canoeists must also be wary of motorboat traffic. As the river emerges from Baseline Lake, there is a portage to the left of a control dam and then to the right of a rock barrier.

Huron River

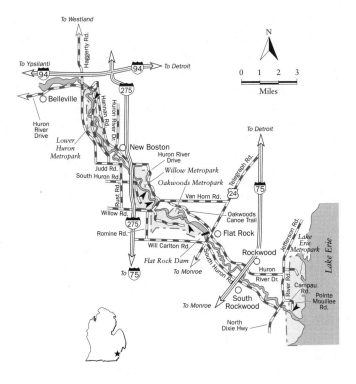

At this point the river enters scenic Hudson Mills Metropark. In about 2 miles, paddlers will reach another HCMA canoe camp on the left bank. At this point the river remains 1 to 3 feet deep but widens to between 70 and 90 feet. Over the next 0.5 mile it passes through an area of shallows, then enters a stretch of light rapids at an old mill site near Territorial Road Bridge. Paddlers with basic maneuvering skills should have no trouble negotiating the clear chute through the rapids, although standing waves may develop during periods of high water. Beginners can portage to the right if necessary. Immediately below the rapids is the main access site for Hudson Mills. For the next 2 miles the river remains wide and mellow with few obstacles. As the Huron exits the metropark, you will begin to see scattered homes along the high bluffs overlooking the river. It is about 4 miles to the access site and riverside picnic area in Dexter-Huron Metropark, and then 2 more miles to Delhi Metropark.

Delhi Metropark is the site of the only notable rapids on the Huron River. Delhi Rapids, a 200-foot run of class II rapids just above the East Delhi Road bridge, can be run on the right by intermediate paddlers. The left side is more technical, with larger drops between boulders, and is a popular training ground for local whitewater kayakers. Anyone in doubt can portage about 400 feet along the right bank to the downstream side of the bridge, where there is another metropark boat launch site.

Taking advantage of the early arrival of spring on the Huron River.

Over the next 5 miles, the Huron slows down and winds through mostly private property—punctuated by occasional small parks—on the outskirts of Ann Arbor. It then enters Barton Pond, which has a city park along its southern shoreline. After crossing the narrow backwaters, paddlers can portage Barton Dam to the right of the powerhouse. Over the next 2 miles you will cross under M–14 and enter Argo Pond, where you might see the University of Michigan rowing team practicing. After portaging around Argo Dam at the end of the left channel, it is another mile to the access site at Island Park in Ann Arbor. The following 2-mile stretch of river offers a unique perspective on the city, as it flows through several city parks and the University of Michigan's lovely Nichols Arboretum. Picnic spots are plentiful along the way.

We recommend ending your trip on the Upper Huron at Gallup Park, a City of Ann Arbor facility with several access sites located where the river opens into Geddes Pond. For the next 12 miles, the Huron runs through the urban/industrial areas of Ypsilanti, Rawsonville, and Belleville. It alternates between stretches of shallow water and the impoundments created by five dams. Winds can make for difficult paddling across the largest two of the man-made lakes—Ford Lake and Belleville Lake.

There is another stretch of good paddling on the Lower Huron, downriver from Belleville Lake. The river maintains its mild character, although the water tends to be less clear than it was in the upper reaches. For the next 17 miles, the Huron meanders through three more metroparks with ample access sites and spots for picnics. The first launch on this stretch is located in Lower Huron Metropark near New Boston, just off of Hannan Road. Within 2 miles you come to the fourth and final HCMA canoe camp on the left bank. About 3 miles later the river exits the metropark and passes through the city of New Boston. In another 3 miles it crosses under Interstate 275 and enters Willow Metropark. This park boasts two launch sites with water and toilets, about 2 and 3 miles downstream from the Interstate 275 bridge. Upon crossing under Willow Road, the Huron enters Oakwoods Metropark. In addition to a launch site and picnic area about 3 miles downstream, Oakwoods also offers a marked canoe nature trail through the marshy backwaters of Flat Rock Dam.

At this writing, there is some uncertainty surrounding the portage for Flat Rock Dam. Although portaging is legally permitted, the trail on the right side of the river goes through a factory gate that is sometimes locked. Paddlers may wish to call ahead to Oakwoods Metropark for information or simply take out there and put in again at the Flat Rock city park below the dam. For the next 10 miles, the Huron passes through another urban/industrial area with scattered parklands. About halfway through this stretch, after crossing under I–75, it begins to spread into marshy braids. We recommend taking out at the headquarters to Pointe Mouillee State Game Area, about 1 mile downstream from the Jefferson Avenue Bridge. Although canoeing is possible through the game area to the river's mouth on Lake Erie, high winds and large waves on the lake can be hazardous.

Access: To reach the boat launch on the northeastern shore of **Proud Lake**, take I–96 to Wixom Road and go north about 7 miles to Sleeth Road. Take Sleeth Road east about 2 miles to Bass Lake Road, then follow Bass Lake Road south about 1 mile to the entrance to Proud Lake Recreation Area. There is a second access site in Proud Lake off of **Wixom Road** about 0.5 mile south of Sleeth Road. To reach the **Kensington Metropark canoe camp**, take I–96 to Milford Road and go north about 3 miles. Jog west on Dawson Road about 0.5 mile, then continue north on Martindale Road about 0.5 mile. Turn west into the metropark and follow the signs. **Dawson Road Bridge**, which offers good access and parking, is located about 0.5 mile west of the intersection with Martindale Road. There are two boat launches on **Kent Lake** in Kensington Metropark. To reach the **east boat launch**, take I–96 to Kent Lake Road (also known as Huron River Drive), go northeast about 1 mile into the metropark, and follow the signs. To reach the **west boat launch**, exit I–96 at Kensington Road and go north less than 0.25 mile to the metropark entrance. Follow the park road west about 1 mile to the boat launch. There are three potential access sites in Island Lake Recreation Area. Exit I–96 at Kensington Road and go south about 0.5 mile. Turn left at the entrance to the recreation area, immediately after crossing over the river, then take the first right. This park road leads to the **Island Lake boat launch** in 1 mile, to the **Island Lake canoe camp** in 2 miles, and to the **Bridge Picnic Area** in 3 miles. To reach the access site in **Huron Meadows Metropark**, take U.S. 23 south 4 miles from Brighton and exit at Silver Lake Road. Turn west onto Winans Lake Road for about 0.5 mile, then go north on Rickett Road about 1 mile. Turn west on Hammel Road immediately after crossing over the river, and after about 0.5 mile turn south into the picnic area.

The only public access to the Huron over the next 10 miles is via a DNR boat launch on **Portage Lake**. Take U.S. 23 to M–36 and go west about 9 miles. Turn south on McGregor Road and follow it about 3 miles to the boat launch. Portage Lake connects to the Huron via a short channel in the southeast corner. **Hudson Mills Metropark** is located on North Territorial Road about 8 miles west of U.S. 23. After turning south into the park, take the first right and follow the signs to the boat launch. To reach **Dexter-Huron Metropark**, exit I–94 at Zeeb Road and go north about 2 miles. Turn west onto Huron River Drive and follow it about 1 mile to the park entrance. **Delhi Metropark** is located about 2 miles east of Zeeb Road off of Huron River Drive. There is a take-out above Delhi Rapids on the west side of the Delhi Road Bridge, and another access site and picnic area on the east side of the bridge. To reach the City of Ann Arbor's **Argo Park**, take M–14 to U.S. 23 South and exit at Plymouth Road. Follow Plymouth west about 3 miles and turn north on Pontiac Trail; the park is on the west side of the road. **Island Park** is located off of Plymouth Road about 1 mile east of Pontiac Trail. To reach **Gallup Park**, exit U.S. 23 at Geddes Road and go west about 1 mile to the park entrance. There is one boat launch to the west of Huron Parkway, and two more to the east of Huron Parkway. In addition to these access sites, many of which require fees, there is access at many of the dozens of bridges that cross the Huron, including Milford Road, McCabe Road, Bell Road, and Zeeb Road.

The first good access on the Lower Huron is at **Lower Huron Metropark**. From I–94 near Belleville, exit at Haggerty Road and go south 0.5 mile. The metropark entrance is straight ahead at the intersection of Huron River Drive. The first launch site is about 1 mile down the park road, the **Lower Huron canoe camp** is about 2 miles down, and the second launch site is about 3 miles down. To reach **Willow Metropark**, exit I–275 at South Huron Road and go east 0.25 mile to the park entrance. The two launch sites are located at Big Bend Picnic Area, about 2 miles down the park road, and Chestnut Picnic Area, about 3 miles down. To reach **Oakwoods Metropark**, exit I–275 at Will Carleton Road and go east 0.5 mile to Romine Road. Follow Romine north about 1.5 miles to Willow Road, then take Willow east about 0.5 mile to the park entrance. The boat launch and canoe nature trail are located about 2 miles down the park road. To reach the take-out at **Pointe Mouillee State Game Area**, exit I–75 at South Huron Road and go east about 3 miles. Travel north on Jefferson for 0.5 mile, then east on Campeau for another 0.5 mile, and south on Pointe Mouillee Road for another 0.5 mile.

Additional Help

MA & G grid: 41, D5; 32, A2–A4 and B2–B4; 33, C5, C6, and D7; 34, D1.

Camping: The Huron-Clinton Metropolitan Authority maintains canoe campgrounds on the Huron at Kensington Metropark, Island Lake State Recreation Area, Hudson Mills Metropark, and Lower Huron Metropark. Paddlers must call ahead to obtain a permit for these campsites. There is also a campground along the river at Proud Lake State Recreation Area. Nearby camping options include Brighton, Pinckney, and Waterloo State Recreation Areas.

Food, gas, and lodging: Commerce, Wixom, Milford, Brighton, Hamburg, Pinckney, Dexter, Ann Arbor, Belleville, New Boston, Flat Rock, Rockwood.

For more information: Huron-Clinton Metroparks (including Proud Lake Recreation Area, Kensington Metropark, Island Lake Recreation Area, Huron Meadows Metropark, Hudson Mills Metropark, Lower Huron Metropark, Oakwoods Metropark).

Canoe liveries: Heavner, Wolynski, Skip's, Argo Park, Gallup Park.

Access Point	Float Distance To Next Access Point
Upper Huron	
Proud Lake, northeast shore	3 miles
Proud Lake Recreation Area, Wixom Road	6 miles
Kensington Metropark Canoe Camp	1 mile
Dawson Road Bridge	3 miles
Kent Lake, east boat launch	1 mile
Kent Lake, west boat launch	2 miles
Island Lake Recreation Area	2 miles
Island Lake Canoe Camp	2 miles
Island Lake Bridge Picnic Area	5 miles
Huron Meadows Metropark	10 miles
Portage Lake	2 miles
Hudson Mills Canoe Camp (no vehicle access)	1 mile
Hudson Mills Metropark	6 miles
Dexter-Huron Metropark	2 miles
Delhi Metropark	6 miles
Argo Park	1 mile
Island Park	3 miles
Gallup Park	None

A whitewater kayaker practices his moves in Delhi Rapids on the Huron River. Photo by Deb Hausler.

Access Point	Float Distance To Next Access Point
Lower Huron	
Lower Huron Metropark	2 miles
Lower Huron Canoe Camp	2 miles
Lower Huron Metropark	6 miles
Willow Metropark	1 mile
Willow Metropark	4 miles
Oakwoods Metropark	11 miles
Pointe Mouillee State Game Area	Take Out

6 Pinckney Recreation Area "Chain of Lakes"

Character: Pinckney's rolling woodlands feature a cluster of interconnected small lakes that offer a mellow afternoon of paddling.

Location: 15 miles northwest of Ann Arbor in Washtenaw County.

Size: Seven small lakes on 11,000 acres.

Skill level: Beginner.

Hazards: Deep water, motorized boat traffic.

Fishing: Bass, northern pike, and assorted panfish.

Maps: USGS 1:25,000 - Chelsea-MI, Dexter-MI, Gregory-MI, Pinckney-MI; 1:100,000 - Jackson-MI, Detroit-MI; 1:250,000 - Grand Rapids-MI, Detroit-MI.

The paddling: This chain of small lakes nestled in southeast Michigan's Pinckney Recreation Area will never be mistaken for rugged and remote canoeing meccas like the U.P.'s Sylvania Wilderness. Homes and cottages line the shores of many of Pinckney's lakes, and motorized boat traffic is permitted throughout the area. Nonetheless, Pinckney's picturesque waters do provide canoeists in Michigan's heavily populated southeastern region with a relaxing alternative to the usual river trips.

Motorboats swarm over Pinckney's lakes on summer weekends, making them unsuitable for paddling at those times. But if you can escape to the recreation area during the week or after the summer crowds have dissipated, the only folks you'll have to share the waters with are a smattering of anglers tucked away in their favorite fishing holes. On such days, you can glide peacefully through shallow but wide channels that take you from one lake to the next. Even if you take time to throw a line in the water along the way, the relatively small size of the lakes makes it possible to explore the entire chain in a matter of hours. Keep in mind, though, that a good portion of the shoreline along these lakes is marshy or privately owned. This state of affairs can make leg-stretching spots somewhat hard to find.

The westernmost of the Pinckney lakes is Bruin Lake. Bruin's western edge is home to a shady shoreline campground and a boat launch. Most of the rest of the shoreline is undeveloped, but the lake's accessibility and accommodations make it very popular with weekend motorboaters. To the east of Bruin lies Watson Lake. The northern shoreline of Watson is developed, but its southern half is a little nugget of woodsy peacefulness.

Two of the chain's larger lakes lie north of Watson Lake. The shorelines of these lakes—Woodburn Lake and Patterson Lake—are primarily privately owned, and have seen a lot of development. Unless you're in the mood to scan the homes that sit along these lakes for redecorating or landscaping ideas, you may as well stick to the chain's more southern sections.

Halfmoon Lake is a very popular destination for visitors to the recreation area. Its developed shoreline includes a boat launch and large picnic area that attract hordes of folks

Pinckney Recreation Area "Chain of Lakes"

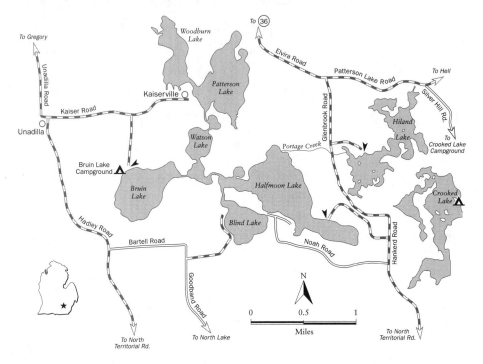

on summer weekends. But the lake does feature a pretty little cove on its western side that remains undeveloped. This cove provides paddlers with access to Blind Lake. Portions of Blind Lake's shoreline are developed as well, but the channel connecting it to Halfmoon Lake is very small. This dramatically curtails the amount of motorized boat traffic that it sees.

Hiland Lake is the easternmost lake in the Pinckney chain. Connected to Halfmoon Lake (and thus the rest of the chain) by Portage Creek, the lake also offers access to the Portage River at its northern end. Hiland Lake's northern shoreline lies outside of the recreation area's boundaries, so it bristles with pricey cottages and homes. Its southern shoreline, however, is nestled within the park's boundaries, and remains heavily wooded and undeveloped.

Access: Much of the land along Pinckney's Chain of Lakes is privately owned, but visitors can access the waterways from several launch points. To reach the boat launch area at **Bruin Lake**, hop on North Territorial Road from M–52 or U.S. Highway 23 to Hadley Road. Take Hadley Road north for 4 miles, then turn east on Kaiser Road, which is equipped with signs that will direct you to the launch site. To put in at **Halfmoon Lake**, take North Territorial Road to Hankerd Road and turn north; the lake's boat launch and day-use area lie 2 miles up the road on the left. To launch your canoe at **Hiland Lake**, take

Hankerd Road north past Halfmoon Lake to Glenbrook Road. The boat launch is located on Glenbrook about 1 mile farther north, on the right.

Additional Help

MA & G grid: 32, A1 and A2.

Camping: Pinckney Recreation Area maintains two campgrounds. Bruin Lake Campground features 180 modern sites, while Crooked Lake Campground contains 25 rustic sites.

Food, gas, and lodging: Chelsea, Dexter, Ann Arbor, Pinckney, Stockbridge, Hell.

For more information: Pinckney Recreation Area.

Canoe liveries: Hell Creek Ranch; the state also maintains a canoe rental concession at the day-use area of Halfmoon Lake.

A pair of swans on Halfmoon Lake, one of the chain of lakes in Pinckney Recreation Area.

7 Pointe aux Barques

Character: A varied piece of Lake Huron coastline that allows kayakers to view lighthouses, beaches, sand dunes, and rugged sandstone cliffs.

Location: On the tip of Lower Michigan's Thumb, where Saginaw Bay meets Lake Huron.

Size: Approximately 20 miles of coastline, from Port Crescent State Park to the Pointe aux Barques Lighthouse.

Skill level: Intermediate.

Hazards: North winds can create high waves; shallow, rocky shoals extend far offshore; waves reflecting off cliffs and caves can create dangerous seas; private property limits landing options in some areas.

Maps: USGS 1:25,000 - Rush Lake-MI, Kinde West-MI, Port Austin West-MI, Port Austin East-MI, Huron City-MI; 1:100,000 - Tawas City-MI, Pointe aux Barques-MI; 1:250,000 - Tawas City-MI. NOAA chart 14863.

The paddling: The Pointe aux Barques area, at the very tip of the Thumb, has a number of interesting features that invite exploration by kayak. There are two historic lighthouses, miles of sandy beach, the largest sand dunes on the east side of the state, and an area of sandstone cliffs and caves that seems to have been transplanted from the rocky shores of Lake Superior.

Appropriately enough, the name "Pointe aux Barques" is French for "point of little boats." Kayakers can launch their little boats at the public access site on rocky Eagle Bay. From here, one possible trip heads west 12 miles past Pointe aux Barques and the city of Port Austin to the dunes of Port Crescent State Park. From the launch site, you paddle northwest through long fingers of submerged rocks around Burnt Cabin Point. About 2.5 miles west—across Alaska Bay and a stretch of sandy beach that is punctuated by cottages—you reach the rock formations of Pointe aux Barques.

For the next mile, the shoreline consists of rugged sandstone cliffs that have been worn into unusual shapes by the action of wind and waves. Examples include a sea stack known as Turnip Rock and a finger-like projection called Thumbnail Rock. There are also several small sea caves and overhanging ledges that can be experienced close-up in calm water. The point is exposed to north winds, however, and even moderate chop can reflect off the cliffs and underlying shoals to make paddling tricky.

After rounding Pointe aux Barques, kayakers will be treated to a view of the Port Austin Reef Light about 1.5 miles offshore. This lighthouse was built in 1878 to mark the end of a shoal that extends out from the point. It is a bit unusual in that it sits on top of a 30-foot pier, making the entire structure over 75 feet tall.

Continuing westward, kayakers will pass a 2-mile stretch of undeveloped sand beach before reaching the city of Port Austin, about 6 miles from Eagle Bay. The marina and public boat ramp on the west side of town is a potential put-in/take-out spot for day trips east-

Pointe aux Barques

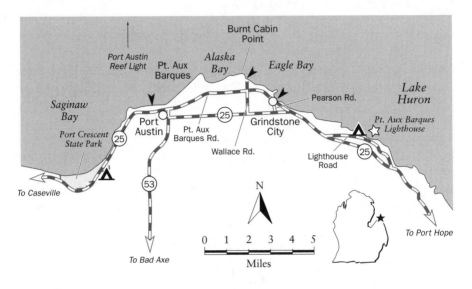

ward to Pointe aux Barques or westward to Port Crescent State Park. The state park is located 5 miles west of Port Austin. It offers a popular campground at the east end (call in advance for reservations), 7 miles of hiking trails, and 3 miles of beach that include the largest sand dunes on the Lake Huron coast.

Another possible kayak excursion in the Pointe aux Barques area heads eastward 5.5 miles from Eagle Bay to the Pointe aux Barques Lighthouse and Museum. From the launch site, paddle east 1.5 miles along the rocky shoreline to Grindstone City, which has a public boat ramp that is another option for putting in or taking out. Continue east about 4 miles to the historic Pointe aux Barques Lighthouse, which was built in 1847 to warn ships of the shallow waters at the approach to Saginaw Bay. The lighthouse is now part of a 7-acre county park that includes a museum and camping facilities.

Access: To reach the hand-carry public boat launch in **Eagle Bay**, take M–25 east 4 miles from Port Austin, then turn north on Wallace Road. Follow Wallace Road 1.5 miles to the access site. To reach the **Grindstone City** boat ramp, continue east 2 miles past Eagle Bay on M–25, then head north 0.5 mile on Pearson Road. The **Port Austin** boat ramp is located just off M–25; take the highway into town and follow the signs to the marina.

Additional Help

MA & G grid: 62, A1–A2; 63, A5–A7.

Camping: Camping is available at Port Crescent State Park (137 modern sites), 5 miles west of Port Austin on M–25, and Albert E. Sleeper State Park (280 modern sites), 13 miles west of Port Austin on M–25. Huron County also operates a small campground just east of the Pointe aux Barques Lighthouse, about 10 miles east of Port Austin via M–25 and Lighthouse Road.

Food, gas, and lodging: Port Austin, Harbor Beach, Caseville.

For more information: Port Crescent State Park.

Rogue River

Character: A quiet western Michigan river easily accessible to Grand Rapids–area paddlers.
Location: Kent County.
Length: 42 miles.
Run: 21 miles, from Grange Road to rivermouth.
Average run time: 4–6 hours.
Class: Flatwater.
Skill level: Beginner.
Optimal flow: May–October.
Average gradient: 2 feet per mile.
Hazards: Occasional fallen trees at upper end of run; deep water at dam reservoirs.
Fishing: Rainbow and brown trout above Rockford.
Maps: USGS 1:25,000 - Sparta-MI, Cedar Springs SW-MI, Cedar Springs-MI, Rockford-MI; 1:100,000 - Cedar Springs-MI; 1:250,000 - Midland-MI.

The paddling: The Rogue River is a peaceful, unassuming stream that is ideally suited for an easy morning or afternoon paddle. Its upper reaches are too shallow and narrow for canoeing or kayaking. But after passing by Sparta, the river picks up sufficient volume from various tributaries to coalesce into a scenic and undemanding float that can be tackled by novice paddlers. This lower section of the Rogue (about 21 miles) is generally divided into two distinct destinations by two dams (Rockford and Childsdale) that sit midway down its length. The river above these dams is quiet and murky, while the water below Childsdale Dam moves at a livelier—but still relatively undemanding—clip.

Paddlers interested in exploring the Rogue above the dams can put in at Grange Road or Algoma Road. This section of the river is murky and heavily shaded, with a slow current. Fallen trees create occasional obstacles through this stretch, which is 40 to 50 feet wide and 2 to 4 feet deep at normal water levels. Most of the limbs can be easily negotiated, but you may have to scramble over or around one or two deadfalls in these first few miles. Much of the shoreline is developed through here, but the homes are well spaced and most are set back some distance from the river.

Below 12 Mile Road Bridge, the Rogue widens (60 to 80 feet) and exchanges forest canopy for open sky. Signs of civilization remain common, however, from the continued presence of homes on shore to the distant roar of the U.S. Highway 131 expressway. From the U.S. 131 bridge to the backwaters of Rockford Dam, the river's current is barely perceptible. Most paddlers who float the Rogue complete their trip at this dam (take out on the left), but if you are intent on exploring all 21 miles of this run, use the portage trail on the right.

Immediately downstream from Rockford Dam, the river is shallow and quick. It slows and deepens again, however, as it approaches Childsdale Dam, another 2 miles downstream. You can portage this second dam on the left side.

Rogue River

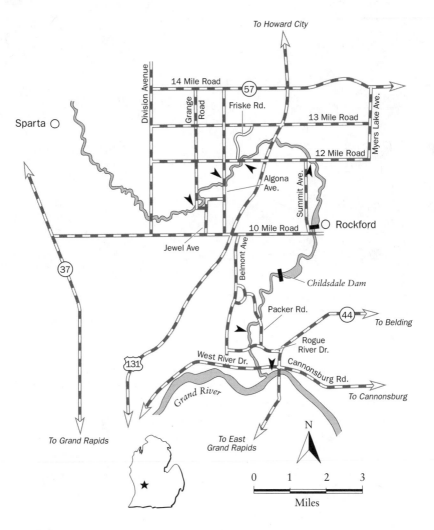

To Howard City

Division Avenue

14 Mile Road

57

Grange Road

Friske Rd.

13 Mile Road

Sparta

12 Mile Road

Myers Lake Ave.

Algona Ave.

Summit Ave.

Jewel Ave

10 Mile Road

Rockford

37

Belmont Ave

Childsdale Dam

Packer Rd.

44

To Belding

Rogue River Dr.

West River Dr.

Cannonsburg Rd.

131

Grand River

To Cannonsburg

To Grand Rapids

To East Grand Rapids

N

0   1   2   3

Miles

The Rogue River provides an easy afternoon escape for residents of the bustling Grand Rapids area. Photo by Dwight W. Hillstrom.

The 7-mile section of the Rogue from Childsdale Dam to the Grand River moves at a moderate pace past a mixed bag of woodlands and homes. It also passes under two bridges (Packer and Rogue River) and winds past a shoreline park on its way southward. This park, located about 4 miles south of Childsdale Dam, provides a nice setting for a picnic or snack break. Summertime paddlers should note, however, that these last few miles can get shallow and scrapy during low-water periods. The last public take-out on the stream is a DNR access site located on the Grand River just upstream from the mouth of the Rogue.

Access: To reach the bridge on **Grange Road**, take U.S. 131 to 10 Mile Road, go west for 1 mile to Jewel Avenue. Follow Jewel north for 1 mile, then turn west on Grange for a few hundred feet. The bridge at **Algoma Road** is 1.5 miles north of 10 Mile Road. **12 Mile Road Bridge** is 3 miles northwest of Rockford. The **Summit Road** access is a small park located at the juncture of Summit and 12 Mile Road. **Rockford Dam** is in downtown Rockford on Bridge Street. The **Childsdale Dam** is on Childsdale Avenue, 2 miles north of M–44. The DNR site at the mouth of the Rogue is located off West River Drive, less than 0.5 mile west of M–44.

Additional Help

MA & G grid: 46, C2–D2.

Camping: No public camping in the immediate area. A privately owned campground is situated at the mouth of the Rogue, 4 miles west of U.S. 131 on West River Drive.

Food, gas, and lodging: Rockford, Sparta, Grand Rapids.

For more information: Contact area liveries.

Canoe liveries: AAA Rogue River Canoe Rentals, Grand Rogue Campgrounds and Canoe.

Access Point	Float Distance To Next Access Point
Grange Road	1.5 miles
Algoma Road	1.5 miles
Friske Road	4 miles
Summit Road	5 miles
Rockford Dam	2 miles
Childsdale Dam	7 miles
DNR site at rivermouth	Take Out

St. John's Marsh

Character: A labyrinth of reeds and cattails teeming with wildlife.
Location: Near Algonac in the St. Clair Flats.
Size: One mile wide and 2.5 miles long.
Skill level: Beginner.
Hazards: Deep water in drainage ditches; part of area open to hunting in season.
Maps: USGS 1:25,000 - Algonac-MI, St. Clair Flats-MI; 1:100,000 - Lake St. Clair North-MI; 1:250,000 - Detroit-MI.

The paddling: Paddlers entering the expanse of wetlands known as St. John's Marsh can lose themselves—and all their worries—in a watery maze of swaying grasses and aquatic plants. Although you can see most of the area within two to three hours of casual paddling, its location less than an hour northeast of Detroit makes it a pleasant escape from the urban grind.

St. John's Marsh is part of the St. Clair Flats—a cluster of islands, wetlands, channels, and shallow bays that have formed where the St. Clair River empties into Lake St. Clair. The Department of Natural Resources manages St. John's Marsh as part of the St. Clair Flats Wildlife Area, which also includes portions of nearby Harsens Island and Dickinson Island. Two sections of the marsh are designated as a wildlife refuge. The marsh's sheltered waters provide migration stopping points and nesting sites for a wide variety of birds, including swans, herons, cranes, Canada geese, ducks, and terns. The upland fields and woods are also home to deer, raccoons, muskrats, squirrels, and other animals.

The main access point for St. John's Marsh is a DNR boat launch off M–29 about 3 miles west of Algonac. Launching here puts you in the extreme southwest corner of the marsh. We recommend following the channel to the right (north), toward the back of the marsh, where traffic sounds fade away and wildlife sightings become more likely. Paddlers can follow this narrow channel through reeds, flowering lilypads, wild rice beds, and scattered hardwood trees for about 2 miles, then turn left (east) and follow the northern boundary of the wildlife refuge 1 mile to M–29. From here you can either turn around and retrace your previous route back to the launch, or work your way southward through the reeds near the highway. Paddlers should note, however, that some areas of the marsh can be shallow and mucky during low-water periods. In very dry years, much of the marsh even becomes impassable.

Access: To reach the **boat launch** for St. John's Marsh, take M–29 east about 14 miles from Interstate 94, or west about 3 miles from Algonac.

St. John's Marsh

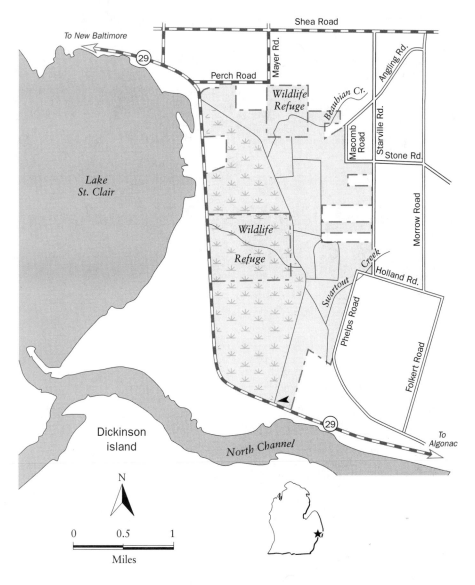

Mute swans are one of the many species of waterfowl that nest in St. John's Marsh.

Additional Help

MA & G grid: 43, C6.

Camping: Algonac State Park (220 modern sites on the St. Clair River and 76 modern sites inland), about 2 miles north of Algonac on M–29.

Food, gas, and lodging: Algonac, New Baltimore, Marine City.

For more information: St. Clair Flats Wildlife Area office, Department of Natural Resources Mount Clemens office.

Rentals/guided trips: Great Lakes Docks and Decks.

Thornapple River

Character: An easygoing stream that meanders through low southwest Michigan woodlands.
Location: Barry County.
Length: 100 miles.
Run: 14 miles, from Charlton County Park to Airport Road Canoe Landing.
Average run time: 5–6 hours.
Class: Flatwater.
Skill level: Beginner.
Optimal flow: May–June, September–October.
Average gradient: 2 feet per mile.
Hazards: Occasional fallen trees.
Fishing: Primarily smallmouth bass through this section of the river.
Maps: USGS 1:25,000 - Maple Grove-MI, Dowling-MI, Hastings-MI, Middleville-MI; 1:100,000 - Grand Rapids-MI; 1:250,000 - Grand Rapids-MI.

The paddling: The Thornapple River is one of the Grand River's major tributaries, but only a small portion of its 100-mile length is good for float trips. Its upper sections—from its origins in Eaton County to Thornapple Lake—are too small and tangled for enjoyable canoeing, while the river below Irving consists of a series of dam-created reservoirs that are heavily developed. In between, however, is a 14-mile stretch of river that is suitable for family outings.

Paddlers interested in exploring the Thornapple can put in at Charlton County Park, a sprawling facility that sits on the river's northern bank. As you begin your float downstream, you will pass under Charlton Park Road and by myriad cottages and homes. The water here is fairly slow and moderately deep (5 to 8 feet) as it passes between banks that range from 40 to 60 feet across.

After passing under McKeown Road Bridge, the Thornapple picks up the pace a bit and most of the shoreline cottages disappear. Occasional fallen trees in the woodsy river corridor will require basic maneuvering skills, but the stream retains a forgiving temperament throughout. River Road Bridge offers good access to the Thornapple (as does Center Road Bridge, another mile and a half downstream), and it can be used by parties who only want to spend an hour or two on the river.

Below River Road Bridge, the Thornapple delivers paddlers through Hastings neighborhoods to a nice city park and then out of town again. This section of the river was disappointingly cluttered with tires, ugly concrete slabs, and other trash when we passed through, but our understanding is that local conservation groups are working hard to address this problem. In Hastings and immediately downstream, the river is fairly tight (it averages 20 to 30 feet across), shady, and rocky, with long stretches of gravelly riverbed. Midway between Hastings and the Airport Road take-out is a golf course that fetches up against the Thornapple's right bank.

Thornapple River

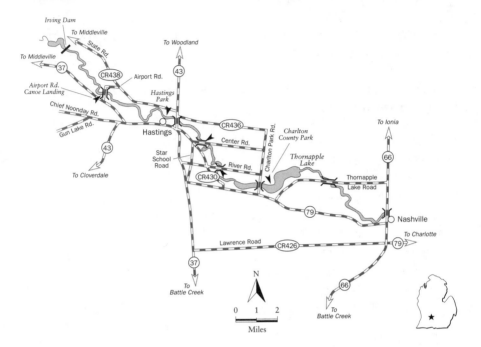

A short distance downstream from Airport Bridge Road, you will find a sandy DNR canoe landing on the left bank. This is a good place to conclude your float because the backwaters of Irving Dam lie a few miles farther downriver. If you decide to press on, you will find a large island a short distance downstream from the canoe landing. Slip past this island on the right; the left channel is impassable. The portage around Irving Dam—actually two closely spaced dams—is a difficult one (on the left), but if you hump it, the nearly 10-mile float from Irving to Middleville offers a mix of riffles and quiet water. You can take out at Middleville Dam on the left.

Access: You can reach **Charlton County Park** from Hastings by taking M–37 south for 2 miles, M–79 east for 3 miles, and Charlton Park Road north for less than 1 mile. **River Road Bridge** lies 2 miles southeast of Hastings, 0.25 mile east of State Road (County Road 430) on River Road. **Hastings City Park** is on M–43 in Hastings. The canoe landing at **Airport Road** is 3 miles west of Hastings, about 0.5 mile north of M–37.

Additional Help

MA & G grid: 37, C5–C6.

Camping: Privately owned riverside campgrounds are located across the stream from Charlton County Park and on Irving Road (just north of M–37) a few miles east of Irving Dam.

Food, gas, and lodging: Hastings, Middleville.

For more information: Contact area canoe liveries.

Canoe liveries: Indian Valley, Whispering Waters Campground and Canoe.

Access Point	Float Distance To Next Access Point
Charlton County Park	2 miles
River Road Bridge	5 miles
Hastings City Park	7 miles
Airport Road DNR Landing	Take Out

⊞ Au Sable River

Character: One of America's legendary trout streams, the Au Sable has cool, clear waters and an attractive shoreline—bristling with launch sites, campgrounds, and forestland—that make it tremendously popular with canoeists as well as anglers.

Location: Begins in Crawford County and winds through Oscoda, Alcona, and Iosco Counties before emptying into Lake Huron.

Length: 135 miles.

Run: 115 miles, from Grayling to Lake Huron.

Average run time: 35–50 hours.

Class: Flatwater.

Skill level: Beginner.

Optimal flow: May–October.

Average gradient: 3 feet per mile.

Hazards: Occasional fallen trees and logjams require basic maneuvering skills; deep water, especially below Wakely Bridge.

Fishing: Michigan's best-known fishing river, with nearly 100 miles of the mainstream classified as Blue Ribbon Trout Stream (the river's major tributaries chalk up an additional 50 miles of Blue Ribbon water). The premier fly fishing destination in the state.

Maps: USGS 1:25,000 - Grayling-MI, Wakeley Lake-MI, Luzerne NW-MI, Red Oak-MI, Mio-MI, Fairview-MI, McKinley-MI, Alcona Dam Pond-MI, Hale-MI, Loud Dam-MI, Sid Town-MI, Foote Site Village-MI, Oscoda-MI; 1:100,000 - Grayling-MI, Hubbard Lake-MI, Tawas City-MI; 1:250,000 - Traverse City-MI, Tawas City-MI.

The paddling: The Au Sable is Michigan's most beloved river. Rich in history, scenic beauty, and recreational opportunities, it is regarded by thousands of anglers and paddlers as the brightest star in Michigan's galaxy of sparkling streams and bustling rivers. The birthplace of Trout Unlimited and the current home of the famous Au Sable Canoe Marathon, the Au Sable holds a special place in the heart of every Michigan sports enthusiast.

The Au Sable first emerged as a destination for anglers in the nineteenth century, when wealthy sportsmen converged on its waters to fish for grayling. As the years passed, however, the river suffered mightily as the timber industry used it to transport vast stands of virgin white pine downstream to waiting ships. By the early twentieth century, the grayling had vanished from the river's waters, the region's forestlands had been decimated, and the stream's banks and river bottom were riddled with heavy scars. Over time, however, the "river of sand," as the Au Sable was called by early explorers, was nurtured back to health. Today, the grayling remains a ghost, a reminder of an earlier era's carelessness. But brook, brown, and rainbow trout roam up and down the stream today in mouth-watering numbers, silently

A team of racers compete in qualifying sprints for the Au Sable River Canoe Marathon.

passing along wooded shorelines that once again rustle and sway on windy afternoons. Paddlers, meanwhile, visit the Au Sable not only because of its clear water and scenic shoreline, but also because of its myriad access sites and plentiful camping alternatives. These attributes make the river one of the state's best choices for extended canoe tripping.

The Au Sable originates at the confluence of Kolka and Bradford Creeks, about 20 miles north of Grayling. Good paddling conditions begin in Grayling, home to numerous canoe liveries. If you don't need to use one of these liveries for a boat or car spotting, your best put-in bet in the area is at Burton's Landing, less than 5 miles downstream. This upper section of the river is narrow (30 to 45 feet) and shallow (1 to 4 feet), with a sandy bottom, a moderate current, and a shoreline that blends cottages with low woodlands.

From Burton's Landing—where an 8-mile stretch of flies-only, no-kill water begins—to Stephan's Bridge, day paddlers and fly fishers can sometimes combine to create a crowded feeling. The 18-mile stretch from Stephan's Bridge to Parmalee Bridge, on the other hand, is far more peaceful. River traffic thins considerably along this segment, which features generally slower water, excellent camping options (at White Pine Canoe Camp, Rainbow Bend, and Parmalee), and increased opportunities for spotting deer, bald eagles, and other wildlife.

The river below Parmalee Bridge is fun to run, with several sections of lively water that alternate with placid stretches. Twelve miles below Parmalee Bridge, however, is Mio Dam, the first of the half-dozen dams that were built on the Au Sable during the 1910s and 1920s. As you approach the Mio Pond impoundment, the current slackens and the char-

Au Sable River

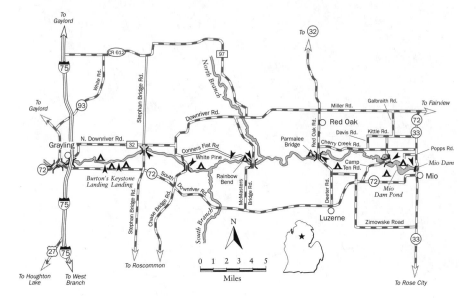

acter of the river corridor changes to marshland. The dam can be portaged on the right via a metal platform.

The 20-mile run below Mio Dam is a particularly lovely section of the Au Sable. The area immediately below the dam sees lots of use from anglers and day paddlers using area liveries. As you continue downstream past McKinley Bridge, however, the crowds diminish and peace descends once again over the river, which continues to display a classic pool-and-riffle character. The ever-widening river corridor passes through Huron National Forest along here, unveiling numerous great shoreline campsites along the way. The relative dearth of access points through this segment acts to cull river traffic down to paddlers on extended trips.

Good canoeing comes to an abrupt end at Alcona Dam Pond, a 4-mile-long impoundment that is heavily developed. Cottages and campgrounds crowd its shores, and powerboats and personal watercraft criss-cross the pond in noisy herds. Rather than brave this crossing, you can instead take out at the Forest Service bridge on Forest Road 4001 and put in below Alcona Dam (which can be portaged on the right if necessary). You can then return to the water either immediately below the dam or at nearby Bamfield Road Bridge.

From Alcona, the Au Sable continues for another 40 miles to the rivermouth at Oscoda. But while the span between Alcona Dam and Loud Dam offers about a dozen miles of moderate current through pleasantly hilly and wooded terrain, it is not representative of points farther downstream. In fact, the eastern reaches of the Au Sable are domi-

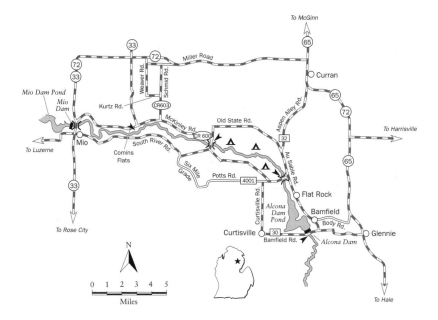

nated by dams and their attendant backwaters. Consequently, this last section of the river may not appeal to canoeists who are partial to moving water.

The four dams that lie downstream from Alcona (Loud, Five Channels, Cooke, and Foote) all include impoundments of significant size. These waters are deep and may be difficult for beginning paddlers to manage on windy days. Portages are clearly marked, however, and the river winds through National Forest land for much of this section, providing paddlers with plenty of nice scenery and primitive shoreline campsites (the lone established campgrounds below Alcona are located on Loud Dam Pond, Cooke Dam Pond, and Foote Dam Pond). The final take-out spot on the Au Sable lies in Oscoda, at a public boat launching site located at the mouth of the river.

Access: Launch sites from Grayling to Mio are numerous. All of these spots can be reached from M–72, which parallels the river corridor. Au Sable River Canoe Campground is 3 miles east of Grayling, 1 mile south of North Downriver Road on Headquarters Road. **Burton's Landing** lies 4 miles east of Grayling off M–72 on Burton's Landing Road. **Keystone Landing** is located 5 miles east of Grayling via M–72 and Keystone Landing Road. **Stephan's Bridge** is located on Stephan's Bridge Road, 2 miles north of its junction with M–72. The launch area lies 200 yards below the bridge on the right. **Wakeley Bridge** lies 9 miles east of Grayling on Wakeley Bridge Road, 2 miles north of M–72 (south of M–72, the road is called Chase Bridge Road). The actual put-in spot at this bridge is located about 30 yards downstream. To reach **Conners Flat**, take FR–32 north from M–72 for 4 miles,

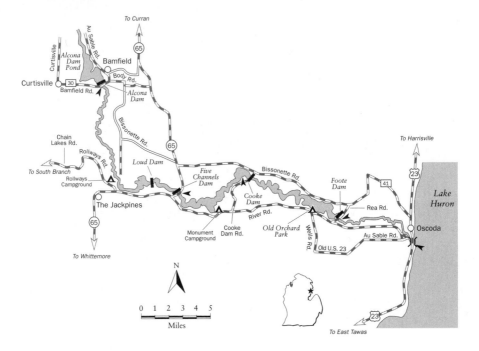

then go east on Conners Flat Road for about 5 miles. The **Rainbow Bend State Forest Campground** is located another mile east on Conners Flat Road. This campground can also be reached by taking McMasters Bridge Road (FR–97) north from M–72 for 5 miles, then turning west on Conners Flat Road and continuing for 1 mile. **McMasters Bridge**, meanwhile, lies 5 miles north of M–72 on McMasters Bridge Road (FR–97). **Parmalee Bridge** lies on Red Oak Road (County Road 489), 5 miles north of M–72. Luzerne Township Park is 3 miles north of downtown Luzerne on Deeter Road off CR–489. **Camp 10 Bridge** is located on Camp 10 Road (CR–609), 4 miles north of M–72 outside of Mio. Sportsman's County Park is located just east of Mio off M–72. It sits on the south shore of Mio Pond. A canoe take-out is also maintained on **Mio Pond**, a few hundred yards above the dam on the left bank. To reach this area by car, take M–72 north out of Mio to Popps Road and go west for 1 mile or so.

Access sites in the Mio area include the **M–72/M–33 Bridge** and **Comins Flats**, located 4 miles east of Mio on CR–600 (also known as FR–32 and McKinley Road). **McKinley Bridge** is located just outside of McKinley on CR–602. The forest service bridge on **FR–4001** lies 5 miles north of Curtisville; take Curtisville Road north for 3 miles, then go east on FR–4001 (Potts Road) for 2 miles to reach the bridge. **Bamfield Road Bridge** is located downstream of Alcona Dam on Bamfield Road (FR–30). **Rollways Campground** is located 7 miles east of South Branch on Loud Dam Pond, just off M–65 on Rollways Road. The **M–65** Bridge just below Five Channels Dam also provides good access.

Primary launch sites from Five Channels Dam to Oscoda include the **Monument Campground**, which lies off River Road on Cooke Dam Pond; a public access site above Cooke Dam on **Cooke Dam Road**; and **Rea Road Bridge**, 0.5 mile east of Foote Site Village on Rea Road. The public launch in **Oscoda** is located near the mouth of the river where it empties into Lake Huron.

Paddlers should also note that in 2000, the USFS began requiring vehicle passes for the use of access and camping sites on national forest land.

Additional Help

MA & G grid: 76, C3 and C4; 77, C5–C7; 78, C1–C2, and D3; 70, A3–A4; 71, A5–A7.

Camping: In its upper reaches, from Grayling to Mio, the Au Sable shoreline is dotted with state forest campgrounds. These include Au Sable River Canoe Camp, Burton's Landing (12 sites), Keystone Landing (18 sites), White Pine Canoe Camp (accessible by canoe only), Rainbow Bend (6 sites, including group sites), Parmalee Bridge (7 sites, including group sites), and Mio Pond (24 sites, including group sites). In addition, three small USFS campgrounds are located between McKinley Bridge and Alcona Dam Pond. Municipal parks with camping facilities include Luzerne Township Park (below Paramlee Bridge) and Sportsman's County Park (on the south shore of Mio Dam Pond). Below Mio, canoeists pass through long stretches of Huron National Forest, where they can choose from plentiful shoreline campsites. In addition, established national forest campgrounds can be found on Loud Dam Pond (Rollways Campground, 19 sites) and Cooke Dam Pond (Monument Campground, 20 sites). Camping is also available at Old Orchard County Park on Foote Dam Pond.

Food, gas, and lodging: Grayling, Mio, South Branch, Oscoda.

For more information: Huron National Forest, Au Sable State Forest.

Canoe liveries: Alcona Canoe Rental, Au Sable Canoes, Bear Paw Canoe Livery, Borcher's Canoe Livery, Carlisle Canoes, Gott's Landing, Hinchman Acres Canoes, Hunt's Canoes, Jim's Canoe Livery, Penrod's Paddlesports Center, Oscoda Canoes, Ray's Canoeing, Watters Edge Livery.

Access Point	Float Distance To Next Access Point
Grayling	5 miles
Burton's Landing	3 miles
Keystone Landing	3 miles
Stephan's Bridge	3 miles

Access Point	Float Distance To Next Access Point
Wakeley Bridge	7 miles
Conners Flat	1 mile
Rainbow Bend	4.5 miles
McMasters Bridge	3.5 miles
Parmalee Bridge	9 miles
Camp 10 Bridge	4 miles
Mio Pond	0.5 mile
M–72/M–33 Bridge	6 miles
Comins Flats	9 miles
McKinley Bridge	11 miles
FR–4001 Bridge	5 miles
Bamfield Road Bridge	11.5 miles
Rollways Campground	5 miles
M–65 Bridge	3 miles
Monument Campground	5 miles
Cooke Dam Road	8 miles
Rea Road Bridge	8 miles
Oscoda Landing	Take Out

Au Sable River, South Branch

Character: A pleasant, slow-moving stream that is popular with canoeists and fly fishermen alike.

Location: Begins at Lake St. Helen in Northern Roscommon County and flows into southeastern Crawford County before joining the mainstream of the fabled Au Sable River.

Length: 37 miles.

Run: 24.5 miles, from Roscommon to Conners Flats public access site on Au Sable mainstream.

Average run time: 7–10 hours.

Class: Flatwater.

Skill level: Beginner.

Optimal flow: May–October.

Average gradient: 2 feet per mile.

Hazards: Occasional fallen trees and logjams create tight squeezes in the Mason Tract section.

Fishing: Prized destination for trout fishermen who flock to the river's "flies-only" Mason Tract segment. Special flies-only fishing regulations are enforced from Chase Bridge downstream to the mainstream, including 4 miles of no-kill fishing immediately below Chase Bridge.

Maps: USGS 1:25,000 - Roscommon North-MI, Eldorado-MI, Luzerne NW-MI; 1:100,000 - Grayling-MI; 1:250,000 - Traverse City-MI.

The paddling: The South Branch of the Au Sable River is an appealing stream for paddlers looking for an undemanding and scenic float. It proceeds at a sleepy pace for its entire length, passing through the heart of the Mason Tract Wilderness Area before joining with the Au Sable mainstream. The Mason Tract is a sanctuary of several thousand acres that was bequeathed to the state back in the mid-1950s by George Mason, an auto executive and outdoor enthusiast. Per Mason's instructions, the entire area—including the river corridor—has been kept in a natural state for successive generations of paddlers and anglers to enjoy. Today, its woodlands of cedar, pine, and hardwoods support good populations of deer, woodcock, ruffed grouse, and other wildlife.

Paddlers utilizing Roscommon-area liveries for canoe rental or car spotting typically begin their trips in town. Here the river is slow and moderately wide (30 to 60 feet) and its shoreline is heavily built up with cottages, many of them sporting canoes and rowboats on their lawns and docks. If you do not require the services of a livery, you can put in about 4 miles downstream from Roscommon at popular Mead's Landing (also known as Steckert Road) or another mile downstream at Deerheart Valley Road, which has limited parking. From here to Chase Bridge, the river remains lazy and open as it passes through a pleasant blend of cottages and woodlands.

The Chase Bridge access site marks the upstream boundary of the Mason Tract. Paddlers navigating the next several miles of river will have to negotiate a greater number of obstacles than they faced upstream. These obstacles take the form of both fly fishermen, who regard this section of the river as "holy waters," and fallen trees and logjams, reminders of terrific storms that have passed through the region in recent years. Slots have been carved

Au Sable River, South Branch

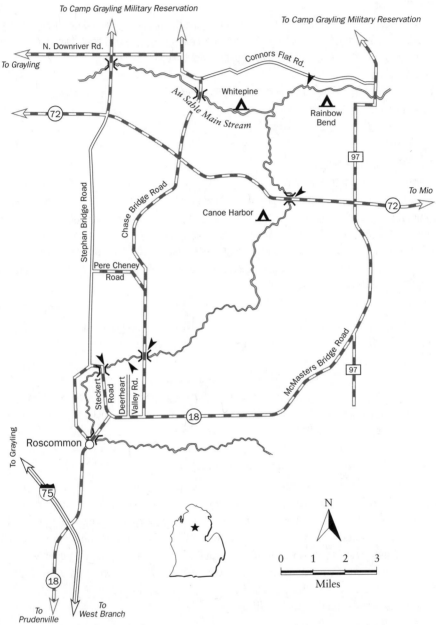

To Camp Grayling Military Reservation

To Camp Grayling Military Reservation

N. Downriver Rd.

To Grayling

Connors Flat Rd.

72

Au Sable Main Stream

Whitepine

Rainbow
Bend

97

To Mio

72

Canoe Harbor

Stephan Bridge Road

Chase Bridge Road

Pere Cheney
Road

McMasters Bridge Road

97

Steckert
Road

Deerheart
Valley Rd.

18

Roscommon

To Grayling

75

18

To
Prudenville

To
West Branch

N

0   1   2   3

Miles

through these downed trees and logjams, allowing canoeists to pass through. But some of these slots are only about 4 or 5 feet wide, making them a challenge for novice paddlers despite the forgiving current. Canoeists with basic abilities should press on, however, for this section of the South Branch is the stream's most scenically rewarding stretch.

The Canoe Harbor Campground, located approximately 9 miles downstream from Chase Bridge, marks the downstream boundary of the Mason Tract. This Au Sable State Forest campground features forty-four rustic sites and is the only legal camping spot on the South Branch. It is ideally situated for parties planning multi-day trips that extend on to the mainstream of the Au Sable. Another mile below Canoe Harbor is Smith Bridge on M-72. This access site is the last remaining one on the South Branch before it joins with the Au Sable mainstream.

From Smith Bridge down, the river passes by shady woodlands and pretty cottages and homes. As with the rest of the South Branch, the river here is moderate in width (60 to 80 feet) and depth (2 to 4 feet with deeper holes) and languid in temperament. Immediately upstream from its confluence with the mainstream, the South Branch current slows to a crawl. Once you reach the mainstream, you can either push upstream a half mile or so to Whitepine Canoe Forest Campground or paddle downstream to the Conners Flat public access site (to take out) or Rainbow Bend State Forest Campground (to camp). The campground, managed by Au Sable State Forest, lies on the left (northern) bank of the river up a sandy trail.

Access: Several liveries in the Roscommon area—located off I–75 in Roscommon County—offer access to the South Branch. **Mead's Landing** (also known as Steckert Road Access) is located 1 mile north of Roscommon off Steckert Bridge Road. To reach the access site on **Deerheart Valley Road**, take M–18 1.5 miles northeast out of Roscommon to Deerheart Valley Road, then turn north for 2 miles until it comes to an end at the river. **Chase Bridge** is located on Chase Bridge Road, 9 miles south of where it meets M–72 or 2 miles north of the intersection of Chase Bridge Road and M–18. **Smith Bridge** is located on M–72, 14 miles east of Grayling and 9 miles west of Luzerne. To reach **Conners Flat**, take FR–32 north from M–72 for 4 miles, then turn east on Conners Flat Road for about 5 miles. The **Rainbow Bend State Forest Campground** is located another mile east on Conners Flat Road. This campground can also be reached by taking McMasters Bridge Road (FR–97) north from M–72 for 5 miles, then turning west on Conners Flat Road for 1 mile.

The Mason Tract section of the river also features numerous foot trails that are used by anglers to reach favorite fishing holes. Some of these paths, which are accessible via area forest roads and two tracks, are occasionally used by locals as put-in spots for canoes, but visitors are advised to stick to the established access sites.

ADDITIONAL HELP

MA & G grid: 76, D4 and 77, D5 and C5.

Camping: Camping on the Au Sable's South Branch is limited to the Canoe Harbor State Forest Campground, which has 44 rustic sites (including 10 canoe group campsites). Other shoreline camping in the Mason Tract is prohibited, and most of the remainder of the river corridor is privately owned. The mainstream of the Au Sable, though, also features campgrounds near its confluence with the South Branch. These include White Pines State Forest Campground and Rainbow Bend State Forest Campground; consult the entry on the Au Sable River for additional information.

Food, gas, and lodging: Grayling, Roscommon, Luzerne, Mio.

For more information: Huron National Forest, Au Sable State Forest.

Canoe liveries: Watters Edge Canoe Livery, Hinchman Acres Canoe Rental, Hiawatha Canoe Livery, Campbell's Canoe Livery, Paddle Brave Canoe Livery & Campground.

ACCESS POINT	FLOAT DISTANCE TO NEXT ACCESS POINT
Roscommon	4 miles
Mead's Landing (Steckert Road)	1 mile
Deerheart Valley Road	1.5 miles
Chase Bridge	10 miles
Smith Bridge (M–72)	8 miles
Conners Flat	Take Out

Betsie River

Character: The upper reaches of this pleasant stream encompass a range of paddling options, from sections of swift, twisting river to quiet marshlands teeming with wildlife.

Location: Southern Benzie and northern Manistee Counties.

Length: 50 miles.

Run: 41 miles, from Grass Lake Campground to Elberta.

Average run time: 15–18 hours.

Class: Flatwater.

Skill level: Intermediate (Beginner in Grass Lake Wildlife Flooding).

Optimal flow: May–September.

Average gradient: 4 feet per mile.

Hazards: Submerged logs, fallen trees, and sweepers appear throughout river corridor; deep holes on outer bends; class I rapids at Thompsonville Dam.

Fishing: Salmon and trout glide through the waters of the stream itself, while bass, pike, and bluegill can be found in the Grass Lake Flooding.

Maps: USGS 1:25,000 - Benzonia-MI, Thompsonville-MI, Karlin-MI, Lake Ann-MI; 1:100,000 - Crystal Lake-MI, Manistee-MI, Traverse City-MI; 1:250,000 - Manitowoc-MI, Traverse City-MI.

The paddling: The Betsie River is navigable by canoe for its entire 50-mile length, from its origin at Green Lake to its terminus at Betsie Lake, just south of Frankfort. The finest segment of this river for paddling is probably the 27-mile, two-day stretch that runs from the Grass Lake Wildlife Flooding to Dair's Mill Landing. Visitors who tackle this section of the Betsie will be rewarded with tranquil marshlands, abundant bird-watching opportunities, and obstacle-studded runs of faster water that will challenge but not overwhelm canoeists with basic skills. But the entire river is open to canoeing, and its lower reaches see a good deal of paddling traffic on summer weekends.

The Grass Lake State Forest Campground in eastern Benzie County is an ideal launching spot for folks interested in exploring the Betsie. This campground is the gateway both to the upper section of the Betsie and the Grass Lake Wildlife Flooding, a watery haven of reeds and cattails that supports swans, loons, bald eagles, ospreys, songbirds, Canada geese, and other waterfowl. Deer, mink, beaver, and otter also make their home in this tranquil marshland area. The flat, currentless water of the flooding makes it an excellent destination for beginning paddlers on all but windy days, when children and novice canoeists might get pushed into the reeds. Landing spots are practically nonexistent, though, so make sure that you attend to rest-room requirements before setting out.

The Grass Lake Wildlife Flooding is separated from the Betsie by a small dam that can be easily portaged on the right (paddlers choosing to forego the Grass Lake Flooding can launch from below the dam). Much of the upper river flows through Pere Marquette State Forest, meandering through hardwood forests, meadows, and marshlands that offer a number of potential campsites. From Grass Lake Campground to Wallin Road Bridge, the

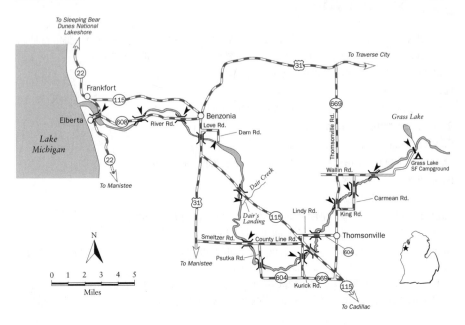

river is narrow (30 feet wide), shallow, and lined with alders and thick brush. Half-submerged logs and tree limbs are scattered throughout the river corridor, but the barely perceptible current that prevails through here makes navigation an easy task except during low-water periods, when carry-overs might be necessary.

From Wallin Road Bridge to Thompsonville Dam, the sleepy current gives way to a faster one that delivers paddlers past attractive meadows, lowland forests, and the odd cottage. The river remains narrow (30 to 40 feet) and winding through here, and its surface is pocked with half-submerged logs and branches that have to be negotiated. In addition, bump-and-scrape conditions prevail at several points during low-water periods. But the surrounding countryside is lovely and unspoiled, making this 7-mile stretch of river a fine one for paddlers with basic skills and a good camping option for overnight trippers.

The Betsie churns up a brief section of standing waves at the site of the former Thompsonville Dam. Paddlers wishing to avoid this section can take out at Carmean Road Bridge or Thompsonville Road Bridge, both located above the washed-out dam. As you make your way downstream to Kurick Road Bridge, the river widens (45 to 60 feet) and maintains a moderate current as it passes over a mix of gravel and sand. The river corridor continues to feature a nice mix of woodlands, but shoreline thickets of alders and high banks of clay and sand make suitable landing and campsites more difficult to find. The Betsie is also deeper in this section, with depths ranging from 2 to 3 feet in midstream to holes of 6 feet or more on the stream's outer bends. The river passes under bridges at both Lindy Road and M–115 on its way to Kurick Road, but neither of these sites offers good access.

The 6-mile section from Kurick Road Bridge to County Line Bridge features a moderately wide streambed (50 to 60 feet), mild current, and one intermediate access point (at rustic Psutka Road Bridge). The river valley, meanwhile, remains largely undeveloped, with alders and cedars crowding the shoreline against a backdrop of rolling hardwood forest. From County Line Bridge to Dair's Mill Landing, the Betsie rolls along in much the same manner, offering up many productive fishing holes on its outer bends. You can take out on the right at Dair's Mill Landing, which is marked by a small wooden footbridge that spans the river. If you decide to cruise on downstream, public boat launches can be used 4 miles downstream at Homestead Dam (portage on the right) or 8 miles downstream at the River Road access site west of Benzonia. The river winds through privately owned lowlands throughout this latter section, severely limiting camping opportunities. Paddlers interested in putting in at Homestead Dam should prepare for big crowds of steelhead fishers immediately downstream during the spring and fall seasons.

Canoeists who float the Betsie between Homestead Dam and the M–22 Bridge at Elberta will find a slower river that passes through marshy lowlands. Submerged deadheads and other snags lurk throughout the streambed, which features a mix of sand, clay, and gravel, but the mellow current takes the teeth out of these obstacles. Again, private land and brushy shoreline effectively negate camping through here until you reach the Betsie River State Game Area. This section of public land begins about 3 miles above Elberta and continues to the outskirts of the town. The river slows to a crawl as you approach Elberta. Take out at the railroad trestle, just upstream from the M–22 Bridge (there is no access at the bridge itself).

Access: Grass Lake State Forest Campground is located 10 miles northeast of Thompsonville. Follow County Road 669 (Thompsonville Road) north out of town for 4 miles, then go east on Wallin Road for 5 miles. The roads leading to the campground are poorly marked. **Wallin Road Bridge** is 2 miles east of CR–669 on Wallin Road. To get to **Carmean Road Bridge**, take CR–669 north from Thompsonville for 2 miles, turn right on King Road and go 1 mile, then head north on Carmean Road for 1 mile. **Thompsonville Road Bridge** is located 2 miles north of Thompsonville on CR–669 (Thompsonville Road). **Kurick Road Bridge** is located 4 miles southwest of Thompsonville via CR–602 (Lindy Road) and Kurick Road. **County Line Road Bridge** is located on County Line Road (Smeltzer Road), 3 miles east of U.S. Highway 31. To reach **Dair's Mill Landing**, follow M–115 (Cadillac Highway) southeast from U.S. 31 for 5 miles to Dair's Mill Road. Travel south on Dair's Mill Road for a few hundred yards, then turn west on Old King Road. The parking lot, which is surrounded by private property, lies at the end of Old King Road. The **Homestead Dam** access site is located just south of Benzonia. Take U.S. 31 south out of town for 1 mile, go east on Love Road for 1 mile, then south on Dam Road for about 1 mile. **Smith Bridge** and **Lewis Bridge** are both located on River Road (CR–608), 1 and 3 miles west of Benzonia, respectively. The railroad trestle access site in Elberta is located on M–22, near the M–22 Bridge.

Additional Help

MA & G grid: 74, D1; 65, A6; 73, D6–D7.

Camping: Shoreline camping in Pere Marquette State Forest; Grass Lake State Forest Campground has 15 rustic sites and provides good access to the river and the Grass Lake Wildlife Flooding.

Food, gas, and lodging: Traverse City, Thompsonville, Benzonia, Frankfort, Elberta.

For more information: Pere Marquette State Forest.

Canoe liveries: Alvina's Canoes.

Access Point	Float Distance To Next Access Point
Grass Lake Campground	3 miles
Wallin Road Bridge	5 miles
South Carmean Road Bridge	2 miles
Thompsonville Road Bridge	5 miles
Kurick Road Bridge	6 miles
County Line Road Bridge	5 miles
Dair's Mill Landing	3 miles
Homestead Dam	3.5 miles
Smith Bridge (River Road)	3.5 miles
Lewis Bridge (River Road)	5 miles
Elberta	Take Out

The Betsie River provides a pleasant float through northern Michigan woodlands.

14 Boardman River

Character: A spirited, attractive stream that flows past conifer forests and northcountry cottages before emptying into Grand Traverse Bay.

Location: Grand Traverse County.

Length: 27 miles.

Run: 20 miles, from the Forks Campground to Boardman Pond.

Average run time: 6–9 hours.

Class: I (class II below Beitner Bridge).

Skill level: Beginner/intermediate.

Optimal flow: April–June, September–October.

Average gradient: 8 feet per mile.

Hazards: Fallen tree limbs and pilings of numerous footbridges require basic maneuvering skills; occasional deep holes; class II water at Beitner Rapids.

Fishing: A highly regarded river for trout fishing, the Boardman includes an 18-mile section—from the Forks to Boardman Pond—that has been formally designated as a state Blue Ribbon Trout Stream.

Maps: USGS 1:25,000 - Jacks Landing-MI, Mayfield-MI; 1:100,000 - Traverse City-MI; 1:250,000 - Traverse City-MI.

The paddling: The Boardman ranks as one of the Lower Peninsula's finest rivers for paddling. Possessed of a moderate current and a winding river corridor that passes through a broad valley of cedar, pine, and assorted hardwoods, it also features one of Lower Michigan's rare bursts of light whitewater. Summer cottages line its banks as well, especially below Brown Bridge Dam. But despite these and other signs of civilization, the river still manages to conjure up a remote and peaceful vibe along a surprising amount of its length.

The mainstream of the Boardman begins at an area known as "The Forks" in Pere Marquette State Forest, where the river's two primary tributaries—the North Branch and the South Branch—meet. A state forest campground located at this junction provides a good launching spot for paddlers interested in exploring the river's upper reaches. The river here is narrow (25 to 35 feet) and lined with tag alders, but it possesses sufficient volume for floating. From here to Scheck's Place State Forest Campground, the Boardman passes through a scenic mix of evergreen and hardwood forest. Fallen cedars are commonplace through here and may require occasional portages. This section is a favorite haunt of trout anglers as well, so keep your eyes peeled at riverbends.

From Scheck's Place to the backwaters of Brown Bridge Dam, the river remains narrow (20 to 40 feet) and twisty and moves at a moderate clip. Occasional cottages pop up along the shoreline, but much of the area remains undeveloped. The entrance to Brown Bridge Pond, meanwhile, is guarded by extensive, shallow sandbars. You may have to drag your boat across these sandbars at low-water levels. The pond itself is quite pretty. Its northern shoreline is a high valley ridge thickly carpeted with forest, while the woods on its

Boardman River

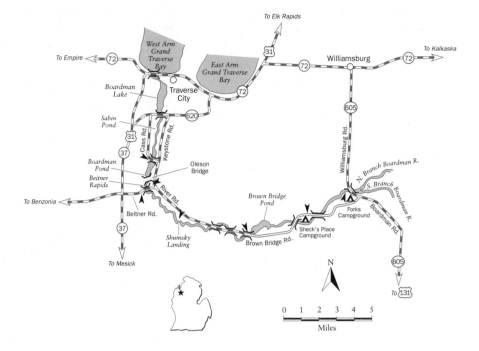

southern side offer many sun-dappled spots for picnicking. Once you reach the dam, you can portage on the left at the stairs if you are continuing downstream.

The first hour or so below Brown Bridge Dam, summer homes line both sides of the Boardman. Many footbridges span the river through here as well, some of which provide very little clearance at high water levels; portage if uncertain of your ability to pass under. This section serves up a steady diet of footbridge supports and riverbends that require basic maneuvering abilities to negotiate. At times it feels a little like a downhill slalom course at half-speed.

As you continue downstream, the Boardman widens somewhat (to 30 to 60 feet) and riffles begin to appear. The shoreline also gradually changes in character, as high, wooded hillsides become more frequent. But private property remains the rule, severely limiting your rest options (an island located about a half hour above Shumsky Landing is your best bet in this regard). From Shumsky Landing to Beitner Road, the stream runs through mostly undeveloped land, skirting occasional meadows and tall banks of cedars and hardwoods. The Boardman maintains its slalom character through here, with pilings of private footbridges the primary obstacles.

Inexperienced paddlers floating this section of the Boardman should conclude their trips at Beitner Road Bridge, which provides good access. Immediately below the bridge is Beitner Rapids (also sometimes known as Keystone Rapids), a 0.5 mile section of class II

Negotiating the rapids below Beitner Bridge on the Boardman River. Photo by Deb Hausler.

whitewater. This fun run features standing waves, rock gardens, and tight turns in pushy water, and is especially challenging during early spring and after big storms. Eddies and patches of calmer water are interspersed, though, providing opportunities for breathers. Oleson Bridge, a footbridge that spans the river at the end of these rapids, is a good take-out spot. Otherwise, you can continue on for another 1.5 miles and take out at the northern end of Boardman Pond, on the west side of the dam.

It is possible to paddle the final 7 miles or so from Boardman Dam to the rivermouth at Grand Traverse Bay. But this stretch is marked by two more dam reservoirs (Sabin Pond and Boardman Lake) and passes through Traverse City's residential and downtown area, making it less appealing than the river's upstream sections.

Access: Forks Campground lies 7 miles south of Williamsburg off Williamsburg Road. To reach **Scheck's Place Campground**, follow Williamsburg Road south out of Williamsburg for 8 miles to Brown Bridge Road, then go west for 4 miles. The access site at **Brown Bridge Dam** is directly off River Road, about 10 miles southeast of downtown Traverse City. The **Shumsky Landing** site is 7 miles south of Traverse City and also is accessed from River Road. To reach **Beitner Road Bridge**, take Beitner Road east from M–37 for 2 miles. The parking area for **Oleson Bridge** is located less than 0.5 mile north of Beitner Bridge, on the west side of Beitner Road. A well-maintained path leads from the parking lot down to the riverside. **Boardman Dam** is on Cass Road, on the southern outskirts of Traverse City.

Additional Help

MA & G grid: 74, C2–C4.

Camping: Pere Marquette State Forest maintains two campgrounds on the upper Boardman. **Forks Campground** (eight rustic sites) is 7 miles south of Williamsburg off Williamsburg Road. **Scheck's Place Campground** (thirty rustic sites) is 12 miles south of Williamsburg; take Williamsburg Road south for 8 miles to Brown Bridge Road, then turn west for 4 miles.

Food, gas, and lodging: Traverse City, Williamsburg.

For more information: Pere Marquette State Forest.

Canoe liveries: None.

Access Point	Float Distance To Next Access Point
Forks Campground	4 miles
Scheck's Place Campground	4 miles
Brown Bridge Dam	6 miles
Shumsky Landing	4 miles
Beitner Road Bridge	0.5 mile
Oleson Bridge	1.5 miles
Boardman Dam	Take Out

15 Chippewa River

Character: A pleasant, scenic river that winds through the fields and forests of Michigan's heartland.
Location: Isabella County.
Length: 85 miles.
Run: 51.5 miles, from Coldwater Road Bridge to Magruder Road Bridge.
Average run time: 14–18 hours.
Class: I.
Skill level: Beginner/intermediate.
Optimal flow: May–October.
Average gradient: 4 feet per mile.
Hazards: Occasional fallen trees and small rock gardens; sections of deep water; potentially confusing route in downtown Mount Pleasant area.
Fishing: Known for its smallmouth bass, the river also supports northern pike and walleye.
Maps: USGS 1:25,000 - Winn-MI, Mount Pleasant-MI, Shepherd-MI, Pleasant Valley-MI; 1:100,000 - Midland-MI; 1:250,000 - Midland-MI.

The paddling: The Chippewa River is a pretty and easily accessible stream that slices through the midsection of Michigan's Lower Peninsula. It actually runs for more than 80 miles from its origins in Mecosta County to Midland, where it joins the Tittabawassee River. But the best paddling is found in its middle reaches, where the river moves at a soothing pace through countryside that remains surprisingly unspoiled, especially above Mount Pleasant.

Many paddlers begin their excursions on the Chippewa at Coldwater Road Bridge in order to avoid the portages at Drew Dam and Isabella Dam immediately upstream. You cannot launch directly below the latter dam because of private property, but this bridge offers good access. Once you are underway, you will find a shallow (2 to 3 feet) and clear stream that passes through meadows and woodlands at a steady but unhurried clip. The banks—generally spaced 40 feet apart or so—feature dense vegetation and occasional homes and cottages. At several points, openings between the shoreline and fallen trees are pretty narrow, but paddlers with basic maneuvering abilities should be able to glide through without difficulty.

Below Deerfield County Park—which is just about the only good camping spot above Mount Pleasant because of the prevalence of private property along much of the river corridor— the Chippewa widens (to 50 to 75 feet) and deepens a bit as it passes over sandy riverbed. For an hour or so below the park, large homes appear periodically along the shoreline. But the river then quickens and enters less developed woodlands. This faster water subsides again, but the surrounding countryside remains quiet and pretty, with an abundance of waterfowl. About 5 miles above Mount Pleasant, Meridian Park appears

Chippewa River

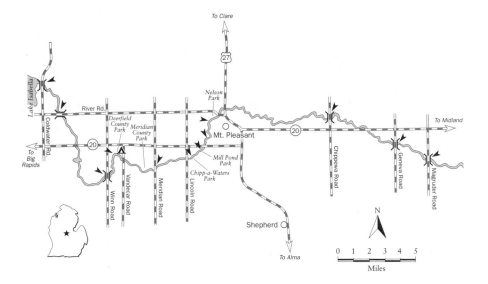

along the northern (left) shoreline. This is a good launch/picnic site that is sometimes used as a take-out by day-trippers who want to avoid entering the Mount Pleasant area.

Below Meridian Park, you will pass under one more bridge (Lincoln Road) before hitting Chipp-A-Waters Park, the first of several Mount Pleasant–area parks. This park on the town's western outskirts provides good access and picnicking facilities. The second of the city's shoreline parks—Mill Pond Park—lies 0.5 mile or so farther downstream. The main parking area at Mill Pond is actually located on satellite ponds of the river itself. The inlet to these ponds is not marked on the river, however, so paddlers who intend to use this spot as a take-out need to pay attention. As you pass under M–20, look for an inlet on the left. If you see a wooden bench platform on the left, you've gone too far. Turn back and look for a watery corridor connecting the river and the ponds a few hundred feet upstream.

If you are continuing downstream, however, take out on the left just past the aforementioned platform, where a dirt road swoops down near the river. Just downstream from this take-out spot, the Chippewa forks into two streams, with dams on both forks. Use the dirt road as a portage trail, following the river as it flows downstream. After passing through a gravel parking lot at the top of a hill, you can put in just below the lowhead dam that blocks the left fork.

The Chippewa's two forks rejoin again a short distance downstream. At that point, you will have a 0.5-mile float to reach Island Park, another island that splits the river in two. Negotiating your way past this popular and attractive park is also a little tricky. During our last paddle through this section of the Chippewa, a massive tree had fallen across the stream 100 feet or so upstream of the island, completely blocking the river corridor. Strong paddlers can lift their canoe and gear over the tree, but the trunk's enormous size does make this a difficult task (especially if you are paddling a loaded boat). The only other option as long as this monster tree remains in place is to make an illegal portage on the left shoreline (this land is railroad property that has been posted).

If this tree is eventually removed, the final approach to Island Park can still be recognized by the presence of a railroad bridge that spans the river just upstream of the island. At the island itself, the left channel of the Chippewa veers off at a 90-degree angle and rushes over a rocky riverbed for 50 feet or so. This jumbled water offers a class II ride at high water, but should be portaged at all other times. Most canoeists take the right channel around the island anyway. This route is cluttered with tree limbs initially, but as you float downstream, the river clears and provides easy access to several nice picnic sites. The forks then reunite at the north end of the 50-acre island.

The last of the city parks—Nelson Park—appears on the left bank of the Chippewa less than 0.5 mile later, just below the Broadway Road Bridge. From Nelson Park to the outskirts of Mount Pleasant proper, the river runs slow and deep and the roar of traffic is ever-present. The river then changes its northward course and runs east through a region of woodlands and farms, gradually leaving the ruckus of the city behind. Occasional portages around fallen trees and logjams may be necessary in this section, but the river remains generally undemanding.

As the Chippewa continues its eastward passage, it widens to 80 to 100 feet and becomes more gravelly. It also passes under a succession of bridges that provide poor or nonexistent access to the river. Chippewa Road Bridge—located about 12 miles east of Mount Pleasant—offers good access, however, and it is often used as a take-out. Immediately below this bridge is an extended run of light rapids that kick up substantial standing waves during high-water periods. The Chippewa then returns to its laid-back ways, ambling along at a relaxed pace through quiet lowlands dotted with homes. You can then take out a few miles farther downstream, at either Geneva Road or Magruder Road, in order to avoid the long, slow float into Midland.

Access: Coldwater Road Bridge sits just downstream from Lake Isabella Dam; take M–20 west out of Mount Pleasant for 10 miles, then go north on Coldwater Road for 4 miles. The bridge on **River Road** is 10 miles west of Mount Pleasant. To reach **Winn Road Bridge**, take M–20 west from Mount Pleasant for about 6 miles, then travel south on Winn for 2 miles. **Deerfield County Park** is on the south side of M–20, 5 miles west of Mount Pleasant. To reach **Meridian County Park**, follow M–20 west from Mount Pleasant for about 3 miles, then turn south on Meridian Road and go another mile. **Chipp-A-Waters Park** is on M–20 on the west side of Mount Pleasant. **Mill Pond Park** is just north of M–20 on Adams Street in Mount Pleasant. **Island Park** is sandwiched between Mosher and Pickard Streets in downtown Mount Pleasant, 1 mile west of Mission Street. **Nelson**

Fishing from a canoe during a pleasant day trip on the Chippewa River.

Park is located on Broadway Street in downtown Mount Pleasant, about 1 mile west of Mission Street. **Chippewa Road Bridge** can be reached by taking M–20 east for 6 miles, then traveling north on Chippewa for 1 mile. **Geneva Road Bridge** lies 1 mile south of M–20, about 10 miles east of Mount Pleasant. **Magruder Road Bridge** is 2 miles south of M–20, approximately 12 miles east of Mount Pleasant and 14 miles west of Midland.

Additional Help

MA & G grid: 58, C1 and D1–D4; 59, D5.

Camping: Deerfield County Park.

Food, gas, and lodging: Mount Pleasant, Shepherd, Midland.

For more information: Contact area liveries.

Canoe liveries: Buckley's Mountainside Canoe, Chippewa River Outfitters.

Access Point	Float Distance To Next Access Point
Coldwater Road Bridge	3 miles
River Road Bridge	7 miles
Winn Road Bridge	3 miles
Deerfield County Park	5 miles
Meridian County Park	5 miles
Chipp-A-Waters Park	0.5 mile
Mill Pond Park	0.5 mile
Island Park	0.5 mile
Nelson Park	15 miles
Chippewa Road Bridge	8 miles
Geneva Road Bridge	4 miles
Magruder Road Bridge	Take Out

16 Jordan River

Character: A fun, spirited river that winds through the gorgeous Jordan Valley.
Location: Runs from central Antrim County north into Lake Charlevoix in Charlevoix County.
Length: 24 miles.
Run: 9 miles, from Graves Crossing to Rogers Road.
Average run time: 3 hours.
Class: I.
Skill level: Beginner/intermediate.
Optimal flow: April–October.
Average gradient: 6 feet per mile.
Hazards: Occasional deep holes.
Fishing: This Blue Ribbon Trout Stream holds steelhead, brook trout, brown trout, and coho salmon.
Maps: USGS 1:25,000 - Mancelona-MI, Chestonia-MI, Boyne City-MI, Ellsworth-MI; 1:100,000 - Charlevoix-MI; 1:250,000 - Cheboygan-MI.

The paddling: The Jordan River offers one of the finest canoeing experiences in the entire state. Michigan's first federally designated "Wild and Scenic River," the Jordan tumbles through a picturesque valley of maple, aspen, cedar, and birch forestlands that is particularly breathtaking in the fall. Blessed with beautifully clear water and plenty of top-notch fishing holes, the stream also features a swift current and tight bends that will delight experienced paddlers. The Jordan's modest length makes it ideal for a morning or afternoon excursion, and if you're like us, you'll want to return to its waters again and again.

Paddlers can put in at Graves Crossing Bridge, which is within easy walking distance of a Mackinaw State Forest campground. From Graves Crossing to Old State Road, the river is swift and clear and 30 to 40 feet wide. Tight bends and the moderate gradient combine to make this stretch a briskly paced one. The water might lick your gunwales in a couple of spots, but if you have basic maneuvering skills you shouldn't have any trouble. Stands of pine and cedar crowd the shoreline along this section of the river.

As you approach Old State Road, you will spot twin culverts that funnel the river underneath the bridge. Pick one culvert and stick with it. Once you emerge on the other side, you will find yourself in a deep pool of swirling crosscurrents as the river gathers itself together again. This jumble of riffles and eddies may dump inexperienced canoeists on occasion, but capable paddlers will be able to negotiate it without difficulty.

From Old State Bridge (also known as Chestonia Bridge) to the bridge at Webster Road, the river widens to 50 to 60 feet and the forest—composed primarily of hardwoods now—retreats from the Jordan's banks. The current also slows through this low-lying area, making it the mellowest stretch on the river. From Webster Road to Rogers Road, the river narrows to 40 to 50 feet and quickens again. This portion of the Jordan remains a peace-

Jordan River

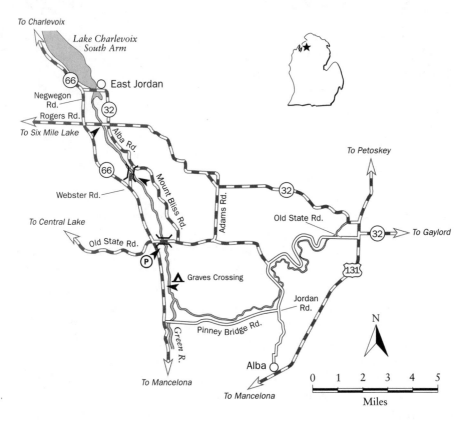

ful and scenic float, but civilization does encroach a bit in the way of scattered cottages and the murmur of distant traffic.

Some paddlers continue on from the Rogers Road Bridge to Lake Charlevoix (where you can take out at a public boat ramp on the left just past the M–32 bridge), but this stretch is not really worth doing. Below Rogers Road the river opens into a marshy area that has little scenery, a mucky bottom, and occasional strong winds that can push weaker paddlers around. Better to take out at Rogers Road, which has easy access and ample parking.

Access: Four major access sites to the Jordan River are all easily reachable from M–66. **Graves Crossing** is located approximately 9 miles south of East Jordan off M–66. **Old State Road Bridge** (also known as **Chestonia Bridge**) lies 0.5 mile east of M–66, about 6 miles south of East Jordan. **Webster Road Bridge** can be reached by taking M–66 south out of East Jordan for about 3 miles, then following Webster Road east for less than 1 mile. **Rogers Road Bridge** lies about 1.5 miles south of East Jordan, approximately 1 mile east of the juncture of Rogers Road and M–66 (also known as Norwegen Road through here).

Much of the scenic Jordan River corridor is lined with cedars.

Additional Help

MA & G grid: 81, 7C and 7D.

Camping: 10 sites are available at the newly refurbished Graves Crossing state forest campground.

Food, gas, and lodging: East Jordan, Mancelona, Boyne City, Gaylord.

For more information: Mackinaw State Forest.

Canoe liveries: Swiss Hideaway, Jordan Valley Outfitters.

Access Point	Float Distance To Next Access Point
Graves Crossing	3 miles
Old State Road Bridge (Chestonia Bridge)	3 miles
Webster Road Bridge	3 miles
Rogers Road Bridge	Take Out

Little Manistee River

Character: A quick and narrow river that winds through Manistee National Forest, this favorite of local anglers sees relatively light paddling traffic.

Location: Begins in northwestern Lake County and passes westward through Mason and Manistee Counties to Manistee Lake.

Length: 67 miles.

Run: 23.5 miles from Fox Bridge to Stronach Bridge.

Average run time: 7–10 hours.

Class: I.

Skill level: Beginner; intermediate between Nine Mile Bridge and Six Mile Bridge.

Optimal flow: May–June.

Average gradient: 6 feet per mile (14 feet per mile between Nine Mile Bridge and Six Mile Bridge).

Hazards: Frequent sweepers and submerged logs; several portages around fallen trees below Nine Mile Bridge.

Fishing: Top-notch habitat for steelhead and brown trout.

Maps: USGS 1:25,000 - Manistee-MI, Star Corners-MI, Udell-MI, Peacock-MI; 1:100,000 - Manistee-MI, Cadillac-MI; 1:250,000 - Manitowoc-MI, Traverse City-MI.

The paddling: The Little Manistee is an attractive stream that offers good paddling for competent canoeists looking to escape for a day trip or overnight excursion. Yet the allure of other nearby rivers (Pere Marquette, Manistee, and Pine) keeps paddling traffic relatively light. Even on summer weekends, the hordes of canoeists that routinely descend on the river's better-known neighbors are absent from the Little Manistee. But you will still need to keep an eye out for anglers, for this is one of the Lower Peninsula's more popular trout streams.

The upper reaches of the Little Manistee are impassable by canoe, but by the time the river reaches Fox Bridge on Bass Lake Road, it has widened and deepened sufficiently for basic maneuvering. In the first half dozen miles or so below Fox Bridge, the river passes through a mix of private and public woodlands. This stretch of shallow water is pocked with sweepers and submerged logs, but also features two scenic U.S. Forest Service campgrounds (Driftwood Valley and Bear Track) that can be utilized for overnight trips.

Below Bear Track, the stream moves along at a moderate clip over a mostly sand river bottom through rugged forestland. Occasional sweepers and low-hanging branches are likely to snare novice paddlers, and the river, which maintains a usual width of 30 to 40 feet, offers only 6 feet or so of passage between obstructions at a couple of spots. Nonetheless, canoeists with basic skills should be able to negotiate this stretch without getting wet. Between Bear Track and Nine Mile Bridge, large tracts of private property severely limit the number of available shoreline campsites. Canoeists determined to progress beyond Bear Track before making camp will find a smattering of good sites on public land through this stretch, but these are located on high bluffs overlooking the river.

Little Manistee River

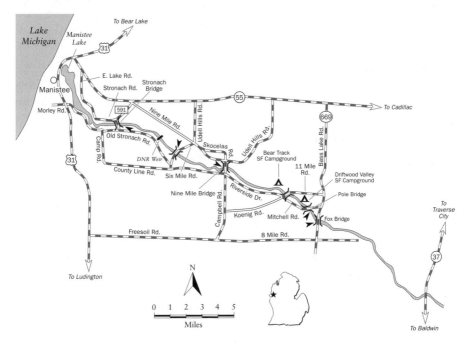

Beginning canoeists will want to take out at Nine Mile Bridge, but for veteran paddlers, the 5 miles between Nine Mile Bridge and Six Mile Bridge are home to the river's most lively and challenging water. The current remains moderate below Nine Mile Bridge for a mile or so, but then picks up markedly. For the next few miles, you can look forward to strong paddling on fast water that features a couple runs of class I rapids, narrow chutes, an array of obstacles (stumps, submerged rocks, and fallen trees), and many tight horseshoe bends. The turns through here are particularly challenging, as the fast current works to push you toward the sweepers and tag alders that lurk on the outside banks. Skilled paddlers will enjoy this portion of the river; beginners who decide to brave it will likely emerge at Six Mile Bridge somewhat worse for wear, and they should tie their gear down so they don't lose it if they dump.

In the last mile or so above Six Mile Bridge, the current slows somewhat, although many obstructions remain. Occasional portages over or around fallen trees will likely be necessary, and thick shoreline vegetation, a still-moderate current, and occasional deeper holes may make such maneuvers trickier than usual.

Many paddlers take out at Six Mile Bridge, in part because the remainder of the Little Manistee can seem anti-climactic after negotiating the challenges of the previous few miles. For those who choose to paddle on, the river offers a slow float through a sand-bottomed riverbed that widens to as much as 100 feet in spots. A DNR weir between Six Mile Bridge and Stronach Road Bridge requires a portage on the right bank. This offers the last decent take-out spot before the stream empties into Manistee Lake.

Access: Paddlers can put in at several points that feature adequate access and parking. To reach **Fox Bridge** from U.S. Highway 31, take Freesoil Road (which turns into Eight Mile Road) 15 miles east from its juncture with U.S. 31 to Bass Lake Road; take Bass Lake north to the bridge. To reach **Pole Bridge**, continue north on Bass Lake Road past Fox Bridge for 1 mile to Mitchell Road and turn west; the bridge lies 0.5 mile down the road. **Driftwood Valley Campground** is directly off Mitchell Road between Bass Lake Road and 11 Mile Road (identified on some maps as 18 Mile Bridge Road). **Bear Track Campground** is on 11 Mile Road, 2 miles west of Bass Lake Road (County Road 669). **Nine Mile Bridge** can be reached by taking Freesoil Road 8 miles east from its juncture with U.S. 31 to Campbell Road. Turn north on Campbell and drive 5 miles to the bridge. If attempting to reach the bridge from the north, take M–55 east from its junction with U.S. 31 for 4 miles to Nine Mile Bridge Road and turn south. Follow Nine Mile Bridge Road for approximately 7 miles to Campbell Road; turn south on Campbell and drive for less than a mile to reach the bridge. Another option is to take M–55 until it meets with Udell Hills Road (note that Udell Hills Road loops to meet M–55 at two different points). Take either loop of Udell Hills Road south to Nine Mile Bridge Road, which connects the two loops. Follow Nine Mile Bridge Road to Campbell Road and turn south on Campbell to reach the bridge. **Six Mile Bridge** is located on Six Mile Bridge Road, 1 mile north from its junction with Old Stronach Road and County Line Road, and less than a mile south from its intersection with Little River Road. To reach **Stronach Road Bridge**, take U.S. 31 south out of Manistee for 1 mile to Stronach Road, then go east for approximately 2 miles.

Additional Help

MA & G grid: 65, B4–B7 and C5–C7

Camping: Driftwood Valley U.S. Forest Service Campground (19 rustic sites) and Bear Track U.S. Forest Service Campground (20 sites) are located on the Little Manistee. Driftwood Valley lies off Mitchell Road between Bass Lake Road and 11 Mile Road (identified on some maps as 18 Mile Bridge Road). Bear Track lies off 11 Mile Road, 2 miles west of its juncture with Bass Lake Road.

Food, gas, and lodging: Manistee, Irons, Stronach.

For more information: Huron-Manistee National Forest.

Canoe liveries: Pine Creek Lodge.

Anglers try their luck on the Little Manistee River.

Access Point	Float Distance To Next Access Point
Fox Bridge	1 mile
Pole Bridge	0.5 mile
Driftwood Valley Campground	3 miles
Bear Track Campground	7 miles
Nine Mile Bridge	5 miles
Six Mile Bridge	7 miles
Stronach Bridge	Take Out

18 # Little Muskegon River

Character: Pleasant and scenic, the Little Muskegon receives little pressure because of its lack of shoreline camping options and log-strewn river corridor.

Location: Southern Mecosta County, northwestern Montcalm County, and eastern Newaygo County.

Length: 44 miles.

Run: 26 miles, from Morley to Croton Dam.

Average run time: 9–12 hours.

Class: I.

Skill level: Intermediate.

Optimal flow: May–October.

Average gradient: 6 feet per mile.

Hazards: Logs and other obstructions; occasional pockets of deep water.

Fishing: Anglers roam the Little Muskegon in search of smallmouth bass, trout, and perch.

Maps: USGS 1:25,000 - Howard City-MI, Tift Corner-MI, Croton-MI; 1:100,000 - Cedar Springs-MI; 1:250,000 - Midland-MI.

The paddling: In some ways, the Little Muskegon River is overlooked among Manistee National Forest rivers. Whereas the Pine, the Pere Marquette, and the Manistee have emerged as major paddling destinations over the years—in part because of the numerous access sites and public campgrounds that are maintained along their shores—the unassuming Little Muskegon has chugged along in peaceful obscurity, relatively unnoticed but for a small contingent of western Michigan paddlers. This state of affairs is unlikely to change anytime soon, especially since the 1999 closure of the Little Muskegon Dispersed Camping Area, an attractive rustic camping facility that fell victim to local complaints about excessive partying.

Nonetheless, the Little Muskegon is worth considering as a paddling destination, especially on those summer weekends when hordes of livery customers clog the Pere Marquette and other streams located farther north. Nestled in the national forest's southernmost ramparts, the river offers extensive woodlands of oak, maple, pine, and aspen, and bountiful opportunities for wildlife viewing (just try to catch a glimpse of a blue heron, deer, or beaver on the Pere Marquette or Pine on a hot summer Saturday afternoon). In addition, the waterway lies only an hour of so north of Grand Rapids, which makes it a great day-trip option for paddlers from that region.

The Little Muskegon is nominally navigable from Altona to Morley, but this 11-mile stretch is shallow and brush-strewn. A wiser course of action is to put in at the Old U.S. Highway 31 (Federal Road) Bridge that runs through Morley or at Tall Pines Campground, located 1 mile west of Morley. From here to Amy School Bridge (Long Road), the river moves at a moderate clip past overgrown shorelines of tag alder, pine, and hardwood forest. The river ranges from 1 to 3 feet deep through this upper portion, and features a

Little Muskegon River

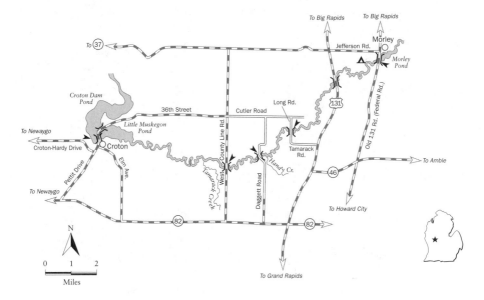

bed of mixed sand, gravel, and stones that is representative of the entire stream. It also has numerous obstacles in the form of fallen trees and logs that sometimes span the entire length of the stream. Paddlers should thus be prepared for occasional portages. Unfortunately, this section of the Little Muskegon also features a disheartening amount of garbage (tires, appliances, Styrofoam fragments, etc.), especially in the first hour or so below Morley Dam.

The put-in spot at the Dagget Road Bridge lies 4 miles downstream from Long Road. This section of the river is extremely twisty and includes a number of spots at which strong current and fallen trees can combine to cause trouble for inexperienced paddlers. Cottages pop up with more frequency along the 3-mile stretch from Dagget Road to West County Line Road (Newcosta Avenue), but this section is relatively clear of obstacles. The bridge at West County Line Road sees a lot of activity from canoeists, as it is the last access site before Croton Pond 9 miles downstream. This latter segment presents the river's best canoeing, as Tamarack Creek gives the stream a notable infusion of water volume. Here the Little Muskegon winds through high, wooded banks, rushing over longish stretches of light rapids and around sharp bends at a brisk pace. This portion of the river is comparatively clear of logjams, too, further adding to the fun. The current slows as you approach Little Muskegon Pond, an area of low marshlands. The Croton Dam Landing site lies on the southwest shore of Croton Pond, which sees a fair amount of motorboat traffic.

All in all, the Little Muskegon's quick current and occasional logjams make it unsuitable for novice paddlers. If you're looking to take a friend or child for their first spin in a

Taking time out to drop a line in the water during a trip down the Little Muskegon River.

canoe, this is not the river to select. For reasonably proficient canoeists who don't mind hoisting their boat over the occasional deadfall, however, this rough little beauty is worth checking out.

Access: To reach the **Old U.S. 31 Bridge**, take the Morley exit off of U.S. 131 and drive east for 2 miles. **Tall Pines Campground** is located midway between Morley and U.S. 131 off Jefferson Road. To reach **Amy School Bridge**, take M–540 (Tamarack Road) west from U.S. 131 for 1 mile, then drive north on **Long Road** for 1 mile. The bridge on **Dagget Road** can be reached by taking U.S. 131 to M–82 at Howard City. Go west on M–82 for 1 mile, then north on Dagget for 3 miles to reach the bridge. **West County Line Road Bridge** lies 3 miles north of M–82, about 5 miles west of Howard City. **Croton Dam Landing** can be reached by taking Croton Drive east out of Newaygo for 7 miles or Elm Avenue north from M–82 for about 5 miles.

Additional Help

MA & G grid: 46, A2–A4.

Camping: Options are very limited, given the closure of the Little Muskegon Dispersed Camping Area, the overgrown shoreline, and extensive private landholdings. The best camping alternative for canoeists is the privately owned Tall Pines Campground, located 1 mile west of Morley off Jefferson Road.

Food, gas, and lodging: Morley, Newaygo, Howard City, Croton.

For more information: Manistee National Forest.

Canoe liveries: Tall Pines Campground.

Access Point	Float Distance To Next Access Point
Old U.S. 31 Bridge (Federal Road)	0.5 mile
Tall Pines Campground	8 miles
Amy School Bridge (Long Road)	4 miles
Dagget Road Bridge	3 miles
West County Line Road Bridge (Newcosta Avenue)	10.5 miles
Croton Dam Landing	Take Out

19 Ludington Canoe Pathway

Character: Located in one of Michigan's most popular state parks, this canoe trail winds through placid marsh waters adorned with tall reeds and floating fields of lily pads.

Location: Ludington State Park's Hamlin Lake, in western Mason County.

Length: Approximately 6 miles round-trip.

Average run time: 2–4 hours.

Class: I.

Skill level: Beginner.

Hazards: Strong north or east winds can create rough paddling conditions on Hamlin Lake.

Fishing: Northern pike, muskie, bass, and walleye.

Maps: Brochures detailing the pathway route available through Ludington State Park.

The paddling: Ideal for a leisurely morning or afternoon paddle, the Ludington Canoe Pathway features a nice blend of open water and marshy waterways. Blessed with abundant populations of waterfowl—including swans, herons, geese, and ducks—the intimate ponds and bayous that comprise the pathway can easily conjure up an atmosphere reminiscent of far more remote northern settings. Of course, you're much more likely to catch a whiff of this northwoods ambience on a cool midweek morning paddle than on a sunny Saturday afternoon, when the trail can get pretty crowded.

The canoe trail begins at the Hamlin Lake canoe concession, located in the park's day-use area. From there you head east across the Big Sable River into Hamlin Lake proper. Keep to the shallow south shore and look for the numbered signs that serve to mark the trail (there are a total of sixteen markers scattered along the pathway). Sign number 4 marks Desperation Point, a hilly, sandy area that is a popular landing spot for swimming. From this point on, the shoreline trails away to the southeast and the lake gives way to shallow, stump-pocked bays and increasing stands of cattails and reeds.

Between markers 6 and 7, you will come to the first of two large, stump-filled coves, both of which are bordered by stands of reeds, pine trees, and white cedar. The first of these bays is a dead end, but the second—lying a short distance beyond marker 7—is the entranceway to the inland portion of the canoe trail. The pathway continues through the back (west) end of the bay to a watery corridor that opens into a small pond. Follow the western shoreline of the pond to a 100-foot portage that takes you into another pond, dubbed "John's Pond." A short paddle across the murky waters of John's Pond brings you to another short portage that offers access to a landlocked pond. Follow the west shoreline to the next portage, which will take you into a cove that is a major spawning area for carp in the spring. Marker 12, which takes you back into Hamlin Lake, sits on the eastern edge of these carp ponds.

Once on Hamlin Lake again, follow the shoreline into the next bay, hugging the south shore. In the area of marker 14, you will encounter a line of cedar trees along an old logging road. You can either push your boat through a stand of dense reeds along the north

Ludington Canoe Pathway

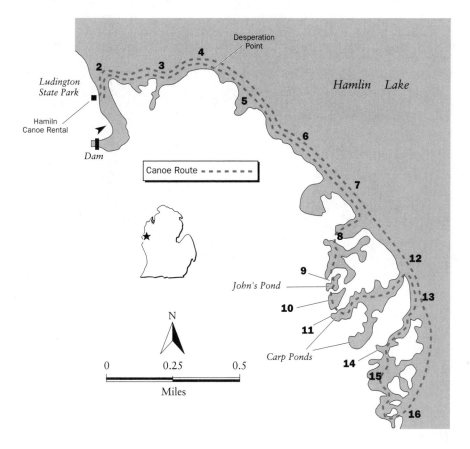

end of the road or make a quick portage across the road itself. From here the water opens up again as the pathway continues southward to the south boundary of the park, where it rejoins Hamlin Lake. When you reach marker 16, you can either turn north and take the shoreline back to the Hamlin Beach area or backtrack through the inland coves and ponds through which you just passed.

On most days, the Ludington Canoe Pathway offers an ideal outing for families and paddlers of limited abilities. The trail is relatively well marked, and the water on Hamlin Lake is often quiet and easy to paddle. The lake does see motorized boat traffic that can churn up the water somewhat, however, and strong winds out of the north and east can create choppy conditions and headwinds that may prove too much for beginning paddlers to handle. Given these realities, a check of the weather forecast prior to departure is a good idea. Finally, deer flies and other insects can be brutal in the marshy inland areas during certain times of year. Make sure your party is well supplied with insect repellent before you head out.

A marker on the canoe trail at Ludington State Park leads paddlers deep into the marsh.

Access: Ludington State Park is located 8 miles north of Ludington at the end of M–116. The Ludington Canoe Pathway begins at the park's canoe livery near the swimming beach.

Additional Help

MA & G grid: 64, D3.

Camping: Ludington State Park (298 sites with modern amenities) and Lake Michigan Recreation Area (99 sites).

Food, gas, and lodging: Ludington, Manistee.

For more information: Ludington State Park.

Canoe liveries: Hamlin Canoe Rental.

20 Manistee River

Character: An undemanding river that features many campgrou
banks, the Manistee is ideally suited for family camping outings.

Location: From headwaters in Antrim and Otsego Counties, the M
ford, Kalkaska, Missaukee, Wexford, and Manistee Counties before

Length: 175 miles.

Run: 160 miles, from Deward to Manistee Lake.

Average run time: 30–40 hours.

Class: Flatwater.

Skill level: Beginner.

Optimal flow: May–October.

Average gradient: 4 feet per mile.

Hazards: Deeper holes of 8 to 12 feet below CCC Bridge, with extended deep stretches in lower reaches.

Fishing: The area below Tippy Dam is known for steelhead and salmon fishing, while upper sections attract anglers on the prowl for brook, brown, and rainbow trout; the river is more difficult to wade below Lower Sharon Bridge and becomes impossible farther downstream.

Maps: USGS 1:25,000 - Lake Arrowhead-MI, Frederic-MI, Lake Margrethe-MI, Fletcher-MI, Sharon-MI, Stittsville-MI, Morey-MI, Arlene-MI, Manton-MI, Mesick, NE-MI, Harrietta-MI, Yuma-MI, Marilla-MI, Brethren-MI, Onekama-MI, Parkdale-MI, Manistee-MI; 1:100,000 - Traverse City-MI, Cadillac-MI, Manistee-MI; 1:250,000 - Traverse City-MI, Manitowoc-MI.

The paddling: A top-tier fishing stream that also ranks as one of Michigan's more popular paddling rivers, the Manistee receives considerable pressure from various users. But the length of the river—which was a major waterway for Native Americans, fur traders, and lumberjacks in centuries past—eases congestion at all but the most popular spots. In addition, the presence of dozens of access sites, a multitude of camping options, and miles of undeveloped shoreline ensure a pretty wide dispersal of people.

The Manistee becomes navigable by canoe downstream from Deward, a ghost town located in the northwest corner of Crawford County. For the next 25 miles or so, you can expect a slow but pretty river with a width that ranges from 35 to 70 feet and a depth of 1 to 4 feet (with occasional deeper holes) over a sand and gravel bottom. Below the CCC state forest campground, the canoe flotillas that populate the upper reaches on summer weekends will likely diminish in number, and you will find yourself floating past rolling hillsides of maple, cedar, birch, and aspen.

As you proceed downstream, the Manistee will continue to widen (to 100 feet in some spots), its slow but heavy current carving swimming holes out of its largely sand bottom on some outside turns. These holes, which can reach depths of 10 to 12 feet during high-water periods, are a common feature of the river from here on out, so parties with poor swimmers should take appropriate precautions. From Lower Sharon Bridge to the U.S.

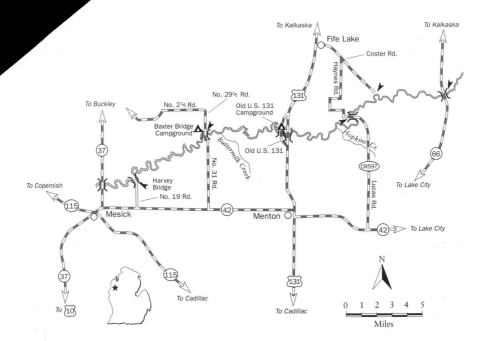

Highway 131 bridge, the Manistee passes through scenic and largely undeveloped terrain that ranges in character from high sandy bluffs to peaceful lowlands. Much of the river corridor here is part of Pere Marquette State Forest, and shoreline camping sites are plentiful.

Below the U.S. 131 bridge, paddlers floating the Manistee can settle into a relaxed routine as the river saunters westward through a valley of sandy bluffs and hardwood forests to the backwaters created by Hodenpyl Dam. This 25-mile stretch features a moderate current as well as occasional sharp turns and strainers on outside bends, but paddlers able to execute basic maneuvers should have little difficulty. Potential riverbank tent sites remain frequent through here as well, although three primitive state forest campgrounds ideally situated between M–66 and M–37 (Smithville, Chase Creek, and Indian Crossing) have all been closed in recent years.

Most paddlers end their Manistee trips before reaching Hodenpyl Dam Pond, an 1,800-acre impoundment that is enormously popular with panfish anglers. If you are interested in continuing on or beginning a trip from this point, keep in mind that the pond is about 6 miles long and can be troublesome for novice paddlers on windy days. The portage at the dam lies on the north side of the impoundment. After lugging your canoe to the other side of the dam and returning to the water, you'll continue southward through the scenic woodlands of Manistee National Forest.

Ten miles downstream from Hodenpyl Dam is Tippy Dam Pond, the backwater for

Manistee River

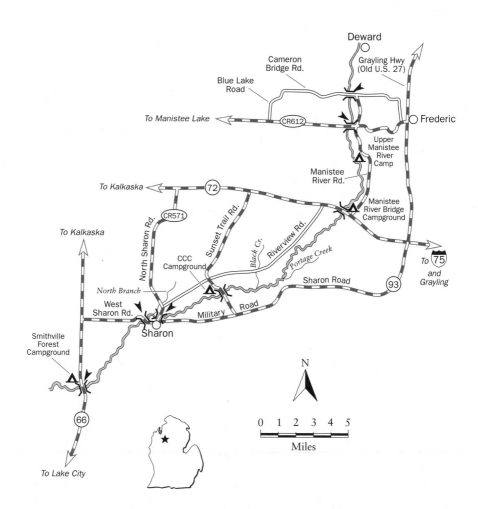

Tippy Dam. At this point the Manistee joins with the Pine River, its cousin to the south. You can either take out at Red Bridge or continue on across the pond's 6-mile length to the dam. The Tippy Dam portage lies to the right. From Tippy Dam to Manistee Lake, the river continues to widen and deepen. This lower section of the river, which winds through broad marshlands, is popular with boating anglers. Paddlers without a big interest in fishing are unlikely to be enthralled by this final stretch of the stream, although the area does support a wide variety of waterfowl and other wildlife. Please note that if you plan to use any of the main access sites below Tippy Dam Pond (High Bridge, Blacksmith Bayou, Bear Creek), you will first need to obtain a vehicle pass from the Forest Service offices (these access sites are part of Manistee National Forest's recreation fee demonstration project).

Manistee River

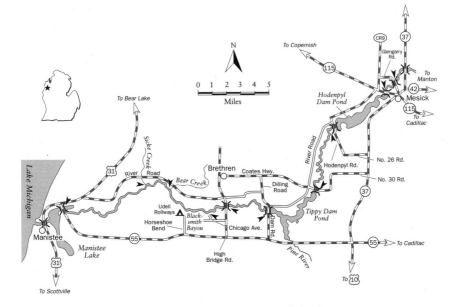

All in all, the Manistee is an attractive destination that accommodates both afternoon paddles and camping expeditions of a week or more. The river corridor remains largely undeveloped along much of its length, and the Manistee's mild temperament makes it an attractive alternative for groups with members of varying abilities. But you should keep in mind that the river's undemanding nature, its accessibility, and the presence of several canoe liveries make it one of the state's more popular waterways with rowdy weekend partiers.

Access: Put-in/take-out spots with good parking are numerous. To reach **County Road 612 Bridge** or **Cameron Bridge** from Grayling, drive 7 miles west out of town to Manistee River Road and turn north; CR–612 lies 7 miles up the road, and Cameron Road an additional 2 miles beyond that. Both bridges are located less than a mile to the west on their respective roads. To drive to **Upper Manistee River Campground**, follow CR–612 west out of Frederic for 3 miles, then drive south on Manistee River Road for 2 miles. **Manistee River Bridge Campground** lies 3 miles south of Upper Manistee River Campground on Manistee River Road. To reach **CCC Bridge** from Grayling, take M–72 west for 6 miles to Sunset Trail Road; the bridge (and the CCC Campground) lie 8 miles south on Sunset Trail. The access sites at **Upper Sharon Bridge** and **Lower Sharon Bridge** are close to one another; the first bridge is on North Sharon Road, 9 miles south of its juncture with M–72, while Lower Sharon Bridge is on West Sharon Road, 4 miles east of its juncture with M–66. The **M–66 Bridge** lies 15 miles south of Kalkaska on M–66. To reach **Baxter Bridge**, take M–42 west out of Manton for 6 miles to No. 31 Road; turn north and follow for 5 miles, after which the road curves west and joins with No. 29½ Road; the bridge lies less than a mile north on No. 29½ Road. The **M–115 Bridge** lies 1 mile west of Mesick on M–115. The parking area at **Hodenpyl Dam** can be reached from Mesick by taking M–115 west for 2 miles to Hodenpyl Road; the lot lies 5 miles west on the south side of Hodenpyl Road. **Red Bridge** lies 8 miles east of Brethren on Coates Highway.

In addition to the above-mentioned access sites, you can also put in or take out at **Coster Road Bridge, Lucas Road Bridge, Harvey Bridge, Glengary Bridge, M–37 Bridge, Tippy Dam, Rainbow Bend, Blacksmith Bayou, High Bridge**, and **Bear Creek**. Consult the map for directions to these sites.

Additional Help

MA & G grid: 65, B4–B7; 66, B1 and A2–A4; 67, A5; 75, D5–D7; 76, C1–C2.

Camping: Upper Manistee River State Forest Campground (30 sites) and Manistee River Bridge State Forest Campground (23 sites) are maintained by Au Sable State Forest. CCC Bridge Campground (32 sites), Old U.S. Highway 131 State Forest Campground (26 sites), and Baxter Bridge State Forest Campground (21 sites) are all managed by Pere Marquette State Forest. In addition, Seaton Creek National Forest Campground (17 sites) and Udell Rollways National Forest Campground (23 sites) can be used by paddlers exploring the lower Manistee. Finally, primitive shoreline camping is available on public land along much of the river corridor.

Food, gas, and lodging: Grayling, Manton, Mesick, Manistee, Kalkaska.

For more information: Huron-Manistee National Forest, Au Sable State Forest, Pere Marquette State Forest.

Canoe liveries: Chippewa Landing, Pine Creek Lodge, Pine River Paddlesports Center, Smithville Landing, Wilderness Canoe Trips.

Access Point	Float Distance To Next Access Point
Cameron Bridge	2 miles
County Road 612	3.5 miles
Upper Manistee CG	5 miles
Manistee River Bridge CG	0.5 mile
M–72 Bridge	14 miles
CCC Bridge	8 miles

Access Point	Float Distance To Next Access Point
Upper Sharon Bridge	2 miles
Lower Sharon Bridge	9 miles
M–66 Bridge	11 miles
Lucas Road Bridge	13 miles
U.S. 131 Bridge	10 miles
Baxter Bridge	20 miles
Harvey Bridge (No. 19 Road)	5 miles
M–37 Bridge	1.5 miles
Glengary Bridge	1.5 miles
M–115 Bridge	5 miles
Hodenpyl Dam	10 miles
Red Bridge (Coates Highway)	5 miles
Tippy Dam	6 miles
High Bridge	8 miles
Bear Creek	14 miles
M–55 Bridge	Take Out

21 Manitou Islands

see map on page 134

Character: Two rugged wilderness islands within the Sleeping Bear Dunes National Lakeshore.

Location: These Lake Michigan islands lie about 8 miles northwest of Sleeping Bear Dunes mainland shoreline.

Size: North Manitou Island is nearly 8 miles long and a little over 4 miles wide and boasts 20 miles of shoreline. South Manitou Island is 3 miles long and about 2.5 miles wide, with approximately 12 miles of coastline.

Skill level: Intermediate.

Hazards: Heavy winds can create very rough conditions along exposed shoreline.

Maps: USGS 1:25,000 - South Manitou Island-MI, North Manitou Island-MI; 1:100,000 - Washington Island-MI, Charlevoix-MI; 1:250,000 - Escanaba-MI, Cheboygan-MI. NOAA chart 14912.

The paddling: North and South Manitou Islands are wonderful destinations for intrepid sea kayakers with a taste for solitude and exploration. Indeed, the size and remote location of these rugged islands make them ideal for multi-day or week-long excursions. South Manitou is the more developed and more frequently visited of the two islands, but both hold the promise of peaceful paddling and quiet camping under the stars.

The coastline of South Manitou is shaped like a lobster claw. It features fine sandy beaches, a nineteenth-century lighthouse, and the carcass of an old steel-hulled freighter—the *Francisco Morazan*—that ran aground in a 1960 storm on the southwest end of the island. Four decades later, Lake Michigan winds still whip through the exposed upper sections of the wreck. The island's interior, meanwhile, includes the remains of an 1800s-era farm settlement—including an old schoolhouse and cemetery—and miles of hiking trails that wind through picturesque woodlands. A special attraction for hikers is the so-called "Valley of the Giants," a stand of old-growth cedars on the island's southwest end.

Drumstick-shaped North Manitou Island, located northeast of its little sister, is girded by miles of low shoreline sand dunes backed by forests and overgrown orchards. These orchards are a reminder of an earlier era in the island's history, when it housed both farming homesteads and summer cottages. Today, the crumbling remains of these buildings and nineteenth-century lumber camps can still be found scattered across the island's interior, which is criss-crossed with 25 miles of unmaintained trails. A couple of these trails lead deep into the island's interior to Lake Manitou, a picturesque lake that is home to big bass (valid state fishing license required; daily limit of one bass, 18-inch minimum). Paddlers exploring North Manitou's coastline typically gravitate to the big dunes on the isle's northwest end or the fine beaches at its south end. You should note, however, that Dimmick's Point is a nesting area for endangered piping plovers and is thus off-limits from May 1 to August 15.

The picturesque South Manitou Island Light dates from the mid-1800s.

Finally, some paddlers plan trips that enable them to explore both of these scenic islands. But North and South Manitou are separated by 4 miles of open water. Great Lakes crossings of this length should only be attempted by sea kayakers with advanced skills.

Access: The Manitou Islands are separated from the Michigan mainland by the Manitou Passage, a watery expanse that has claimed dozens of ships over the centuries. This passage, which was a main route for Great Lakes steamers and other vessels of yesteryear, is now a state-protected preserve that is popular with scuba divers. Only expert sea kayakers should even consider making the 8-mile crossing from the mainland to the islands. This is especially true when winds sweep through the passage out of the southwest or northeast. You're better off to instead take advantage of the Leland-based ferry service that makes regular runs to and from both islands. Round-trip ferry rates are $22 per person and $20 per kayak.

The ferry makes daily trips to South Manitou throughout the summer, weather permitting (10:00 A.M. departure from mainland). It also visits the island in May, September, and October, but on a less frequent basis. The ferry service also goes to North Manitou seven days a week throughout the summer (10:00 A.M. departure from Leland). It also offers limited service to North Manitou in late spring and during the autumn months (an annual fall deer hunt on the island attracts heavy interest). As with the South Manitou ferry, service is occasionally suspended when storms roll through, so make sure you pack sufficient provisions for an extra day or two. Contact Manitou Island Transit for more information on ferry schedules for both islands.

Additional Help

MA & G grid: 72, A1–A2 and B1–B2.

Camping: Village Campground is the only established camping facility at North Manitou Island. It has eight campsites, an outhouse, and two fire rings (open fires are not permitted elsewhere on the island). The rest of the island is open to wilderness camping provided you obtain a backcountry camping permit on the mainland and set up camp at least 300 feet away from the shoreline's high-water mark or the island's inland waters and buildings. You should hang your food if you hope to outwit the racoons that prowl the island's interior. These bandits have a well-deserved reputation for both boldness and ingenuity, so take appropriate precautions. Finally, campers on North Manitou should note that potable water is available only at the ranger station.

On South Manitou Island, overnight visitors are limited to three campgrounds along its shoreline. The northernmost of these is Popple Campground (six sites), located about 3.7 miles from the island's lone dock facility. Bay Campground (twenty-two sites) lies only 0.5 mile northwest of the dock. The last facility, Weather Station Campground (seventeen sites), sits about 1.3 miles from the dock on the island's southern shore. All three of these rustic campgrounds are suitable for use by kayakers (Popple offers the most peace and quiet), but potable water is available only at the Weather Station and Bay facilities. Call ahead for reservations.

Food, gas, and lodging: Empire (on mainland).

For more information: Sleeping Bear Dunes National Lakeshore.

22 Muskegon River

Character: A sleepy section of Michigan's second-longest river that is ideal for family camping trips.

Location: Originates in central northern Michigan and flows through eight counties before emptying into Lake Michigan (the run described below passes through Roscommon, Missaukee, Clare, and Osceola Counties).

Length: 230 miles.

Run: 85 miles, from M–55 to Evart.

Average run time: 26–30 hours.

Class: Flatwater.

Skill level: Beginner.

Optimal flow: May–October.

Average gradient: 2 feet per mile.

Hazards: Occasional fallen trees in upper sections; deep water.

Fishing: Campers on the Muskegon can augment their dinner menu with fresh-caught brook and brown trout or smallmouth bass.

Maps: USGS 1:25,000 - Meads Landing-MI, Houghton Lake-MI, Merritt-MI, Moddersville-MI, Cooperton-MI, Prestle Creek, MI, Temple-MI, Lake NE-MI, Sears-MI, Evart-MI; 1:100,000 - Houghton Lake-MI, Cadillac-MI; 1:250,000 - Traverse City-MI.

The paddling: The Muskegon River is the friendly giant of Michigan rivers. It is the state's second-biggest river (next to the Grand), snaking its way for nearly 230 miles through the green forests of the northwestern Lower Peninsula before discharging into Lake Michigan. But despite its great size—it ultimately drains a watershed of more than 2,300 square miles—the Muskegon is a placid and peaceful waterway that doesn't want to make trouble for anyone. Instead, its mild current delivers paddlers through miles of quiet woodlands bursting with deer, otter, beaver, and assorted waterfowl. This is especially true in the stream's upper sections, where it runs through large tracts of state forestland. Indeed, the Muskegon's best extended canoe camping opportunities can be found in the 85-mile segment of river that stretches from M–55 to Evart.

A roadside park at the M–55 bridge offers good access to paddlers interested in exploring the Muskegon's uppermost reaches. From here to Cadillac Road, a dozen miles downstream, you will have to maneuver around blowdowns in the narrow (30 to 45 feet) river corridor. But below Cadillac Road, fallen trees and other obstacles begin to disappear, and the lackadaisical current takes the teeth out of the stray limbs that do remain.

As you continue downstream to Leota Bridge, the Muskegon has an average width of 50 to 60 feet and depth of 2 to 4 feet. Shoreline tent sites can be found through here amid the waterway's banks of dense green foliage, but this area is also popular with ORV users. Below Leota, however, paddlers have the riverbanks all to themselves.

Muskegon River

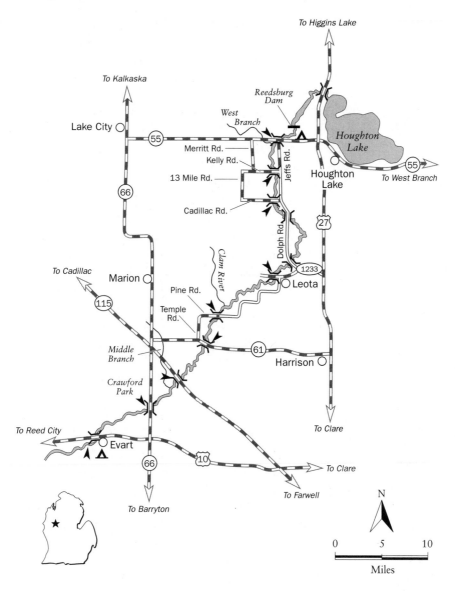

From Leota to Church Bridge on Pine Road, the river passes through heavily wooded lowlands and collects water from several creeks and streams, including the Clam River. The Muskegon's depth in this stretch ranges from 2 to 6 feet at normal water levels, and its width ranges from 60 to 80 feet. This is a pretty and peaceful stretch of water that can be completed in four to five hours of steady paddling, but you may have trouble capturing any vibes of serenity and well-being through here in midsummer, when biting flies and mosquitos can be merciless.

Summertime canoe and tubing traffic picks up on the Muskegon below M–61 and remains fairly strong all the way to M–115. But even so, pressure on the river does not approach what you will see on an average summertime Saturday on the Au Sable, the Rifle, or the Pine. The Muskegon continues to widen through here (to 150 feet or more), and some areas of the riverbed get very shallow during midsummer and other low-water periods (you may have to walk your boat through several extended sections if you're floating down the river in July or August). The river also exits Au Sable State Forest around M–115, severely diminishing shoreline camping opportunities farther downstream.

The Muskegon receives a big infusion of water just below M–115 from the Middle Branch River, but this does nothing to change the mainstream's dawdling character. In fact, the river slows to a real crawl between M–115 and M–66, an 8-mile section dotted with shoreline cabins and cottages. The current picks up a bit below the M–66 bridge, but remains mild-mannered as it continues on to Evart. You can take out in Evart at the township park, which is located between the first and second bridges spanning the river.

Below Evart, the Muskegon continues to offer easy paddling all the way to the rivermouth, 150 miles away. The river remains placid and undemanding (with the exception of a brief dose of class I–II water in Big Rapids), and much of the time it runs through quiet, attractive woodlands. But large dam reservoirs mar the section from U.S. Highway 131 to M–37, and camping options become less frequent as you move downstream.

Access: The roadside park at **M–55** is 6 miles west of Houghton Lake. To access the river at **Kelly Road (Hi-Lo Bridge)**, take Jeffs Road south from M–55 for 3 miles, then drive west on Kelly for a hundred yards or so. The **Cadillac Road** access at **Lowell Bridge** (also known as Dolph Bridge) also lies just a short distance west of Jeffs Road, about 6 miles south of M–55. **Dolph Road Bridge** is 0.5 mile south of the small village of Dolph. To reach **Jonesville Road Bridge**, take County Road 1233 west from U.S. Highway 27 for 4 miles, then go northwest on Jonesville for less than a mile. **Leota Bridge** is also on CR–1233, just west of Leota. To get to **Church Bridge**, follow M–61 west out of Harrison for 13 miles, then travel north on Temple Road for 3 miles and east on Pine Road for 1 mile. The **M–61 Bridge** is 12 miles west of Harrison. The **M–115 Bridge** is about a dozen miles northwest of the junction of M–115 and U.S. 10. **Crawford Park** is just downstream from the M–66 bridge, 3 miles north of U.S. 10. **Riverside Park** in Evart is sandwiched between 6 Mile Road and Main Street, just south of U.S. 10.

Additional Help

MA & G grid: 68, B2, C2, and D1; 67, D7; 57, A5–A7.

Camping: Shoreline camping spots can be found along much of the upper section of the river, which runs through large areas of state forest land. In addition, Pere Marquette State Forest maintains a campground at Reedsburg Dam that has 42 rustic sites, and several privately owned campgrounds line the river. A municipal campground can also be found in Evart, at Riverside Park.

Food, gas, and lodging: Houghton Lake, Evart.

For more information: Au Sable State Forest, Pere Marquette State Forest.

Canoe liveries: Duggan's Canoe Livery, Muskegon River Camp and Canoe, Old Log Resort, Sawmill Tube and Canoe Livery, Vic's Canoes, White Birch Canoe Trips.

Access Point	Float Distance To Next Access Point
M–55 Roadside Park	6 miles
Kelly Road (Hi-Lo Bridge)	6 miles
Cadillac Road (Lowell or Dolph Bridge)	2.5 miles
Dolph Road Bridge	9.5 miles
Jonesville Road Bridge	2 miles
CR–1233 (Leota Bridge)	18 miles
Pine Road (Church Bridge)	8 miles
M–61 Bridge	13 miles
M–115 Bridge	8 miles
Crawford Park (M–66)	12 miles
Evart (Riverside Park)	Take Out

The sleepy Muskegon River promises ample opportunities for viewing wildlife.

23 Negwegon State Park

Character: Remote and largely undeveloped, this park of sandy beaches and low-lying woodlands of pine and cedar is an outstanding day-trip option for Lake Huron paddlers.

Location: Lake Huron shoreline in southeastern Alpena County and northeastern Alcona County.

Size: This 1,800-acre park includes 6.5 miles of Great Lakes shoreline.

Skill level: Beginner/intermediate.

Hazards: Heavy winds from the north and east can create rough water offshore; shallow shoals and boulders along sections of the shoreline and around Bird and Scarecrow Islands.

Maps: USGS 1:25,000 - Black River-MI, South Point-MI; 1:100,000 - Hubbard Lake-MI; 1:250,000 - Tawas City-MI. NOAA chart 14864.

The paddling: Negwegon State Park stands as one of the last unspoiled stretches of Lake Huron shoreline in Michigan's Lower Peninsula. Named after a former Chippewa Indian chieftain, the park remains a quiet haven of woodland trails, sandy beaches, and shallow coves. This is due in large part to the state's laudable decision to go easy on amenities. Camping is prohibited in the park, and facilities amount to little more than vault toilets, a water spigot, trail signs, and a big gravel parking lot that remains half-empty on the park's busiest days.

Negwegon State Park will appeal to a variety of kayakers, but it is particularly welcoming to beginning paddlers. The shoreline consists of sand and cobblestone beaches for much of its 6.5-mile length, while the shallow waters of its coves and bays offer an ideal training ground. Paddlers exploring the coastline, however, do need to remain vigilant for shallow boulders and shoals that in some areas extend far from shore. Other popular destinations in the vicinity of the park include rocky South Point, a promontory that forms the southern boundary of Thunder Bay, and Hardwood Point, 3 miles farther up the coastline. In addition, some kayakers use the Ossineke State Forest Campground on Thunder Bay as a base camp from which to explore Negwegon. The 6-mile stretch from Ossineke Campground to South Point takes kayakers past an attractive wooded shoreline that includes portions of Mackinaw State Forest. Finally, some paddlers put in at the DNR access site at the mouth of the Black River, about 1 mile south of the state park. From here, you can paddle northward along the park shoreline all the way to Ossineke campground, 10 miles up the coast.

Negwegon is particularly appealing to paddlers whose outdoor interests include birding. South Point is an important stopover along the North American migratory flyway during the spring and fall, while the small islands of Bird Island and Scarecrow Island are designated bird sanctuaries that support rookeries of gulls, cormorants, and great blue herons. Loons and eagles frequent the area as well, adding to the wonderful avian mix. Bird Island lies only a few hundred yards offshore from the mainland, northwest of South Point. Scarecrow Island, however, sits approximately 2 miles northwest of South Point and should only be targeted by experienced paddlers. Both islands are girded with shoals that can

Negwegon State Park

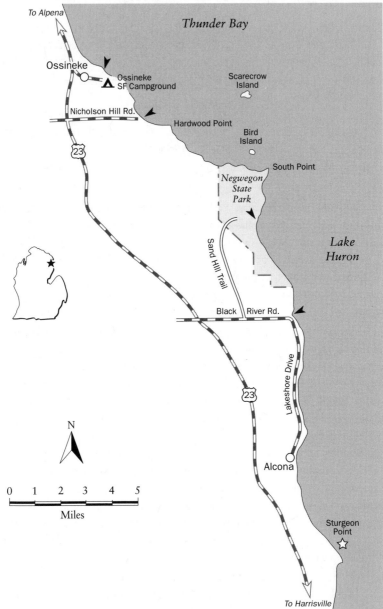

To Alpena

Thunder Bay

Ossineke

Ossineke
SF Campground

Scarecrow
Island

Nicholson Hill Rd.

Hardwood Point

Bird
Island

South Point

23

Negwegon
State
Park

Lake
Huron

Sand Hill Trail

Black River Rd.

Lakeshore Drive

23

N

Alcona

0 1 2 3 4 5

Miles

Sturgeon
Point

To Harrisville

churn up lumpy water on windy days. People are prohibited from setting foot on these islands, and kayakers interested in circling them should be sensitive to maintaining an appropriate distance between themselves and the islands' feathered inhabitants.

Access: To reach **Negwegon State Park**, take U.S. Highway 23 north from Harrisville about 12 miles to Black River Road. Drive east on Black River Road for 1.5 miles, then north on Sand Hill Trail (a two-track) for about 2.5 miles to the park entrance. Visitors should note, however, that two-wheel vehicles can become mired in Sand Hill Trail's sandy tracks during the summer months. The **Ossineke State Forest Campground** is located 2 miles east of Ossineke off U.S. 23 on Nicholson Hill Road. The **Black River** access site can be reached by taking U.S. 23 north out of Harrisville for 12 miles to Black River Road. Take Black River Road east for about 3 miles, then south on Lakeshore Drive for a few hundred feet to the parking lot.

Additional Help

MA & G grid: 79, A6–A7.

Camping: Camping is not permitted at Negwegon State Park. A few miles up the Lake Huron shoreline, however, Ossineke State Forest Campground maintains 42 sites for area visitors.

Food, gas, and lodging: Harrisville, Ossineke, Alpena.

For more information: Harrisville State Park.

Rentals/guided trips: None.

24 Old Mission Peninsula

Character: This scenic area near Traverse City offers several outstanding day trips with views of lighthouses, beaches, and hillsides covered with orchards and vineyards.

Location: Grand Traverse Bay north of Traverse City in the northwestern Lower Peninsula.

Size: Over 40 miles of coastline.

Skill level: Beginner/intermediate.

Hazards: Cold, deep water; northerly winds can create high waves.

Maps: USGS 1:25,000 - Traverse City SE-MI, Williamsburg-MI, Mapleton-MI, Elk Rapids-MI; 1:100,000 - Traverse City-MI; 1:250,000 - Traverse City-MI. NOAA chart 14913.

The paddling: The Old Mission Peninsula, which juts 15 miles north into Grand Traverse Bay from bustling Traverse City, is a lovely area known for its cherry and apple orchards, vineyards, sandy beaches, and historic lighthouse. One of the best ways to view the peninsula's many charms is by sea kayak. Its protected location—sandwiched between the Leelanau Peninsula to the west and the mainland of Lower Michigan's mitten to the east—means that the waters surrounding the peninsula remain relatively undisturbed except by strong northerly winds.

One possible launch spot is Lighthouse Park at the very tip of the peninsula. The highlight of this park is the original Mission Point Light, which dates from 1870. Although the old lighthouse on shore is no longer operational, paddlers can put in at the beach and head north 1.5 miles for a close-up look at its working replacement. Heading east from the park, it is a scenic 3-mile paddle to Haserot Beach in Old Mission Harbor. Heading west, it is an 8-mile paddle past rolling hills and sandy beaches to the public boat launch in Bowers Harbor. The water is often quite shallow, even some distance from shore, but most of the land along the coastline is privately owned.

A notable exception is Power Island, a 200-acre offshore parcel that belongs to Grand Traverse County. The island lies 2.5 miles southwest of Bowers Harbor. Kayakers can head across from the boat launch and spend an afternoon exploring its sandy beaches and forested interior. There is a dock on the east side of the island, and a popular boaters' beach on the west side. A network of hiking trails begins near the dock. Just north of Power Island is tiny Bassett Island, which features five boat-in campsites that can be reserved in advance by calling the Grand Traverse Parks and Recreation Department.

Access: To reach **Lighthouse Park** at the tip of the peninsula, follow U.S. Highway 37 north 17 miles from Traverse City. To reach the public boat launch at **Bowers Harbor**, take U.S. 37 north about 8 miles from Traverse City, then continue north on Seven Hills Drive about 1 mile. Turn west on Peninsula Drive and follow the signs to the boat launch on Neah-ta-wanta Road. Another potential launch site is **Haserot Beach** on Old Mission Harbor. Take U.S. 37 north about 14 miles to Swaney Road and turn east. Follow the shoreline about 2 miles to the beach.

Old Mission Peninsula

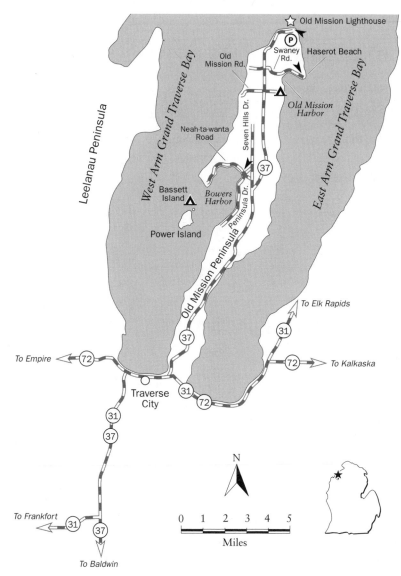

Old Mission Lighthouse

Swaney Rd.

Haserot Beach

Old Mission Rd.

Old Mission Harbor

West Arm Grand Traverse Bay

East Arm Grand Traverse Bay

Leelanau Peninsula

Neah-ta-wanta Road

Seven Hills Dr.

Bassett Island

Bowers Harbor

Power Island

Peninsula Dr.

Old Mission Peninsula

To Elk Rapids

To Empire

Traverse City

To Kalkaska

To Frankfort

To Baldwin

N

0 1 2 3 4 5

Miles

Additional Help

MA & G grid: 74, B3–A4.

Camping: Bassett Island (5 rustic boat-in sites); Old Mission Inn Campsites (29 modern sites) near Old Mission Harbor.

Food, gas, and lodging: Traverse City.

For more information: Traverse City Convention and Visitors' Bureau.

Rentals/guided trips: Northwest Outfitters Kayak Tours.

Pere Marquette River

Character: Michigan's first National Wild and Scenic River, the beautiful Pere Marquette winds gently through the wooded hills of Manistee National Forest.

Location: Lake and Mason Counties in the western Lower Peninsula.

Length: 56 miles.

Run: 42 miles, from M–37 near Baldwin to Custer Bridge near Custer.

Average run time: 15–18 hours.

Class: I.

Skill level: Beginner/intermediate.

Optimal flow: May–October.

Average gradient: 4 feet per mile.

Hazards: Occasional fallen trees and light rapids; high water levels can create strong current in early spring.

Fishing: The Pere Marquette is known for its plentiful brown trout, steelhead, and salmon; a 39-mile section above Indian Bridge has been designated a Michigan Blue Ribbon Trout Stream; the stretch between the M–37 Bridge and Gleason's Landing is restricted to the use of flies only.

Maps: USGS 1:25,000 - Ludington-MI, Scottville-MI, Custer-MI, Tallman-MI, Townsend Lake-MI, Baldwin-MI; 1:100,000 - Ludington-MI, Big Rapids-MI; 1:250,000 - Milwaukee-MI, Midland-MI.

The paddling: The Pere Marquette—or "PM," as it is known to its legions of fans—well deserves its designation as a National Wild and Scenic River. Its crystal clear waters wind through the sandy bluffs and dense woods of Manistee National Forest, offering paddlers ever-changing views of great natural beauty. The PM's moderate pace and relative lack of obstacles make it suitable for all but absolute beginners, while its occasional sharp bends and light rapids will entertain intermediate paddlers.

The PM is one of the finest rivers in the state for canoeing as well as for fishing. Large numbers of anglers ply its waters for brown trout, steelhead, and salmon. As a result, the river tends to become quite crowded on summer weekends. The U.S. Forest Service attempted to address the traffic problem in 1983 by instituting a permit system for watercraft. Paddlers must have a permit to launch any craft on the river between May 15 and September 10 each year. Permits cost $2.00 per craft per day and are available at the ranger station on M–37 south of Baldwin or through area canoe liveries. The Forest Service also charges a modest user fee for parking at its many well-maintained access sites along the PM. A vehicle pass for Manistee National Forest costs $3.00 per day, $5.00 per week, or $20.00 annually. Finally, canoeing hours are limited to between 9:00 A.M. and 6:00 P.M. daily during the summer months.

In exchange for their fees, paddlers are treated to a series of public landings that are very nice and well maintained. Some of the landings include camping facilities, some are accessible by car and feature parking areas and boat launches, and some are only accessible by river and consist of a picnic area and pit toilets. Despite all the restrictions on river use,

Pere Marquette River

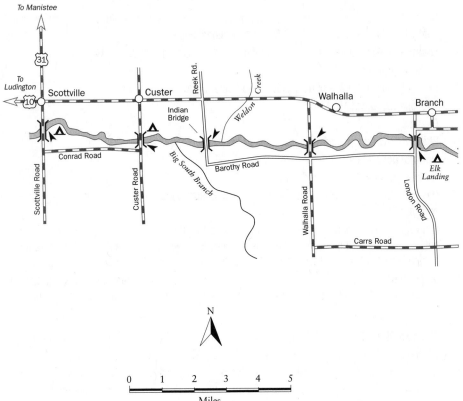

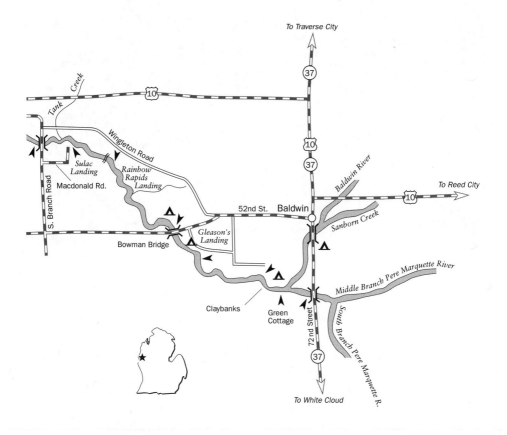

To Traverse City

37

10

Tank Creek

10

Wingleton Road

37

10

Baldwin River

Sulac Landing

Macdonald Rd.

Rainbow Rapids Landing

To Reed City

10

S. Branch Road

Sanborn Creek

52nd St.   Baldwin

Bowman Bridge

Gleason's Landing

Middle Branch Pere Marquette River

Claybanks

Green Cottage

72nd Street

South Branch Pere Marquette R.

37

To White Cloud

The Pere Marquette is one of Michigan's most popular and beloved rivers.

however, some of the more popular landings for livery trips (like Gleason's Landing) can assume a frat party atmosphere on summer Saturdays.

There is a well-maintained put-in with ample parking on M–37 south of Baldwin. A short distance above this spot, the PM divides into the Middle Branch and the Little South Branch—both of which are popular with anglers but not suitable for canoeing. In the 8-mile stretch between M–37 and Gleason's Landing, the river is 40 to 60 feet wide and flows with a moderate current over a mostly sand bottom. The depth ranges from 1 to 3 feet with some deeper pockets. Paddlers will encounter few fallen trees or other obstacles along this stretch, but should be prepared to do some basic maneuvering around winding turns. The shoreline varies from sandy bluffs to shady hardwood forests. The scattered cottages immediately below the bridge soon give way to unobstructed views of national forest lands.

Gleason's Landing is a popular take-out for day trips arranged through local canoe liveries, as well as a good midpoint for overnight trips on the PM. It features a well-maintained boat launch, ample parking, and a walk-in campground. Campers must make reservations through Ivan's Canoe Rental. The sites with the best view of the river are F3, F4, and G2.

From Gleason's Landing to Bowman Bridge (about 3 miles), the current remains moderate but the increased presence of sweepers and other obstacles makes things a bit more interesting. In the 7-mile stretch between Bowman Bridge and Rainbow Rapids, the river widens and picks up pace as it enters a patchwork of public and private land. The depth remains 1 to 3 feet but deeper pockets of 8 to 10 feet become more prevalent, and the bottom gradually changes from sand to gravel and rocks. This stretch of the PM includes several fun runs of mild rapids. Paddlers will encounter a few standing waves, but all the runs are straightforward with clear passages that should not pose a problem for anyone with basic maneuvering skills.

Immediately below the Rainbow Rapids landing is the stretch of river that gives it its name. Rainbow Rapids is a sweeping turn with a couple hundred yards of class I water. Although absolute beginners might feel a little intimidated, the run is straightforward with very few obstacles. The 3-mile section between Rainbow Rapids and Sulak Landing features five or six more short stretches of mild rapids that will delight intermediate paddlers. Equally beautiful and a bit more challenging than the upper section of the river, this part of the PM also seems to receive a bit less pressure from both canoeists and anglers. Sulak provides a good take-out spot for paddlers who like their rivers lively, as the PM's character changes farther downstream.

Over the 13-mile stretch between Sulak Landing and Walhalla Bridge, the river slows down and widens to between 60 and 80 feet. It also increases in depth and returns to a mostly sand bottom. Between Walhalla and Indian Bridge (5.5 miles), the PM enters a section known as the "spreads." It divides into multiple channels and meanders through a marshy area full of cattails and tag alders. The channels can be shallow and difficult to follow. Shortly below Indian Bridge, the Big South Branch of the PM flows into the mainstream and doubles its size. The river becomes slow and wide, and is generally more attractive to motorboats than to canoes. The next take-out is Custer Bridge, about 2.5 miles downstream. The PM is canoeable from Custer Bridge all the way to the M–31 Bridge near Ludington—another 15 miles—but it continues to be wide, slow, and marshy through this stretch.

Access: The **M–37 Bridge** is located 2.5 miles south of Baldwin on M–37. To reach the **Green Cottage** access site, take M–37 south 3 miles from Baldwin, then turn left on Seventy-second Street. Follow Seventy-second Street west 1.5 miles to Peacock Road, then go north 0.25 mile. To reach Claybanks USFS Campground, go west out of Baldwin on Fifty-second Street (Carrs Road) to Aster Road. Turn left, then take the next dirt road on the right. To reach **Gleason's Landing** from Baldwin, take Seventh Street west to Fifty-second Street (Carrs Road) and proceed west 4.5 miles. Turn left onto Clay Banks Road and go south 1 mile to Shortcut Avenue. Take Shortcut southeast another mile to Gray Road, then turn right and follow the signs to the landing. **Bowman Bridge** is located 5 miles west of Baldwin on Fifty-second Street (Carrs Road). To reach the **Rainbow Rapids** access site, take Fifty-second Street west from Baldwin for 2.5 miles, then continue northwest on Wingleton Road for 4 miles. The landing is on the south side of the road, across the railroad tracks. To reach **Sulak Landing**, continue west on Fifty-second Street (Carrs Road) for 4 miles past Bowman Bridge. Turn right onto South Branch Road, and proceed north 2 miles until the road forks. Sulak is about 0.5 mile down the right fork. **Upper Branch Bridge** is located about 0.5 mile farther down the left fork on South Branch Road. Alternately, take South Branch Road south and east 2.5 miles from U.S. 10 in Branch. To reach **Lower Branch Bridge**, take U.S. 10 west from Branch about 0.5 mile, then go south

Enjoying an afternoon paddle on the beautiful Pere Marquette River.

1 mile on Langdon Road. **Walhalla Bridge** is located 1.5 miles south of Walhalla on Walhalla Road. To reach **Indian Bridge**, take U.S. 10 east 2 miles from Custer, then go south 1 mile on Reek Road. **Custer Bridge** is located 1 mile south of Custer on Custer Road.

Additional Help

MA & G grid: 54, A3–A4; 55, A5, A6, and A7.

Camping: The Forest Service maintains canoe campgrounds at several access sites along the Pere Marquette, including Claybanks, Gleason's Landing (reservations required), Bowman Bridge, and Elk Landing (access by canoe only). Primitive camping is available along the river on federal land at Sulak Landing and Custer Bridge, as well as in the surrounding Manistee National Forest. In addition, the local canoe liveries operate private campgrounds near Baldwin.

Food, gas, and lodging: Baldwin, Ludington, Pentwater.

For more information: Manistee National Forest.

Canoe liveries: Baldwin Canoe Rental, Ivan's Canoe Rental.

Access Point	Float Distance To Next Access Point
M–37 Bridge	6 miles
Green Cottage or Claybanks Campground	2.5 miles
Gleason's Landing	2.5 miles
Bowman Bridge	7 miles
Rainbow Rapids	3 miles
Sulak Landing	3 miles
Upper Branch Bridge	0.5 mile
Elk Landing (canoe access only)	2.5 miles
Lower Branch Bridge	2.5 miles
Log Mark (canoe access only)	4.5 miles
Walhalla Bridge	5.5 miles
Indian Bridge	2.5 miles
Custer Bridge	Take Out

Pigeon River

Character: A beautiful trout stream with a wilderness feeling and an unpredictable character.
Location: Otsego and Cheboygan Counties, northeast of Gaylord.
Length: 35 miles.
Run: 17 miles, from Red Bridge (Webb Road) to Mullett Lake.
Average run time: 6–8 hours.
Class: I–II.
Skill level: Intermediate.
Optimal flow: May–September.
Average gradient: 12 feet per mile.
Hazards: Several unnamed light rapids; swift current around sharp bends; possibility of beaver dams, logjams, and other obstructions requiring liftovers or portages.
Fishing: Brook, brown, and rainbow trout all reside in this designated Blue Ribbon Trout Stream; walleye in the lower river.
Maps: USGS 1:25,000 - Cheboygan-MI; 1:100,000 - Petoskey-MI; 1:250,000 - Hardwood Lake-MI, Afton-MI, LeGrand-MI, Indian River-MI, Mullett Lake-MI.

The paddling: The crystal-clear waters of the Pigeon River flow northward through the 98,000-acre Pigeon River Country State Forest, home to Michigan's thriving elk herd. One of the most remote and unspoiled wilderness areas remaining in the Lower Peninsula, the state forest also provides prime habitat for black bears, deer, bobcats, pine martens, bald eagles, and a variety of other wildlife. The river adds to this wild character with a relatively swift current and a number of sharp bends. It is also subject to fallen trees, logjams, and beaver dams that are no longer cleared regularly, as the main livery that used to service the river quit to focus its business on the nearby Sturgeon.

Most Pigeon River paddling excursions begin at Red Bridge on Webb Road. The Pigeon is nominally navigable by canoe for another 12 miles upstream, beginning at Sturgeon River Valley Road. In fact, there are four state forest campgrounds along this upper stretch that are quite popular with anglers. But the river tends to be shallow in its upper reaches, and it is liberally strewn with fallen trees, beaver dams, and other obstacles that can make passage difficult.

The Pigeon enters its namesake state forest 0.25 mile downstream from the put-in at Red Bridge. At this point the river ranges from 30 to 40 feet wide and 1 to 3 feet deep. The current is moderate over a rocky bottom. Several good backcountry campsites exist along the wooded banks. About a mile downstream is a fishing access off of Montgomery Road known locally as McIntosh Landing. Over the next 5 miles the river gradually slows and the bottom changes to mostly sand. Campsites become less frequent as tag alders begin to dominate along the low banks.

Pigeon River

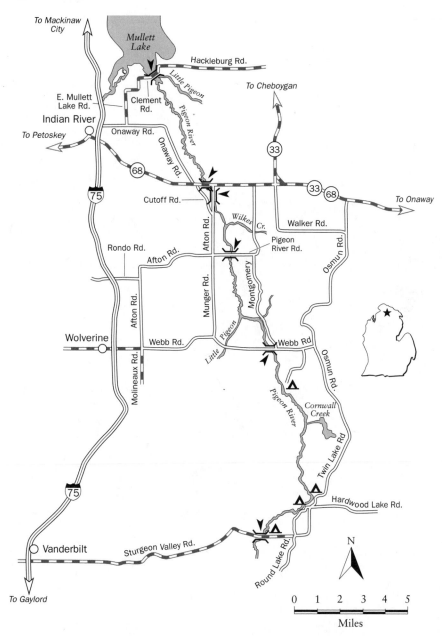

To Mackinaw City

Mullett Lake

Hackleburg Rd.

Little Pigeon

To Cheboygan

E. Mullett Lake Rd.

Clement Rd.

Indian River

Pigeon River

To Petoskey

Onaway Rd.

33

Onaway Rd.

68

33   68

To Onaway

Cutoff Rd.

Wilkes Cr.

Walker Rd.

Afton Rd.

Pigeon River Rd.

Rondo Rd.

Afton Rd.

Munger Rd.

Montgomery

Osmun Rd.

Afton Rd.

Wolverine

Little Pigeon

Webb Rd.

Webb Rd

Molineaux Rd.

Osmun Rd.

Pigeon River

Cornwall Creek

Twin Lake Rd

75

Hardwood Lake Rd.

N

Vanderbilt

Sturgeon Valley Rd.

Round Lake Rd.

To Gaylord

0 1 2 3 4 5

Miles

A lovely fall day on the Pigeon River.

As the river approaches the Pigeon River Road Bridge, however, it widens to between 40 and 60 feet and the bottom once again becomes rocky. The current increases below the bridge to create some riffles that might become light rapids during high water. But this section was quite shallow when we visited; expect some bottom-scraping to occur in late summer. About 3 miles below Pigeon River Road Bridge is Afton Road Bridge, which offers good access and parking. In another mile paddlers reach M–68, which might be a good take-out spot for beginners.

The Pigeon enters its most challenging stretch immediately below the M–68 Bridge. Over the next 3 miles, a series of sharp bends makes the swift current and light rapids significantly more interesting. In addition, fallen trees, sweepers, and other obstacles lurk at the outside of many tight turns, just waiting to swallow wayward canoes. Intermediate paddlers with good maneuvering skills will enjoy testing their abilities on this stretch, while beginners may end up getting wet. The current slows over the final miles before Mullett Lake, and the Pigeon eventually spreads into a series of shallow channels. The take-out is on the right at the Mullett Lake Road Bridge.

Access: To reach the **Red Bridge** access site, exit Interstate 75 at Webb Road and go east about 7 miles. The bridge is 0.25 mile west of the junction with Montgomery Road. To reach the **Pigeon River Road Bridge**, take Webb Road east 1 mile from I–75 and turn north on Afton Road (also known as Molineaux Road). Proceed north 4 miles to Pigeon River Road, then turn east and follow it about 4 miles to the bridge. To reach the **Afton Road Bridge**, exit I–75 at M–68 and go east about 6 miles to Afton Road. Turn south and follow it about 1 mile to the bridge. The **M–68 Bridge** is located about 5 miles east of I–75 on M–68, just past the intersection with Cutoff Road. To reach the bridge access on **Mullett Lake**, take Onaway Road east 1.5 miles from Indian River and turn north on Mullett Lake Road (also known as Bowersock Road and Clement Road). Follow this road north and east about 4 miles to the bridge.

Additional Help

MA & G grid: 83, A5–D5.

Camping: There are 4 rustic campgrounds located along the upper river in Pigeon River Country State Forest: Pigeon Bridge, off Sturgeon River Valley Road; Pigeon River, off Hardwood Lake Road; Elk Hill, off Twin Lake Road; and Pine Grove, off Webb Road. All of these campgrounds lie above the Webb Road put-in, on the stretch of river that is liberally strewn with fallen trees and other obstacles.

Food, gas, and lodging: Vanderbilt, Wolverine, Indian River, Onaway.

For more information: Pigeon River Country State Forest, Mackinaw State Forest.

Canoe liveries: None.

Access Point	Float Distance To Next Access Point
Red Bridge (Webb Road)	6 miles
Pigeon River Road Bridge	3 miles
Afton Road Bridge	1 mile
M–68 Bridge	7 miles
Mullett Lake	Take Out

Pine River

Character: Swift and strong, the Pine River has a North Country ambience and challenging runs that make it one of the Lower Peninsula's top paddling destinations.

Location: Runs through Lake, Wexford, and Manistee Counties.

Length: 60 miles.

Run: 40 miles from Edgetts Bridge to Low Bridge.

Average run time: 12–16 hours.

Class: I–II.

Skill level: Intermediate.

Optimal flow: May–October.

Average gradient: 10 feet per mile.

Hazards: Fast current, tight bends, sweepers.

Fishing: The Pine is a designated Blue Ribbon Trout Stream that supports brown trout, brook trout, and rainbow trout.

Maps: USGS 1:25,000 - Reed City North-MI, Chase-MI, Luther-MI, Stewart Lake-MI, Wellston NE-MI, Wellston-MI; 1:100,000 - Cadillac-MI; 1:250,000 - Traverse City-MI.

The paddling: The Pine River is one of the most appealing streams in the entire state. Passing through Manistee National Forest and other public land for much of its length, the cold, clear river rambles past banks that bristle with towering pines and deep hardwood forests. This natural beauty, combined with the river's reputation as one of the fastest in the Lower Peninsula, makes it a real gem for canoeing and river kayaking enthusiasts. In fact, the Pine's charms attract so many paddling visitors that the U.S. Forest Service instituted a canoe permit system for the river back in 1978 that remains in force today. This system controls overuse somewhat, but be warned that thick clots of paddlers do descend on the river on many summer weekends.

Under the USFS regulations, all paddlers must secure a permit for their canoes to be on the river between May 15 and September 10. Area liveries receive a portion of the daily permit allotment. If you are planning on running the Pine with your own canoe or kayak, make sure that you call ahead to the Manistee National Forest's Baldwin Ranger Station (231–745–4631) for reservations. Finally, paddlers looking to make use of the national forest's four primary access points along the Pine (Low Bridge, Peterson Bridge, Dobson Bridge, and Elm Flats) need to obtain a vehicle pass from Forest Service offices or area vendors (this last hurdle was implemented as part of a national forest recreation fee demonstration project designed to provide perpetually strapped forest managers with funds for maintenance, resource conservation, etc.).

Approximately 40 miles of the Pine's 60-mile length can be paddled, making it a top-tier option for canoeists looking for a two- or three-day trip. Paddlers interested in floating the river's full navigable length can put in at Edgetts Bridge, where the current runs at a moderate clip and the river ranges from 25 to 40 feet wide. About 6 miles downstream is

Pine River

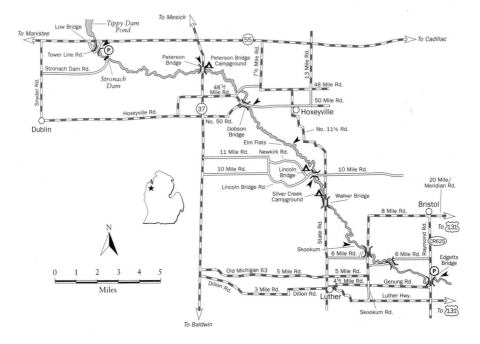

Skookum Bridge, off-limits to paddlers because of surrounding private property. Shortly below the bridge, however, are two public sites with good access and parking. The 8 miles immediately below the Skookum access sites—including Walker Bridge, which lies 6 miles downriver of Skookum—are privately owned. This stretch of water moves at a brisk pace through banks that range from 30 to 45 feet across.

Immediately below Lincoln Bridge, the river enters Manistee National Forest. The remaining portion of the river—all 26 miles of it—has been designated as a National Wild and Scenic River in recognition of its beauty and unspoiled character. Elm Flats lies about 3 miles downstream from the Pere Marquette State Forest campground at Lincoln Bridge. This is a favorite put-in spot for day-trippers looking to float down to Dobson Bridge or Peterson Bridge.

The already lively Pine picks up additional speed below Dobson Bridge, and as you approach Peterson Bridge, you'll encounter water that requires a command of basic paddling strokes. Tight bends, logs and other obstacles, and scattered boulders and rock ledges combine to create light rapids and standing waves that may overwhelm beginners, especially during the spring and other high-water periods. If you're a good paddler, though, you'll love this extended stretch of light whitewater.

The national forest campground at Peterson Bridge sees a lot of use, since camping is prohibited elsewhere along the 26-mile portion of the Pine River corridor designated as

Wild and Scenic. Below Peterson Bridge, the Pine continues to offer exhilarating paddling most of the way to Stronach Dam. Fallen logs, rocky chutes, and hairpin turns are all part of the mix, adding spice to a section that whisks paddlers past tall bluffs adorned with nodding pines and hardwoods.

The Pine slows as you approach Stronach Dam, which can be portaged on the left. It is worth noting that this portage won't be necessary in a few years. In 1997 the U.S. Forest Service and Consumers Power launched a six-year dam removal process in which the Stronach Dam will be removed in increments. Officials indicate that when the dam removal process is complete, the increased flow from Peterson Bridge to Low Bridge may well provide paddlers with another run of genuine class II whitewater. Pine River paddling concludes at Low Bridge, which lies a short distance downstream from the dam site. It offers decent access and parking.

Access: Edgetts Bridge is located on Raymond Road. To reach it, take U.S. Highway 131 to Marion Road (also called 20 Mile Road). Go west for 5 miles to Bristol, then proceed south on Raymond Road for 3 miles. To reach the **Skookum** access from U.S. 131, take Luther Road into Luther (about 6 miles west of U.S. 131), then turn north on State Road. Stay on State for about 2.5 miles, then go east on Six Mile Road for about 1.5 miles; the access sites lie on the north side of the road, less than 0.5 mile west of Skookum Bridge. The **Silver Creek** state forest campground is 5.5 miles north of Luther off State Road. To reach **Lincoln Bridge** state forest campground, drive 2 miles past the Silver Creek campground to Ten Mile Road, then drive west for less than a mile. The access site at **Elm Flats** can be reached by taking State Road north out of Luther for about 9 miles to where it meets 11¼ Road. The access site lies down a gravel road to the south. **Dobson Bridge** is located 2.5 miles south of the juncture of M–37 and M–55. Take M–37 to No. 48½ Road, then go east for 2 miles to No. 50 Road; the bridge lies another mile to the east on No. 50 Road. **Peterson Bridge** and its namesake campground are located right off M–37, about a mile south of M–55. To reach **Low Bridge** from the junction of M–55 and M–37, go west about 5 miles to Low Bridge Road, then travel less than a mile to the Low Bridge landing.

Additional Help

MA & G grid: 65, C7; 66, C1, C2, and D2

Camping: Streamside campgrounds include two Pere Marquette State Forest campgrounds, at Silver Creek (25 rustic sites) and Lincoln Bridge (9 rustic sites). Manistee National Forest also maintains a 20-site campground with 10 walk-in sites at Peterson Bridge. Shoreline camping is prohibited anywhere else along the 26-mile stretch of the river (Lincoln Bridge to Stronach) that has been designated a National Wild and Scenic River.

The swift-paced Pine River pleases paddlers and anglers alike.

Food, gas, and lodging: Luther, Cadillac, Wellston, Baldwin.

For more information: Manistee National Forest, Pere Marquette State Forest.

Canoe liveries: Baldwin Canoe Rental, Bosman's Canoe Rental, Famous Jarolim Canoe Rental, Horina Canoe Rental, Pine River Paddlesport Center, Sportsman's Port.

Access Point	Float Distance To Next Access Point
Edgetts Bridge	7 miles
Skookum	8 miles
Silver Creek SF Camp	1 mile
Lincoln Bridge SF Camp	3.5 miles
Elm Flats	6.5 miles
Dobson Bridge	6 miles
Peterson Bridge	8 miles
Low Bridge	Take Out

28 Platte River

Character: Challenging in its upper reaches, the Platte turns into a placid, family-friendly float as it nears Lake Michigan.

Location: Benzie County in the northwestern Lower Peninsula.

Length: Approximately 30 miles, from Lake Ann in northeast Benzie County to Lake Michigan in Sleeping Bear Dunes National Lakeshore.

Run: 16 miles, from the Veterans Memorial State Forest Campground on U.S. 31 through Platte Lake to Lake Michigan.

Average run time: 6–8 hours.

Class: Flatwater.

Skill level: Intermediate above Platte Lake; beginner below Platte Lake.

Optimal flow: May–October.

Average gradient: 13 feet per mile above Platte Lake; 3 feet per mile below Platte Lake.

Hazards: Above Platte Lake, swift current, frequent turns, occasional logjams and sweepers; below Platte Lake, deep water toward the middle of Loon Lake.

Fishing: A 6-mile section of the Platte above Honor has been designated a Michigan Blue Ribbon Trout Stream. In addition to brown trout, rainbow trout, and brook trout, the river also has impressive spring runs of steelhead and fall runs of coho and Chinook salmon.

Maps: 1:25,000 - Frankfort-MI, Beulah-MI, Platte River-MI; 1:100,000 - Crystal Lake-MI, Traverse City-MI; 1:250,000 - Manitowoc-MI, Traverse City-MI.

The paddling: The Platte River offers two vastly different paddling experiences, depending on whether you put in above or below Platte Lake. For much of the 9-mile segment upstream of the lake, the river races along at a swift pace. Intermediate paddlers will enjoy maneuvering through narrow passages to avoid the logjams, sweepers, gravel bars, and other obstacles that litter this stretch. Beginners, on the other hand, are better off starting downstream of the lake. Over the last 4 miles before it enters Lake Michigan, the Platte flows at a leisurely pace through the sandy paradise of Sleeping Bear Dunes National Lakeshore.

The put-in on the Upper Platte is located at Veterans Memorial State Forest Campground on U.S. 31. At this point, the clear waters of the spring-fed river range from 30 to 50 feet wide and 1 to 3 feet deep. It generally flows between high, wooded banks over a bottom of sand and gravel. About 3 miles downstream is Platte River State Forest Campground, which is another possible access site. From here, the river widens and deepens a bit with the injection of water from Carter and Collison Creeks. Obstacles become less frequent and easier to avoid in this stretch, although the current remains swift.

About 3 miles downstream from the Platte River Campground, the river passes through the small town of Honor, crossing under bridges at South Street (which turns into Zimmerman Street), Henry Street, and U.S. 31. South Street offers good access with limited roadside parking, although the position of the take-out just upstream from a narrow

Platte River

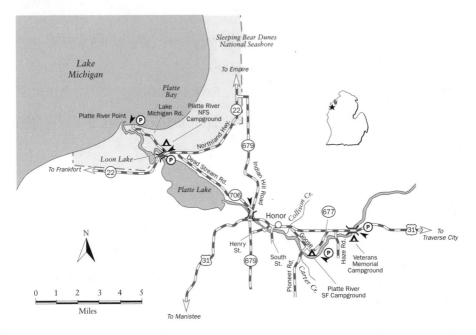

culvert might make it a bit tricky for beginners. There is no access at U.S. 31. The last bridge along this stretch is Indian Hill Road (CR–679), a little over a mile below Honor. There is little room for parking at the bridge, but it is the last take-out option for paddlers wishing to avoid Platte Lake. Below the bridge, the Platte enters a 2-mile stretch of marshy lowlands before reaching the 2,500-acre lake, which can become wavy when winds blow out of the west. Continue paddling along the northern shore about 3 miles to enter the lower section of the river.

Shortly after exiting the lake, the Platte crosses under M–22 and passes the Platte River Campground maintained by the National Park Service. This is the launching spot for the highly popular 4-mile trip down the placid lower Platte through Sleeping Bear Dunes. On summer weekends, expect to see throngs of splashing children and sunburned adults floating along in canoes, kayaks, rafts, and inner tubes. At this point, the river ranges from 50 to 70 feet wide and 2 to 4 feet deep over a sandy bottom. It flows slowly between low, wooded banks.

About 1 mile downstream from the campground, the Platte enters tiny Loon Lake. Paddle along the northern shore about 0.5 mile to pick up the river again. In another 1.5 miles, the Platte begins to widen as the wooded banks give way to open sand dunes. The take-out comes 1 mile later at a public access site on the right side at the mouth of the river. Be sure to leave some extra time to enjoy the beautiful white sand beach along Lake Michigan.

The Platte River winds through a narrow, wooded corridor in its upper reaches.

Access: The put-in on the Upper Platte at **Veterans Memorial State Forest Campground** is located 3.5 miles east of Honor (or 21 miles southwest of Traverse City) on U.S. Highway 31. To reach the access site at **Platte River State Forest Campground**, take U.S. 31 east 1 mile from Honor, then go south 1.5 miles on Goose Road (County Road 677). To avoid paddling across Platte Lake, you can take out at the **Indian Hill Road Bridge**. Take U.S. 31 west 2 miles from Honor, then turn north on Indian Hill Road (CR–679) and proceed 0.25 mile to the bridge. Trips on the Lower Platte put in at the **M–22 Bridge**, located 11 miles north of Frankfort—or the same distance south of Empire—on M–22 (Northland Highway). The take-out at **Platte River Point** on Lake Michigan is located 3 miles northwest of M–22 on Lake Michigan Road.

Additional Help

MA & G grid: 73, C5–C7.

Camping: Veterans Memorial State Forest Campground (24 rustic sites), 3.5 miles east of Honor on U.S. 31; Platte River State Forest Campground (26 rustic sites), 2.5 miles southeast of Honor on Goose Road (CR–677); Platte River Campground (179 modern sites), 0.25 mile west of M–22 on Lake Michigan Road (CR–708) in Sleeping Bear Dunes National Lakeshore.

Food, gas, and lodging: Empire, Honor, Benzonia, Frankfort.

For more information: Pere Marquette State Forest, Sleeping Bear Dunes National Lakeshore.

Canoe liveries: Riverside Canoe Trips.

Access Point	Float Distance To Next Access Point
Veterans Memorial SF Campground	3 miles
Platte River SF Campground	4 miles
Indian Hill Road Bridge (CR–679)	5 miles
M–22 Bridge	0.25 mile
Platte River NPS Campground	3.75 miles
Lake Michigan Public Access	Take Out

Rifle River

Character: Both canoeists and tubers flock to this attractive, easygoing northern river on summer weekends.

Location: Ogemaw and Arenac Counties.

Length: 60 miles.

Run: 47 miles, from the Rifle River Recreation Area to Stover Road near Saginaw Bay.

Average run time: 15–20 hours.

Class: Flatwater.

Skill level: Beginner.

Optimal flow: May–October.

Gradient: 4 feet per mile.

Hazards: Light (class I) rapids below M–55; deep water in lower sections.

Fishing: Steelhead, brown trout, and salmon are among the species that roam this undammed river.

Maps: USGS 1:25,000 - Selkirk-MI, Skidway Lake-MI, Sterling-MI, Omer SW-MI, Omer-MI, Standish NE-MI; 1:100,000 - Tawas City-MI, Bay City-MI; 1:250,000 - Tawas City-MI.

The paddling: The Rifle River is one of the most popular streams in the entire state on summer weekends. It possesses a mild current, long sections of sandy riverbed, and plentiful swimming holes, all of which make the stream a good option for families and other groups looking for an undemanding float. The Rifle is also attractive, winding past pretty woodlands, summer cottages, and quiet farm fields for much of its length as it makes its way to its outlet at Saginaw Bay. And finally, it is easily accessible. Access spots are numerous, and liveries have sprouted all along the stream's length, making it easy for vacationers to organize trips that can range in length from a few hours to a couple of days. All of these factors create flotillas of rental canoes and inner tubes on summer holidays and June-through-August weekends. This state of affairs will undoubtedly delight some folks and irritate others, depending on their personal tastes. Midweek and off-season excursions, on the other hand, offer the prospect of a much quieter paddling experience.

The river is at its most scenic in its upper reaches, at Rifle River Recreation Area and immediately downstream. Here the river is clear and lively, though of modest size (30 to 50 feet wide), as it passes through hardwood forests. The riverbed is rocky through here, and basic maneuvering abilities will come in handy. If you are interested in exploring this area of the Rifle, you can put in either at White Ash Bridge on Sage Lake Road or Ballard Bridge on Peters Road.

Below the M–55 Bridge (no access), the Rifle deepens and slows to a crawl for long stretches. But the section from M–55 to Maple Ridge Road (Moffat Bridge) also features the only rapids on the river. The first of these lies about 4 miles below M–55, while the second appears another 3 miles or so downstream, shortly below Greenwood Road Bridge. Both of these rapids are created by shelves of bedrock that kick up standing waves. They

Rifle River

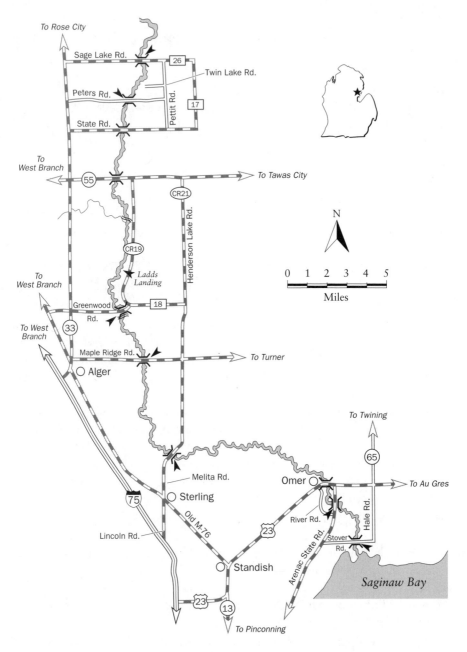

are modest (class I–II) in size and can be walked through during low-water periods, but they may well unnerve (and unseat) beginning paddlers at higher water levels. Portage if in doubt.

As you near Maple Ridge Road, the Rifle remains wide (80 to 100 feet) and slow as it passes over rocky riverbed. Shallow conditions prevail in this area during midsummer, so the screech of aluminum canoes on rock is a common one. But the river also features many deeper stretches that provide relief from the bottom-scraping.

Below Maple Ridge Road, the stream continues to blend light riffles with slow water as it passes through quiet and largely undeveloped woodlands. Downstream from Omer, the Rifle leaves the riffles behind and remains deep, dark, and ponderous as it enters marshlands. The public access sites at River Road and Stover Road are your last take-out options before the Rifle empties into Saginaw Bay.

Access: White Ash Bridge on **Sage Lake Road** (FR-26) is 3.5 miles east of M–33, about 5 miles south of Rose City. To reach the access on **Peters Road** (Ballard Bridge), take M–33 south of Rose City for approximately 7 miles, then go east on Peters for about 4 miles. **Ladds Landing** is located on County Road 19, about 6 miles south of M–55. To reach **Greenwood Road Bridge**, take FR–9 southeast out of West Branch for 8 miles, then travel east on Greenwood for 5 miles. Moffat Bridge on **Maple Ridge Road** is located 4 miles east of M–33, just outside of Alger. The access site at **Melita Road** is a short distance downstream from the bridge, about 3 miles north of Sterling. The **River Road** public access lies on the outskirts of Omer, less than a mile south of U.S. Highway 23. The bridge at **Stover Road** is about 7 miles southeast of Omer. To reach it, follow Arenac State Road south out of town for 4 miles, then drive east on Stover for 3 miles.

In addition to these public access sites, area liveries maintain many private camping areas and access sites all along the Rifle for their clients' use. Contact individual liveries for information on their specific trip offerings.

Additional Help

MA & G grid: 70, A1–D1 and D2–D4.

Camping: The Rifle River Recreation Area is about 5 miles east of Rose City on FR–28 (Rose City Road). It includes a modern campground with 80 sites, as well as 3 rustic campgrounds with a total of 101 sites. One of these is on **Devoe Lake**, while the other two— **Ranch** and **Spruce**—are located right on the shoreline of the Rifle River. You can also camp on the stream's upper reaches on Au Sable State Forest land, but the rustic state forest campground located just upstream from Twin Lake Road closed in the mid-1990s. Finally, many of the liveries that service the Rifle also maintain private campgrounds.

Paddlers flock to the scenic yet undemanding Rifle River on summer weekends.

Food, gas, and lodging: West Branch, Rose City, Sterling, Standish.

For more information: Au Sable State Forest, Rifle River Recreation Area.

Canoe liveries: Rifle River AAA, Riverbend Campground and Canoe, River View Campground and Canoe, Russell Canoes, White's Canoe Livery.

Access Point	Float Distance To Next Access Point
Sage Lake Road (FR–26)	3 miles
Peters Road	17.5 miles
Greenwood Road	3.5 miles
Maple Ridge Road (Moffat Bridge)	7 miles
Melita Road	11.5 miles
River Road	4.5 miles
Stover Road	Take Out

⬛ Sleeping Bear Dunes National Lakeshore

Character: This prized expanse of Lake Michigan shoreline offers lovely sand beaches, towering dunes, and a plethora of launching options for day trips.

Location: Northwestern Benzie County and western Leelanau County.

Size: 35 miles of shoreline along the mainland (approximately 70,000 acres). The National Lakeshore also includes North and South Manitou Islands (see separate entry for paddling information on these destinations).

Skill level: Beginner/intermediate.

Hazards: Winds can create heavy surf along exposed shoreline and churn up rough conditions around Pyramid Point and Sleeping Bear Point.

Maps: USGS 1:25,000 - Frankfort-MI, Beulah-MI, Empire-MI, Glen Haven-MI, Glen Arbor-MI, Good Harbor Bay-MI; 1:100,000 - Crystal Lake-MI, Traverse City-MI; 1:250,000 - Manitowoc-MI, Traverse City-MI. NOAA charts 14902, 14912.

The paddling: Sleeping Bear Dunes National Lakeshore is one of Michigan's natural treasures. The shoreline itself is blessed with miles of inviting beach and gargantuan dunes, while inland areas feature fauna-rich wetlands and rolling forests of beech, maple, oak, and pine. Of course, sampling Sleeping Bear's riches comes at a price. The many and varied charms of the region attract huge throngs of vacationers on hot summer weekends, transforming facility campgrounds and parking lots into hives of activity that can frazzle the nerves of even the most serene individuals. Luckily for kayakers, a vast blue refuge from the din lies waiting offshore.

Highlights of Sleeping Bear Dunes' southernmost shoreline are crescent-shaped Platte Bay and the towering sand walls known as Empire Bluffs. These dunes, their tops graced with windswept stands of trees and hardy grasses, rise steeply from the shoreline to heights of 200 feet or more. Long stretches of sandy beach through here make landings easy. Day-use areas scattered along the shoreline provide you with a range of launch site options. Popular day trips you might want to consider in this area include an excursion from Platte River Point to Otter Creek and back (8 miles round-trip) or a 7-mile round-trip jaunt from Empire Beach to Otter Creek and back.

North of the town of Empire, swimmers, sunbathers, and beachcombers concentrate at several points along the shoreline, providing kayakers with plenty of people-watching opportunities. As you proceed northward, meanwhile, the relatively low shoreline that prevails in the vicinity of the town gives way to massive dunes that dwarf the figures frolicking below. These spectacular bluffs are the lakeshore's namesake Sleeping Bear Dunes. At times they rise to heights of nearly 500 feet, and they guard the coastline for a good 3 miles. They reach their apex about 4 miles north of Empire, then diminish again as you approach Sleeping Bear Point. The east end of the point houses a historic Coast Guard station that is now maintained as a museum. Glen Haven's Cannery Beach, located about 8 miles north of Empire Beach and 0.5 mile east of the station, is the favored put-in/take-out spot in the Sleeping Bear Point area.

Sleeping Bear Dunes National Lakeshore

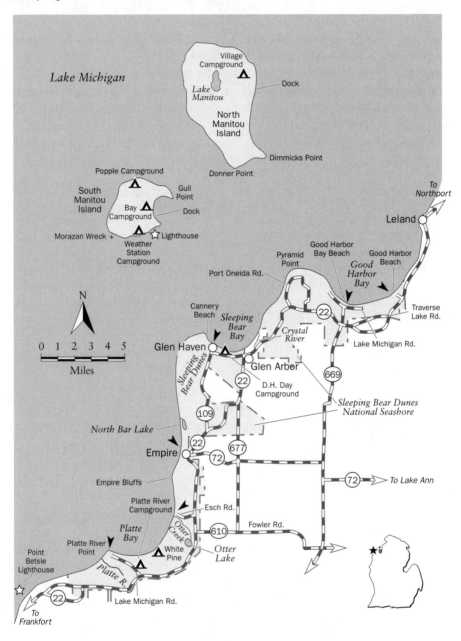

The waters from Sleeping Bear Bay to Good Harbor Bay are also popular with kayakers. The distance from the principal launch sites (Cannery to Good Harbor Bay Beach) in these coves is about 11 miles one way, making it another good day-trip option (you can also add another 3 miles to the trip by using Good Harbor Beach, at the far east end of the national lakeshore). If you decide to explore this area, you'll be treated to a scenic shoreline that gradually changes from high, wooded bluffs to truly imposing dunes at Pyramid Point. Keep in mind, though, that private property prevails along much of the coast both east and west of the point, limiting landing options. But even here the national lakeshore restrictions on personal watercraft use are in effect. These rules, which ban the noisy machines from approaching within 0.25 mile of the mainland, have been essential in maintaining Sleeping Bear's status as a premier Great Lakes paddling destination.

Access: The **Platte River Point** beach area lies at the end of Lake Michigan Road, which is located 10 miles northeast of Frankfort on M–22. The **Otter Creek** access site lies another 5 miles north up M–22, at the west end of Esch Road. The **Empire** public beach lies near the intersection of M–72 and M–22; follow the signs through downtown to the city beach. To reach the **Cannery Beach** put-in, head north out of Empire on M–22 for about 2 miles, then go north on M–109 for 4 miles. When M–109 jogs east, keep going north into Glen Haven and the Old Cannery beach. **Glen Arbor Municipal Beach** is located along the shores of Glen Arbor, on M–22. Both **Good Harbor Bay Beach** and **Good Harbor Beach** are located directly off M–22. They lie 8 and 5 miles southwest of Leland, respectively. Follow the signs to reach either beach.

Additional Help

MA & G grid: 73, A6–A7, B6, and C6.

Camping: Visitors to Sleeping Bear Dunes have numerous camping options from which to choose, although many of them are jam-packed during the summer. You can save yourself grief and almost certain disappointment by calling ahead for reservations. The two primary mainland campgrounds managed by the National Park Service are Platte River Campground, a modern facility with 179 sites (including a limited number of reservable sites), and D.H. Day Campground, which features eighty-eight no-frills sites along the shoreline (proximity to the lake makes this a favorite of kayakers). Another option for paddlers can be found at White Pine Campground on Platte Bay. This is a quiet backcountry campground with 6 sites, but it is about 0.25 mile from Lake Michigan.

Camping alternatives outside the National Lakeshore include Interlochen State Park (490 sites divided between modern and rustic campgrounds), Platte River State Forest Campground (twenty-six sites), and Lake Ann State Forest Campground (thirty sites). Finally, there are a host of privately owned campgrounds scattered across the region.

Food, gas, and lodging: Frankfort, Benzonia, Empire, Honor, Glen Arbor, Traverse City.

For more information: Sleeping Bear Dunes National Lakeshore.

Sturgeon River

Character: A fast and challenging river that promises great fun for experienced paddlers and great misery for beginners.

Location: From Ostego County near Gaylord to Burt Lake in Cheboygan County.

Length: 40 miles.

Run: 17 miles, from Trowbridge Road, south of Wolverine, to Burt Lake.

Average run time: 6–8 hours.

Class: I–II.

Skill level: Intermediate.

Optimal flow: May–October.

Average gradient: 14 feet per mile.

Hazards: Numerous strainers and sweepers, several unnamed rapids, frequent hairpin turns.

Fishing: Designated as a Michigan Blue Ribbon Trout Stream for its lower 21 miles, its waters hold steelhead, brown, rainbow, and brook trout.

Maps: USGS 1:25,000 - Indian River-MI, Wolverine-MI, Green Timbers-MI; 1:100,000 - Petoskey-MI; 1:250,000 - Cheboygan-MI.

The paddling: The Sturgeon is the fastest-flowing river in the Lower Peninsula, and also one of the most challenging for canoeists. You'll encounter obstacles—including strainers, sweepers, rocks, and narrow passages—at an exhilarating pace. Many of these hazards seem to be strategically placed on the outside of tight turns, and the boat naturally wants to follow the strong current right into them. Although the Sturgeon has no true whitewater, bow and stern paddlers will have to communicate early and often to escape unscathed.

From its headwaters near Gaylord in Otsego County, the spring-fed Sturgeon runs northward for 24 miles before it becomes navigable by canoe. Starting at Trowbridge Road, just north of where the river crosses under Interstate 75, the Sturgeon is quite narrow (15 to 20 feet) and overgrown, snaking its way through thickets of tag alders. Typical depth is 1 to 3 feet over a mostly gravel bottom. We came across two 1- to 2-foot drops over fallen trees early on—one with a standing wave that washed over our bow.

About 3 miles downstream, the river widens to 30 to 40 feet after intersecting with the West Branch near Wolverine. On the left bank is a city park that would make a nice spot for a picnic. At the downstream end of the park is a 2-foot drop over an old dam with another sizeable standing wave at the bottom. After leaving town the Sturgeon enters its most challenging stretch. For the next three hours, it races through heavily wooded state forest land, but paddlers won't have much time to enjoy the scenery. You'll be too busy negotiating hairpin turns, avoiding strainers, and lifting over logjams.

About halfway through this stretch is Haakwood State Forest Campground, a favorite of anglers and a good stopping point for an overnight trip on the Sturgeon. It is first visible from the river as a sandy path on the left bank, half an hour or so after you pass the Meadows Bar (orange ribbons may also mark the pathway). Haakwood features twenty

Sturgeon River

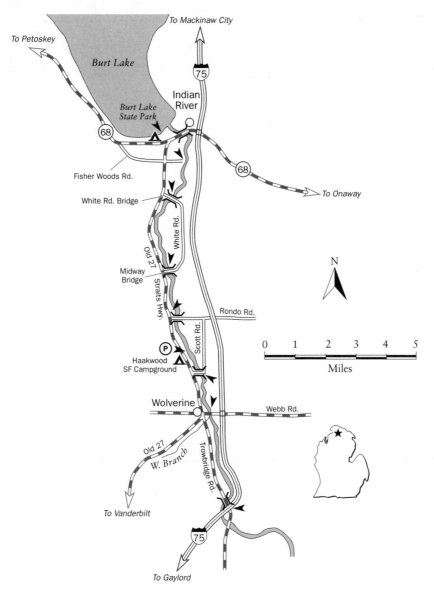

Splashing over one of several short drops on the challenging Sturgeon River.

rustic sites, most relatively secluded and set among stands of birches. The campground is divided into three loops, and it is worth noting that the southernmost loop provides paddlers with the most direct access to the river. The canoe landing for the northernmost loop is in a stagnant pool, while the landing for the middle loop requires hauling gear up a steep bank and along an overgrown anglers' trail. If you're planning an overnight excursion, it may be best to grab a site at Haakwood before hitting the river, because there are few other camping options available along the way. Besides, that way you are guaranteed dry sleeping bags!

The current finally begins to slow around Midway Bridge, as the river gradually becomes deeper (2 to 6 feet) with a mostly sand bottom. There are still turns to negotiate and obstacles to look out for, but in between you'll find straight, flat stretches to catch your breath. During the last 4 or 5 miles on the Sturgeon, the current remains fairly swift but the most frequently encountered obstacles are tubers who put in at White Road Bridge. There is a private landing in Indian River, just before the M–68 bridge (the operators charge a small fee for taking out there), or continue into Burt Lake, paddle along the shoreline to the left, and take out at the public launch in Burt Lake State Park.

Intermediate canoeists with good maneuvering skills will enjoy the Sturgeon. For them, it will be a fun and exciting way to test and improve upon their abilities. But the river is definitely not for everyone—beginners are likely to find canoeing the Sturgeon to be a wet and frustrating experience. In fact, the local liveries report having to retrieve one or two canoes from the Sturgeon per week, abandoned by waterlogged beginners.

Access: Paddlers can access the Sturgeon from a number of locations along its length. To reach the **Trowbridge Road** put-in, exit Interstate 75 at Wolverine, head west into town, and then go south 3 miles on Trowbridge Road to the first bridge. **Wolverine Park** in Wolverine also provides good access and parking. There is another public access site at the **Scott Road Bridge** about a mile north of Wolverine. Take Old 27 Straits Highway north and then turn right on Scott Road. **Haakwood State Forest Campground** is about 2 miles north of Wolverine along Old 27. The next public access site is about 3 miles north of Wolverine along Old 27, just north of **Rondo Road**. To reach the **Midway Bridge** access, continue north 1 mile past Rondo Road on Old 27 and turn right on White Road. Two miles farther north, White Road crosses the Sturgeon again at **White Road Bridge**, where there is access with roadside parking. The final public access before Burt Lake is at the end of **Fisher Woods Road**, 1 mile north of White Road along Old 27. Alternatively, all of these sites may be accessed from the north by exiting I–75 at M–68, heading west into Indian River, then turning south on Old 27.

Additional Help

MA & G grid: 82, A3–B3.

Camping: Haakwood State Forest Campground (twenty rustic sites), Burt Lake State Park (300 modern sites).

Food, gas, and lodging: Indian River.

For more information: Mackinaw State Forest.

Canoe liveries: Big Bear Adventures, Tomahawk Trails Canoe Trips.

Access Point	Float Distance To Next Access Point
Trowbridge Road	3 miles
Wolverine Park	1.5 miles
Scott Road	1 mile
Haakwood Campground	1.5 miles
Rondo Road	2 miles
Midway Bridge	3 miles
White Road Bridge	2 miles
Fisher Woods Road	3 miles
Burt Lake	Take Out

White River

Character: The easy-going White River offers pleasant floats through the southern section of Manistee National Forest.

Location: Originates in central Newaygo County and flows through the southeast corner of Oceana County before emptying into Lake Michigan in Muskegon County.

Length: 80 miles from headwaters to Lake Michigan.

Run: 37 miles from Hesperia to White Lake.

Average run time: 12–16 hours.

Class: I.

Skill level: Beginner; upper river more challenging during high-water periods.

Optimal flow: May–June.

Average gradient: 5 feet per mile (10 feet per mile from Hesperia to Pines Point).

Hazards: None.

Fishing: A productive stream that gives up steelhead, salmon, trout, smallmouth bass, and walleye.

Maps: USGS 1:25,000 - Holton-MI, Big Blue Lake-MI, Montague-MI, Dalton-MI, Michilinda-MI; 1:100,000 - Big Rapids-MI, Ludington-MI, Muskegon-MI; 1:250,000 - Midland-MI, Milwaukee-MI.

The paddling: A mild-mannered and scenic river for much of its canoeable length, the White River is suitable for family outings. Access points are relatively few, however, and several of those that do exist are controlled by local liveries. Make sure to secure permission to use such access sites before setting out.

The most challenging paddling on the White can be found from Hesperia to the Pines Point National Forest campground (above Hesperia, the river's narrow channel is choked with downed trees and logjams). The presence of quick water and rocky obstacles in this section require an understanding of basic paddling strokes, especially during high-water periods. On the other hand, this portion of the river can get very shallow during the summer months, and its gravelly bottom will carve up the underside of a loaded canoe. Campers determined to run this section of the river might want to consider renting at such times. Primary launch points for exploring this upper part of the White are Hesperia Dam and a town park located a short distance downstream.

At Pines Point Campground, which lies about 8 miles below Hesperia, the temperament of the river changes considerably. It deepens and slows, and the rocky bottom gives way to sand. The stream also takes on a meandering quality at this point, ambling through low woodlands that house a variety of wildlife. The width of the river here ranges from 30 to 50 feet.

Most of the river below Pines Point runs through Manistee National Forest, and while the shoreline is often swampy and festooned with thick tag alders, you can find occasional spots suitable for camping. Another option for paddlers looking to camp overnight is Dia-

White River

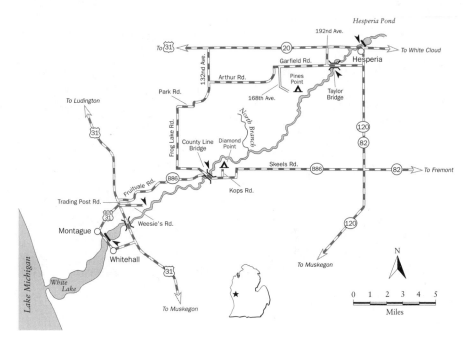

mond Point Recreation Area, a rustic four-site campground located about 1 mile below the White's juncture with its North Branch.

County Line Bridge is the primary take-out spot for trips on the White.

Below County Line Bridge, the river corridor passes through private land once again. It also continues to widen (to 60 to 70 feet) and deepen (to 4 to 6 feet, with deeper holes) before fraying into multiple shallow channels that wind through marshlands. Negotiating this stretch of the river can be a pain, which accounts for the popularity of County Line Bridge as a take-out point. If you choose to press on, however, you can take out at the BR-31 Bridge in Whitehall just before the river empties into White Lake.

Access: Paddlers looking to put in at Hesperia can access the river at **Hesperia Dam**, a local park just downstream from the dam, or **Taylor Bridge**. To reach the bridge take M–20 west out of Hesperia for 2 miles to 192nd Avenue, go south for 1 mile, and turn east on Garfield Road; the bridge lies 0.25 mile down. To reach **Pines Point Campground** from Hesperia, take Garfield Road west for 3 miles to 168th Street. Follow the signs south and east for 2.5 miles into the Pines Point Recreation Area. To reach the **Diamond Point Campground**, take U.S. 31 near Montague to County Road B-86. Follow this east for 9 miles past County Line Bridge to Kops Road. Drive north for 0.5 mile to Forest Road 9403. Continue north for 0.5 mile to the recreation area. **County Line Bridge** is located

Relaxing after a day of paddling on the White River.

on Fruitvale Road. To reach it from Montague and Whitehall, take Whitehall Road (Business U.S. 31) or U.S. 31 north to CR–B-86 and follow it east for 7 miles. To reach the access site at **Weesie's Road**, take Trading Post Road south off B-86 to Weesie's Road, then proceed east for less than 1 mile.

In addition to these access points, several two-tracks provide access to the river from B-86 and other roads. These unmarked sites—known by such colorful names as Loggers Outpost and Jack Drivers Rest—are commonly utilized by area canoe liveries.

Additional Help

MA & G grid: 44, A4; 45, A5.

Camping: Pines Point Campground (33 sites), Diamond Point Campground (four rustic sites).

Food, gas, and lodging: Montague, Whitehall, Muskegon, White Cloud.

For more information: Huron-Manistee National Forest.

Canoe liveries: Happy Mohawk Canoe Livery, Kellogg's Canoes.

Access Point	Float Distance To Next Access Point
Hesperia	4 miles
Taylor Bridge	6 miles
Pines Point Campground	10.5 miles
Diamond Point Campground	5 miles
County Line Bridge	7 miles
Weesie's Road	4.5 miles
White Lake	Take Out

Wilderness State Park

Character: Rugged shoreline and a chain of small islands make Wilderness State Park a notable Lake Michigan kayaking destination.

Location: Northern Emmet County.

Size: This 8,286-acre park includes more than 26 miles of shoreline on Lake Michigan and the Straits of Mackinac.

Skill level: Intermediate.

Hazards: Winds from the north and west can create rough conditions; boaters should also beware of shoals and rocks in shallow waters near Waugoshance Point and around the islands.

Maps: USGS 1:25,000 Waugoshance Island-MI, Big Stone Bay-MI, Bliss-MI; 1:100,000 Beaver Island-MI, Cheboygan-MI; 1:250,000 Cheboygan-MI. NOAA charts 14881 and 14902.

The paddling: Situated on the northwestern tip of Michigan's Lower Peninsula, Wilderness State Park boasts miles of undeveloped Great Lakes shoreline. Both Sturgeon Bay, which lies on the southwestern side of the park, and Big Stone Bay, which opens into the Straits of Mackinac, are fine kayaking destinations. Most paddlers visiting the park, however, concentrate their attention on its northwest side, where Waugoshance Point and a small chain of islands trail away into Lake Michigan's deeper waters.

Paddlers looking to explore westward out to Waugoshance Point can put in at the park's established boat launch (about 10 miles round-trip from the launch to the point) or a small gravel parking lot near the end of Park Drive (about 3.5 miles round-trip from the launch to the point). The shoreline along here is a rugged and rocky one backed by windswept woodlands of evergreens and old hardwoods. Beyond the point lies a group of small islands that can also be explored by boat, including Temperance Island and Crane Island. You should keep in mind, however, that these islands are located on shallow shoals, and that changing Lake Michigan water levels can have a significant impact on the topography. High water levels are capable of submerging some smaller islands and splintering larger ones like Crane Island into smaller clusters, while low-water periods may expose little spits of land that usually lie below the lake surface. Kayakers should exercise appropriate caution while negotiating this area.

A round-trip paddle from the park boat launch to the western tip of Crane Island is about 15 miles, but paddlers can shave 6 miles off that distance by putting in at the aforementioned Park Drive parking lot. Expert kayakers who reach the western end of Crane Island have been known to tack on a visit to an abandoned lighthouse that lies 2 miles to the north. This towering limestone structure is a forbidding and evocative relic of the past, making it an undeniably attractive destination for intrepid kayakers. But reaching it requires traversing 4 miles of open water (round-trip), and the waters surrounding the lighthouse are often far more challenging than those near shore. These factors make the lighthouse an inappropriate destination for all but the most advanced paddlers.

Wilderness State Park

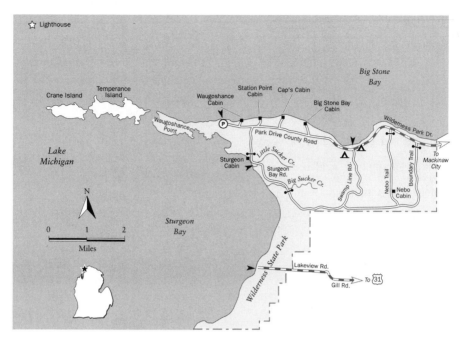

Access: The **east entrance** to Wilderness State Park is located 9 miles west of Mackinaw City. Take County Road 81 west to Wilderness Park Drive, then continue west to the entrance. Good access points along the park's north shoreline include the boat launch just west of the **Lakeshore Campground** and the first of two parking lots off **Park Drive**, a scenic drive that extends westward through the park toward Waugoshance Point. You should be aware, however, that some stretches of shoreline in the park's western reaches are favorite nesting areas of the endangered piping plover and other birds. These nesting areas are off-limits to park visitors. Another park entrance is located at the south end of **Sturgeon Bay**. This entrance can be reached from U.S. Highway 31 by turning west on Gill Road, located 4 miles south of the juncture of U.S. 31 and Interstate 75. Take Gill Road for 5 miles to Lakeview Road, then continue west on Lakeview for 3 miles to the parking lot. This lot can be used by paddlers interested in exploring Sturgeon Bay. In addition, a smaller launch/parking area located near Sturgeon Cabin can also be used for this purpose. The scenic coastline of this bay is cut from the same rough-hewn cloth as Waugoshance Point and its nearby islands, but its shoally, boulder-strewn waters are vulnerable to southerly and westerly winds.

Additional Help

MA & G grid: 93, B8; 94, B1.

Camping: Facilities at Wilderness State Park include 250 modern sites, at Lakeshore Campground (150 sites) and Pines Campground (100 sites), and three rustic bunkhouses, each equipped with twenty-four bunks. The park also maintains six rustic cabins—including four situated on the Straits of Mackinac—that are extremely popular; call well in advance if you hope to use one of these as your kayaking base camp.

Food, gas, and lodging: Mackinaw City.

For more information: Wilderness State Park.

Rentals/guided trips: None.

34 Au Train River

Character: A mellow river that serves as a pleasant outing for families visiting the Pictured Rocks area.

Location: Flows northward through Alger County from Forest Lake to Lake Superior.

Length: 17 miles.

Run: Approximately 10 miles, from the southeast shore of Au Train Lake to the river's mouth at Lake Superior.

Average run time: 4–6 hours.

Class: Flatwater.

Skill level: Beginner/intermediate.

Optimal flow: April–September.

Average gradient: Less than 2 feet per mile.

Hazards: Deep water and possible high winds on Au Train Lake.

Fishing: Good fishing with walleye, perch, northern pike, and suckers available year-round; steelhead runs in spring, salmon runs in fall.

Maps: USGS 1:25,000 - Au Train-MI; 1:100,000 - Munising-MI; 1:250,000 - Marquette-MI.

The paddling: The placid Au Train River got its name from the French voyageurs, who had to drag (or *trainerant*) their canoes over a sandy shoal at the river's mouth on Lake Superior. In the 1880s it served as a major logging run, transporting 10 million board-feet of pine in one year. Today it carries families in canoes from the resorts that line the shores of scenic Au Train Lake to the popular swimming beach at the river's mouth.

The U.S. Forest Service has designated a canoe trail along approximately 10 miles of the Au Train. The route begins at the boat launch on the southeast shore of Au Train Lake. This lake is a popular spot for resort-goers and retirees, so paddlers should be wary of motorboat traffic. In addition, paddling a mile across the lake can be difficult or even dangerous during periods of strong north winds. The canoe route exits the lake in the northeast corner and meanders westward another mile to the southern H-03 bridge access. This section of the river tends to be wide and slow, and passes through banks lined with cottages.

About 0.5 mile past the bridge, the Au Train enters Hiawatha National Forest. The river narrows and begins to twist and turn through this 5-mile section, although it retains its mellow current. Paddlers are likely to see a variety of wildlife, including ducks, herons, kingfishers, muskrats, turtles, and an occasional eagle or osprey. By the time it reaches the northern H-03 bridge access, the Au Train begins to widen into a series of sloughs. The

Au Train River

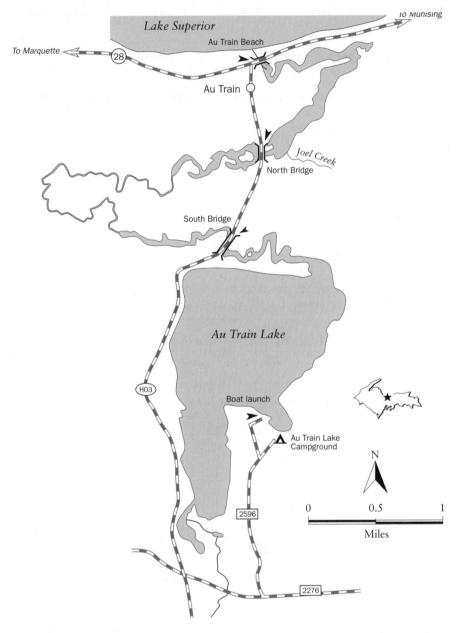

Lake Superior

To Munising

Au Train Beach

To Marquette

28

Au Train

Joel Creek

North Bridge

South Bridge

Au Train Lake

H03

Boat launch

Au Train Lake
Campground

N

2596

0   0.5   1

Miles

2276

remaining 3-mile section takes paddlers through a sandy marsh and past the town of Au Train to Lake Superior.

The mouth of the Au Train, near the M–28 bridge, is a popular swimming spot along the sandy Lake Superior shoreline. The river's waters are warmed by the sun in the shallow upstream marshes, which creates a pleasant alternative to the bracing chill of the big lake.

Access: To reach the U.S. Forest Service boat launch at **Au Train Lake**, take H-03 (Au Train Forest Lake Road) south about 3.5 miles from Au Train. Go east 0.5 mile on FH 2276, then north 1 mile on FH 2596, and follow the signs. The **southern bridge access** is located about 1.5 miles south of Au Train on H-03, while the **northern bridge access** is about 0.5 mile south of Au Train on H-03.

Additional Help

MA & G grid: 102, A2–B2.

Camping: Au Train Lake Campground, 37 rustic sites on Au Train Lake with boat launch, picnic area, and popular songbird trail; Bay Furnace Campground, 50 rustic sites on Lake Superior near Christmas.

Food, gas, and lodging: Au Train, Christmas, Munising.

For more information: Hiawatha National Forest, Munising Ranger District; Au Train Tourist Association.

Canoe liveries: Northwoods Resort, Riverside Resort.

Access Point	Float Distance To Next Access Point
Au Train Lake	2 miles
H-03 South Bridge	5 miles
H-03 North Bridge	3 miles
Au Train Beach (Lake Superior)	Take Out

Bete Grise Bay

Character: A quiet and scenic kayaking destination on the Keweenaw Peninsula's southern shores.

Location: Southeastern Keweenaw County on Lake Superior.

Size: 12 miles round-trip from Bete Grise Beach to the Montreal River Falls; 18 miles round-trip from Bete Grise Beach to Burnette Park.

Skill level: Intermediate (to Montreal River Falls and back); advanced (to Burnette Park and back).

Hazards: Exposure to southerly and easterly winds; sparse landing options along significant sections of coastline, especially in rough seas; boat traffic in Lac La Belle and in vicinity of channel.

Maps: USGS 1:25,000 - Fort Wilkins-MI, Lake Medora-MI, Point Isabelle-MI, Deer Lake-MI; 1:100,000 - Hancock-MI, Copper Harbor-MI; 1:250,000 - Hancock-MI. NOAA chart 14964.

The paddling: Bete Grise Bay is a lovely and tranquil piece of southern Keweenaw shoreline. Sheltered from northerly and westerly winds by the looming ridges that track through the peninsula's midsection, the bay often receives kayakers who have been chased from the Keweenaw's exposed northern coastline. But Bete Grise Bay is a worthy destination in its own right. It features miles of quiet shoreline, offers waterfalls and other interesting natural features, and provides access into the sheltered waters of Lac La Belle. These attributes, coupled with infrequent but easily accessible launch sites, make the bay a great choice for an extended day trip.

Most paddlers who visit these waters begin their excursions at Bete Grise Beach, located in the northern corner of the bay. No defined parking lot exists here, but the shoulder of the road affords plenty of space for parking. From here you can either venture east to the mouth of the Hurricane River, or head south, pushing around Point Isabelle to as far as Burnette Park.

The paddle from Bete Grise Beach east to the Montreal River (not to be confused with the river of the same name that forms the western boundary of Gogebic County) is the most popular one in Bete Grise Bay. This 6-mile jaunt (one-way) takes you past cobblestone beaches, rocky bluffs (look for eagles), and picturesque woodlands to the Montreal's rivermouth, a waterfall that splashes directly into Lake Superior. A small beach next to the falls offers a good resting spot. More experienced kayakers can continue on from here to the cobble beaches of Keystone Bay, where primitive camping can be had on state land. All in all, this is a scenic and often peaceful paddle. This slice of coastline offers protected paddling in northerly or westerly winds, but winds from the south or east can create difficult conditions for landing along rocky sections of shoreline.

Another paddling option for kayakers visiting Bete Grise Bay is to explore its southern ramparts. The first notable attraction along this route is the canal that connects Lac La Belle to Lake Superior proper. Paddlers who turn into the canal will find a peaceful lake, its shoreline dotted with summer cottages. This canal was originally built in 1866 to help transport copper from the Keweenaw mines to industrial ports all along the Great Lakes.

Bete Grise Bay

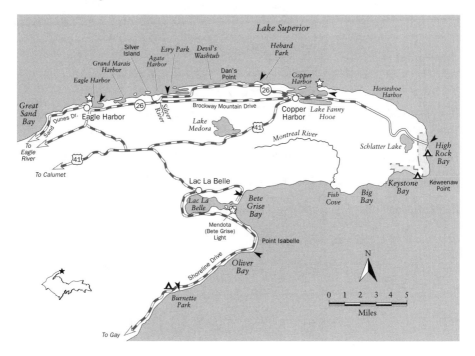

A few years later, the Mendota or Bete Grise Lighthouse was constructed to help guide ships to this remote port. Today, though, the canal is used only by recreational boaters, and the non-operational lighthouse—which sits on the southern bank of the canal near the entrance to Lake Superior—provides a mute reminder of a bygone era in the region's history.

Continuing southward from Lac La Belle, the high ridges that dominate the peninsula's northern interior begin to drop back, giving way to gentler slopes of forest. Monstrous slabs of stone and cobble/sand beaches continue to gird significant pieces of shoreline along here, as do extended stretches of private property. Point Isabelle, which marks the southern end of Bete Grise Bay, lies 3 miles below Bete Grise Beach. Burnette Park, located along Shoreline Drive, sits another 6 miles down the coastline. If the day is a nice one, Burnette Park's sandy swimming beach, attractive picnic area, and toilet facilities make it a good final destination for car-spotting paddlers. In between Point Isabelle and Burnette Park, the shoreline features a blend of sandstone ledges, shallow coves, and sandy beaches.

Access: Bete Grise Beach lies 17 miles south of Copper Harbor. Take U.S. Highway 41 south out of Copper Harbor for approximately 12 miles, then go south on the Lac La Belle road for 8 miles. You can park on the shoulder along the road. A public boat launch site exists on the north end of **Lac La Belle**. To reach it, take U.S. 41 south out of Copper

Harbor for 12 miles, then follow the Lac La Bell Road for 5 miles into the village. **Burnette Park** lies 10 miles north of Gay on Shoreline Drive.

Additional Help

MA & G grid: 118, A1–A2; 119, B8.

Camping: Fort Wilkins State Park in Copper Harbor maintains a modern campground with 165 sites.

Food, gas, and lodging: Copper Harbor, Gay, Lac La Belle.

For more information: Keweenaw Tourism Council.

Rentals/guided trips: Upper Peninsula Adventure Travel.

A remote stretch of coastline along Bete Grise Bay on the Keweenaw Peninsula.

36 | Big Island Lake Wilderness Area

Character: An ideal locale for canoeists who like to catch their supper after a day of paddling and exploration.

Location: Part of Hiawatha National Forest in western Schoolcraft County.

Size: Twenty-three lakes ranging in size from 5 to 149 acres, spread over 5,000 acres.

Skill level: Beginner/intermediate.

Hazards: Orienteering skills are necessary to reach some lakes and for off-trail exploration.

Fishing: Many of the lakes are managed for trophy fishing (both cold- and warmwater species available); anglers should consult the Michigan DNR fishing regulations guide for special fishing regulations in the Big Island Lake Area.

Maps: USGS 1:25,000 - Juniper-MI, Corner Lake-MI; 1:100,000 - Munising-MI; 1:250,000 - Marquette-MI.

The paddling: The inland lakes comprising Big Island Lake Wilderness Area attract paddlers from all over the region. Home to a wide range of wildlife, the lakes and their surrounding hillsides of white birch, aspen, and maple offer visitors a pristine and secluded setting in which to explore and enjoy the outdoors. Canoeists who enjoy putting a line in the water are particularly fond of the Big Island Lake Area, for its streams and lakes offer terrific sport-fishing opportunities.

While twenty-three lakes lie within the boundaries of the wilderness area, nine of them receive nearly all the paddling pressure. Connected by a series of maintained portage trails, these lakes run through the midsection of the area, from Big Island Lake in its northwest corner to Byers Lake in its southeast section. Three major footpaths lie along the wilderness area's western boundary (County Road 445) and serve as the primary access routes to these portage-connected lakes. The paths are clearly marked, and each has a parking area at the entrance.

The northernmost of these paths (less than 0.5 mile in length) will take you to the western corner of Big Island Lake, the namesake for the entire wilderness area. A gorgeous lake framed by shining stands of trees, Big Island Lake is the most heavily visited of all the lakes in the area. But even here, paddlers will be able to find a secluded stretch of shoreline for themselves on all but the most crowded of weekends. From Big Island Lake, portages can deliver you to Mid Lake, Townline Lake (which boasts a number of picturesque coves and peninsulas), and points south.

A second trail leads from the road to Neds Lake, a quiet beauty with a lone designated campsite but no established portage trails linking it to the rest of the wilderness. Another Big Island Lake Wilderness footpath, which formerly delivered paddlers to the south end of Coattail Lake, has reportedly been closed.

The southernmost of the trails into Big Island Lake Wilderness is more than a mile long, so the bulk of its traffic is comprised of hikers unencumbered by canoes. If you're

Big Island Lake Wilderness

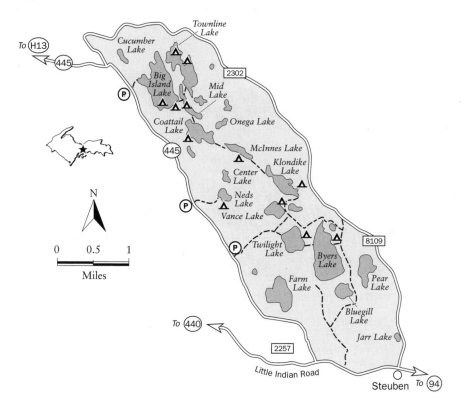

willing to make the haul, though, the trail will take you to scenic Twilight Lake, which in turn is connected by a short portage to Byers Lake, which rivals Big Island Lake in size.

If you decide to light out for Big Island Lake Wilderness, keep in mind that mechanized equipment, bikes, motors, carts, trailers, and other wheeled devices are not allowed in the wilderness area. In addition, you should be prepared for primitive camping conditions; the absence of garbage cans means that you should adhere to the "pack-it-in, pack-it-out" method of handling trash. Finally, the interior of the wilderness area includes a sometimes-confusing maze of old two-tracks and other trails that wander off in all directions, and some maps of the area include misleading or out-of-date information. Visitors without a compass and good orienteering skills can become lost, so use good judgment when exploring the region.

Access: The Big Island Lake Wilderness Area is located about 22 miles northwest of Manistique and about 15 miles southeast of Munising. It is bounded on the south by CR–437, on the west by CR–445, on the northeast by Forest Road 2303, and on the south by FR–8109 (an abandoned railroad grade also known as Haywire Grade).

A serene lake within the Big Island Lake Wilderness Area.

To reach the wilderness area from Manistique, take M–94 approximately 20 miles north to CR–437. Turn east and follow for 3 miles to CR–445. To reach Big Island Lake from Munising, take Forest Highway 13 south for 12 miles to CR–445 and turn east. If you're making your way on H–13 from Munising, you should be aware of a sign that can be confusing. A sign for Island Lake National Forest Campground lies about 1.3 miles north of the junction of H–13 and CR–445; ignore the sign, for it directs travelers to a Forest Service campground that is not a part of the Big Island Lake Wilderness Area.

All three major trails into Big Island Lake Wilderness Area lie along CR–445. The trail leading to Big Island Lake is located 3.3 miles west of CR–445's juncture with H–13, and the trail leading to Neds Lake lies 3 miles south of the Big Island Lake Trail. The Twilight Lake Trail is located another mile or so south on CR–445.

Additional Help

MA & G grid: 102, C4; 103, C5.

Camping: Overnight camping in Big Island Lake Wilderness Area is permitted at designated sites. These campsites consist of a site post, metal fire ring, and pit latrine. There are currently a dozen campsites scattered across the wilderness. Regulations prohibit camping at sites posted as closed. In addition, groups larger than six may not occupy one individual site. Currently, there are no permits required for camping or day use in the Big Island Lake Wilderness. For more information on camping and day-use regulations, contact Hiawatha National Forest.

Food, gas, and lodging: Munising, Manistique, Steuben.

For more information: Hiawatha National Forest, Munising Ranger District.

Canoe liveries: None.

Portages	Distance and Grade
Big Island Lake–Mid Lake	100 feet; easy
Townline Lake–Mid Lake	200 feet; easy
Mid Lake–Coattail Lake	425 feet; difficult
Coattail Lake–McInnes Lake	1,050 feet; moderate
McInnes Lake–Klondike Lake	1,235 feet; easy
Klondike Lake–Vance Lake	1,799 feet; easy
Vance Lake–Twilight Lake	1,490 feet; easy
Twilight Lake–Byers Lake	780 feet; easy

Brule River

Character: A wild and picturesque river that serves as part of the border between Michigan's Upper Peninsula and northern Wisconsin.

Location: Passes between Iron County, Michigan, and Forest and Florence Counties in Wisconsin.

Length: 48 miles.

Run: 44.5 miles, from M–73 to Brule River Flowage.

Average run time: 15–18 hours.

Class: I–II.

Skill level: Beginner/intermediate.

Optimal flow: April–October.

Average gradient: 6 feet per mile.

Hazards: Relatively remote location; occasional class I–II rapids.

Fishing: Brook and brown trout, walleye, and northern pike (the section from M–73 to M–189 is a designated Blue Ribbon Trout Stream).

Maps: USGS 1:25,000 - Hagerman Lake-MI, Iron River-MI, Tipler-MI, Gaastra-MI, Fortune Lakes-MI, Florence West-WI, Florence East-WI; 1:100,000 - Iron River-MI, Iron Mountain-MI; 1:250,000 - Iron Mountain-MI.

The paddling: The Brule River is an often-overlooked treasure of the North Country. The stream, which defines a 45-mile stretch of border between the states of Michigan and Wisconsin, slices through a vast expanse of near wilderness before joining with the Michigamme River to form the Menominee River. Most of the land on the Wisconsin side of the river is part of Nicolet National Forest, while large sections of the Michigan side are owned by the state. Blessed with cold and clear waters, unbroken pavilions of forestland, and a terrific profusion of wildlife (including osprey, bald eagles, mergansers, mallards, moose, and deer), the Brule is a true pleasure to canoe from spring through fall. Best of all, the Brule receives remarkably little pressure from paddlers or anglers despite its many winning qualities.

With the exception of a few widely spaced spots, the Brule River also offers a placid float that is suitable for canoeists with basic skills. But the stream does include a couple of class II rapids that can challenge paddlers, especially when the water gets pushy at higher volumes. In addition, the river passes through isolated areas where help can be hard to come by. For these reasons, the Brule is not recommended for parties without experienced paddlers.

The Brule is navigable by canoe for much of its length, making it a good choice if you are looking for a two- or three-day excursion. The best launching spot to explore the river's uppermost reaches is the USFS Brule River Campground, on Wisconsin 55 just south of the Michigan border (the bridge itself has no access). The river is narrow and lined with alders in these upper reaches, with a slow but steady current and pleasant riffles. As you make your way downstream, occasional feeder streams add to the Brule's volume, includ-

Approaching Two-Foot Falls on the Brule River, which forms the border between Michigan and Wisconsin.

ing Allen Creek (about 8 miles downstream from W–55/M–73) and Huff Creek (another 5 miles downstream).

As you pass below the M–189/W–139 bridge, the river remains slow and shallow (1 to 3 feet), with an average width of 40 to 60 feet. Numerous riffles murmur over the Brule's rocky bottom through here, and during low-water periods you'll have to stick to deeper channels on the outer bends to avoid bumping and scraping. This section of the river also features some of the Brule's prettiest scenery, for the stream passes through woodlands of pine, maple, and cedar that rise high above the waterway. Birch are particularly numerous and handsome through here, standing sentinel in long and ragged lines that stretch far down the river corridor.

The Iron River joins the Brule from the Michigan side about 6 miles downstream from the M–189/W–139 bridge (this tributary can be identified by the presence of a railroad bridge on the Brule immediately below the mouth of the Iron). The increased water volume from the Iron River deepens the Brule and gives it a reddish hue. The current picks up here as well, while riffles continue to pop up regularly. The alternative landing site on Forest Road 2152 lies about 0.5 mile below the entrance of the Iron, but it is difficult to spot from the river (this makes the site a better bet for putting in than taking out).

About 3 miles below the mouth of the Iron River, you will encounter the first rapids of any consequence on the Brule. Twin Rapids begins with a relatively short class I run through a rock garden. It then offers up a few hundred yards of quiet water before chug-

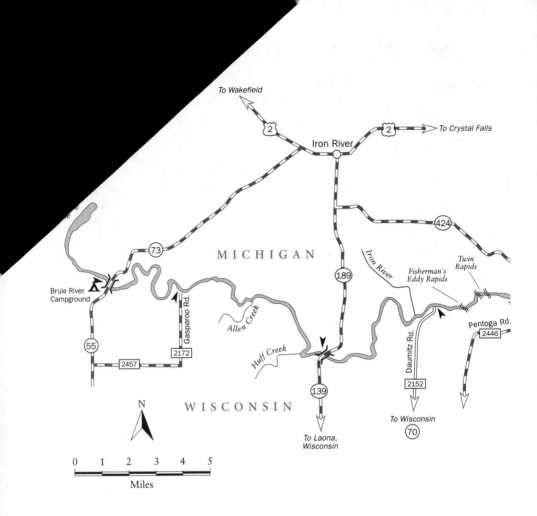

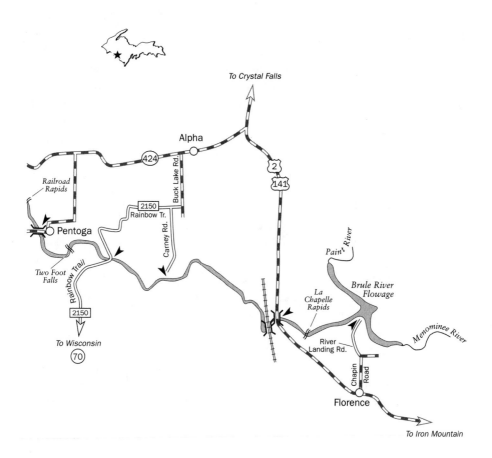

ging into a second run through boulder-strewn waters. This second set of rapids (class I–II) is the more challenging of the two, especially during spring run off and other high-water periods.

Below Twin Rapids, boulders dot the river for the remainder of its length. The Brule also remains a grudging provider of shoreline campsites through here, thanks to the stream's overgrown banks. As you approach Pentoga Bridge, the river averages 60 to 70 feet across and moves at a steady clip. Pentoga Bridge provides relatively low clearance over the river, and paddlers often portage it (on the right) at higher water levels. Two miles downstream from the bridge is Two-Foot Falls (class II), a ledge that spans the entire width of the river. A tongue of water near the right bank provides paddlers with a clear route over the drop, but this run can be tricky for inexperienced canoeists because the river quickly veers to the left immediately downstream. Use the portage trail on the right bank to bypass the drop. This trail also leads to a fine campsite that overlooks the river (white-noise fans will appreciate the churning of the falls immediately upstream, and the site's placement on the Wisconsin side of the river lets campers bask in the sun until dusk).

The 2 miles from Two-Foot Falls to FR 2150 (Rainbow Trail) feature fun riffles over a rocky bottom. Riffles and occasional small boulder fields continue below Rainbow, but as you approach U.S. Highway 2, longer stretches of flatwater appear. Densely wooded islands also become more frequent as you make your way downstream. But most of the land below Rainbow Trail is privately owned on both sides of the river, severely limiting camping opportunities from this point forward.

Carney's Landing is an attractive site that offers access from the Michigan side. It is located about 8 miles downstream from Pentoga Bridge. Paddlers continuing downstream, meanwhile, should keep their eyes peeled for another old railroad bridge. Shortly after passing the bridge, which signals the approach to U.S. 2/U.S. 141, the river divides around a massive island. Stick to the left side, which offers clearer passage. The massive pillars of the interstate bridge lie a short distance downstream. Take out on the left.

From the bridge at U.S. 2/U.S. 141 to Brule River Flowage, the stream continues to feature scattered islands and stretches of riffly water. La Chapelle Rapids (class I–II) appears about 2 miles downstream from the bridge. This is an extended stretch of light whitewater that winds in an S-shape through rock gardens before finally petering out after a hundred yards or so. Portage on the right if the rapids look too daunting.

As the Brule nears the Brule River Flowage, the current slackens and the high banks that predominated farther upstream return. You can take out at the landing that appears just inside the flowage on the right (Wisconsin) bank.

Access: The **USFS Brule River Campground** is located on W–55, just south of the Michigan-Wisconsin state line. The **FR–2172** put-in site can be reached by taking FR–2172 (Gasparoo Road) north from its juncture with W–70 for about 6 miles. The **M–189/W–139 Bridge** lies 6 miles south of Iron River on M–189. The end of **FR–2152** (Daumitz Road) is sometimes used as an alternate access site; it lies 8 miles north of the road's juncture with W–70. **Pentoga Road Bridge** is located 0.25 mile west of the small town of Pentoga, Michigan, on FR–2446 (Pentoga Road). The landing at **FR–2150** (Rainbow Trail) is about 6 miles southwest of Alpha, Michigan; take CR–424 west from Alpha for 0.5 mile, turn south on Buck Lake Road for 2 miles, then west on Rainbow Trail and drive for about 3 miles to reach this access site. The **Carney Road Landing** lies 3 miles south of Alpha on Carney Road. The bridge at **U.S. 2/U.S. 141** lies 10 miles south of Crystal Falls, Michigan, and 4 miles northwest of Florence, Wisconsin. The landing at **Brule River Flowage** is 3 miles north of Florence; take Chapin Road north out of town for 2 miles, then turn left on River Landing Road and follow to the take-out.

Additional Help

MA & G grid: 98, D2–D4; 87, A5–A7.

Camping: Many paddlers set up camp on the banks of the Brule, which runs through national forest land for much of its length. You can camp anywhere along the banks of Nicolet National Forest on the Wisconsin side, but permits are supposed to be secured before camping on Michigan DNR land. Nicolet National Forest also maintains the rustic Brule River Campground (11 campsites). This campground, which provides direct access to the stream, is located just south of the W–55/M–73 bridge and is a good starting point for overnight excursions. Other campgrounds in Nicolet National Forest within reasonable driving distance include Windsor Dam (8 sites), Stevens Lake (6 sites), Chipmunk Rapids (6 sites), and Lost Lake (27 sites).

Food, gas, and lodging: Iron River and Crystal Falls in Michigan; Florence and Conover in Wisconsin.

For more information: Ottawa National Forest (Michigan), Nicolet National Forest (Wisconsin).

Canoe liveries/outfitters: Northwoods Wilderness Outfitters (Michigan), Rohr's Wilderness Tours (Wisconsin).

Access Point	Float Distance To Next Access Point
Brule River Campground	5 miles
FR–2172 (Gasparoo Road)-WI	9.5 miles
M–189/W–139 Bridge	7 miles
FR–2152-WI	5 miles

Access Point	Float Distance To Next Access Point
Pentoga Road Bridge	4.5 miles
FR–2150 (Rainbow Trail)	3.5 miles
Carney Road Landing	6.5 miles
U.S. 2/U.S. 141	3.5 miles
Brule River Flowage-WI	Take Out

(Note: "WI" in above chart designates access sites from Wisconsin side of river only)

Carp River

Character: A pretty, twisty river that passes through the Mackinac Wilderness and Hiawatha National Forest.
Location: Mackinac County.
Length: 50 miles.
Run: 19 miles, from M–123 to St. Martin Bay.
Average run time: 8–10 hours.
Class: Flatwater (with occasional stretches of class I–II water during high-water periods).
Skill level: Intermediate.
Optimal flow: April–June.
Average gradient: 3 feet per mile.
Hazards: Logjams and fallen trees throughout river corridor; occasional light rapids.
Fishing: Known as a good river for brook, brown, and rainbow trout.
Maps: USGS 1:25,000 - Kenneth-MI, Ozard SE-MI, Charles-MI; 1:100,000 - Saulte Ste. Marie South-MI; 1:250,000 - Sault Saint Marie-MI.

The paddling: The Carp River is a designated Wild and Scenic River that is ideal for early season overnight expeditions. Easily accessible (by U.P. standards, at least), the Carp winds through Hiawatha National Forest for nearly all of its canoeable length, offering up numerous shoreline campsites along the way. The surrounding terrain is a pleasant blend of wetlands and dense forest, and the river corridor supports a tremendous variety of wildlife, including beaver, black bear, pine marten, mink, snowshoe hare, bald eagle, osprey, sandhill crane, and great blue heron. The river's temperament, meanwhile, varies with the season, as is the case with so many U.P. streams. During the spring, snowmelt transforms the Carp into a moderately fast river that boasts a couple of fun rapids. The bustling current makes good maneuvering skills a must during this time of the year, for the Carp is narrow (35 to 45 feet), twisty, and cluttered with fallen trees and logjams for much of its length. As the water level drops during the summer months, the current slackens and the stream's obstacles become easier to negotiate. During such periods, the canoe trail can be paddled by less experienced folks. But when water levels get too low—and they often do by midsummer—obstacles increase in number and some sections become too shallow to float.

The Carp River originates in southern Chippewa County, then ambles eastward before emptying into Lake Huron's St. Martin Bay. Some paddlers launch from Forest Road 3458, but the 6-mile stretch from there to M–123 is narrow and overgrown. The river widens and clears somewhat below M–123, making it a better put-in for overnight excursions.

The entire 7-mile run from M–123 downstream to East Lake Road (FR–3119) passes through the Mackinac Wilderness, a lovely and untamed region of Hiawatha National Forest. Motorized equipment and vehicles are prohibited throughout this section of the forest. If you choose to explore this twisty section of the river, you will find plenty of fallen

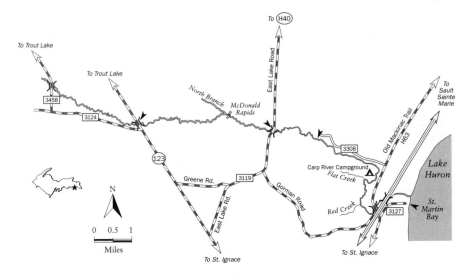

trees, sweepers, and logjams to maneuver around, many of them on the outer bends. You'll also get a dose of light rapids midway through the Wilderness. This run, dubbed McDonald Rapids, is at a washed-out dam located a short distance downstream from the Carp's confluence with its north branch.

From East Lake Road to the Carp River National Forest Campground, the stream runs shallow (1 to 4 feet) over a sandy bottom and receives plenty of shade from shoreline stands of fir, cedar, maple, and birch. Springtime runoff creates class I rapids midway through this section and just above the national forest campground. From the campground to the rivermouth, the Carp continues to offer pleasant paddling through hardy woodlands. The tranquil and remote feel of the stream's upper reaches is hard to maintain, though, as signs of civilization (traffic noises, other river users) multiply. The river's best springtime whitewater, meanwhile, can be found immediately below the Interstate 75 Bridge. This extended run (class II in spring) includes standing waves capable of dousing bow paddlers. During the summer months, however, these rapids subside considerably. A public boat launch at the entrance to St. Martin Bay serves as the final take-out spot on the canoe trail.

Access: To reach the **M–123 Bridge** from St. Ignace, take I–75 north for 2 miles, then follow M–123 northwest for 10 miles. The **East Lake Road Bridge** is located 5 miles north of M–123 on East Lake Road (FR–3119). The access site at the end of **Forest Road 3308** is located 3 miles west of Old Mackinac Trail Road (H–63), approximately 15 miles north of St. Ignace. The **Carp River National Forest Campground** is 8 miles north of St. Ignace off Old Mackinac Trail (H–63). The **rivermouth boat launch** can be reached by taking H–63 to just below the underpass of Interstate 75, then turning right on FR–3127 to the parking lot. In addition to these existing launch/take-out sites, new management plans for the Carp River may include the construction of additional canoe launches in the future. Contact Hiawatha National Forest for more information.

Additional Help

MA & G grid: 106, D1–D3.

Camping: Camping is permitted all along the river corridor in Hiawatha National Forest. In addition, the forest service has designated six specific shoreline spots as dispersed camping sites. Carp River National Forest Campground (located just west of I–75 on H–63) includes 44 rustic sites in a spacious and attractive setting.

Food, gas, and lodging: St. Ignace, Hessel, Trout Lake.

For more information: Hiawatha National Forest.

Canoe liveries: None.

Access Point	Float Distance To Next Access Point
M–123 Bridge	7.5 miles
East Lake Road Bridge (FR–3119)	4 miles
Forest Road 3308 Access	3 miles
Carp River Campground	4.5 miles
Rivermouth	Take Out

Copper Harbor/Eagle Harbor

Character: Two beautiful Keweenaw Peninsula harbors linked by a dozen miles of rugged Lake Superior shoreline.

Location: Northwestern shoreline of the Keweenaw Peninsula in Keweenaw County.

Size: Copper Harbor is 3 miles long and 0.5 mile wide, while Eagle Harbor is 1 mile long and 0.25 mile wide. The bays lie approximately 13 miles apart.

Skill level: Beginner (for paddles inside either bay); advanced (for trips from one harbor to the other).

Hazards: Cold water; exposure to northerly winds; sections of shoreline unsuited for landings, especially in rough weather; light boat traffic in both harbors.

Maps: USGS 1:25,000 - Eagle Harbor-MI, Delaware-MI, Lake Medora-MI, Fort Wilkins-MI; 1:100,000 - Hancock-MI, Copper Harbor-MI; 1:250,000 - Hancock-MI. NOAA chart 14964.

The paddling: The Keweenaw Peninsula is a gorgeous land of rocky ridges, deep forests, and agate beaches that juts far out into the icy waters of Lake Superior. Picturesque and wild, its shoreline abounds with prized kayaking destinations, from Keweenaw Bay all the way up to Keweenaw Point. But few areas of the peninsula can compare to Eagle Harbor and Copper Harbor for sheer paddling pleasure. Both harbors feature sheltered bays, open beaches, and historic lighthouses that conjure up visions of an earlier maritime era, while the shoreline that connects the two harbors is a magnificent expanse of multi-hued boulders and wind-twisted forestlands.

In the 1900s, mining towns sprouted all up and down the remote valleys and ridgelines of the claw-shaped Keweenaw Peninsula, their inhabitants laboring mightily to harvest the region's vast copper reserves. Today, however, the mines of Copper Country—as the peninsula is sometimes called—are silent, and the towns that remain increasingly rely on tourism for their survival. Two of the healthiest villages on the Keweenaw's northern shore are Eagle Harbor and Copper Harbor. Eagle Harbor has emerged as an attractive summer resort destination over the years, while Copper Harbor has become a top tourist attraction, thanks to its proximity to Fort Wilkins State Park, its status as a main launching point to Isle Royale National Park, and its standing as Michigan's northernmost community.

The chief attraction for kayakers in 1-mile-long Eagle Harbor is the large brick lighthouse that sits on its western end. The Eagle Harbor Lighthouse, perched so that it looks out over both the crescent bay and the seemingly limitless waters of Lake Superior, is now part of a small museum complex that covers the mining and maritime history of the region. A sand beach spans the interior of the bay, which is backed by boreal forestlands that march up onto the high hills and ridgelines of the peninsula interior. A parking area and boat launch at the east end of the harbor provide good access to its waters.

Copper Harbor looks out at Lake Superior from the Keweenaw's northern shoreline. Nestled amid steep hillsides of thick forest, the bay features a historic lighthouse at Hayes

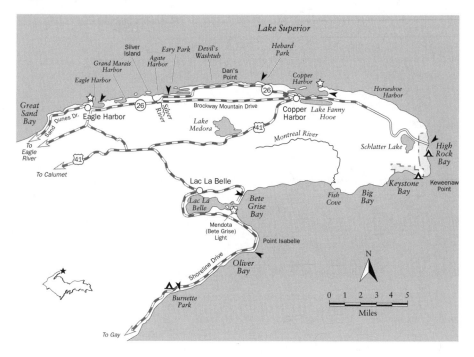

Point on its eastern end and a string of sheltering islands that protect the waters at its western end. The Copper Harbor Marina, which houses the *Isle Royale Queen III* ferry in between voyages to and from Isle Royale National Park, is located in this western section of the bay. The only section of the harbor that is exposed to northern winds is the gap between Hayes Point and the Porter's Island shoals, making much of its length ideal for exploration by novice paddlers. But the harbor is a worthwhile destination for kayakers of all skill levels, for it features lots of scenic shoreline and fine opportunities for viewing loons and other waterfowl.

The 13-mile stretch of Lake Superior shoreline that links Copper Harbor to Eagle Harbor should only be explored by experienced kayakers. The rocky shores that prevail through here severely limit landing options and create reflective waves in rough seas. Advanced paddlers blessed with good weather, however, will be delighted with this slice of Copper Country shoreline. Grand Marais Harbor, located 2 miles east of Eagle Harbor, is a picturesque bay that offers good shelter. The midway point between Eagle Harbor and Copper Harbor is lovely Agate Harbor, which is guarded at its western end by Silver Island and the mouth of the Silver River. Continuing eastward, the 7-mile stretch from Agate Harbor to Copper Harbor is a tremendously scenic paddle past boulder-and-rock shorelines backed by magnificent hillsides of northern forest, but this is the most exposed portion of the journey. The so-called Devil's Washtub, a series of rock outcroppings located

The Copper Harbor area offers a number of possibilities for exploration by kayak.

midway between Agate Harbor and Copper Harbor, can create particularly hazardous conditions in rough seas.

Access: To put in at **Eagle Harbor**, drive east out of town on M–26 to Marina Road and turn north. The parking lot and launch site lie at the end of the road, less than 1 mile from M–26. Kayakers launching in **Copper Harbor** can either use the Copper Harbor Marina, which lies just north of U.S. Highway 41 near the center of the village, or the gravel beach on the south side of Hayes Point, near the lighthouse. Paddlers who choose this put-in can use the lighthouse parking lot, located just north of U.S. 41 on the east end of town, for a small fee (follow the signs to reach the lot). Other access sites located in between the two harbors on M–26 include **Esry Park** and **Hebard Park**, both of which have picnic facilities.

Additional Help

MA & G grid: 118, A1–A2; 119, A7–A8.

Camping: Fort Wilkins State Park, located at Copper Harbor, includes a campground of 165 modern sites that occasionally fills to capacity on midsummer weekends.

Food, gas, and lodging: Copper Harbor, Eagle Harbor, Calumet.

For more information: Fort Wilkins State Park, Keweenaw Tourism Council.

Rentals/guided trips: Keweenaw Adventure Company.

▦ 40 Craig Lake State Park

Character: One of the state's premier destinations for wilderness canoeing and camping.

Location: Eastern Baraga County.

Size: Six lakes spread out over 6,900 acres.

Skill level: Beginner/intermediate.

Hazards: Deep and cold water; windy conditions are capable of kicking up significant waves on bigger lakes.

Fishing: Anglers work the lakes within the park for a wide range of species, including muskellunge, bass, northern pike, and walleye. Fishing permitted only with artificial lures. Catch limits on walleye are two a day (13-inch minimum); fishing for northern pike, bass, and muskellunge is strictly catch-and-release. Statewide possession and size regulations apply for all other species. No motors—including electric motors—are permitted on the lakes with the exception of Keewaydin Lake, which extends outside the park's boundaries. Contact Van Riper State Park for information on additional regulations.

Maps: USGS 1:25,000 - Three Lakes-MI; 1:100,000 - L'Anse-MI; 1:250,000 - Iron River-MI.

The paddling: Even in a state bristling with quality paddling options, Craig Lake State Park stands as one of Michigan's great destinations for canoeing and kayaking. Remote and undeveloped, it is a true northcountry paradise. The lakes of the park feature ruddy shorelines of weathered boulders and windswept forest that are ideal for afternoon hikes, while the waters themselves are clear and quiet and dotted with rugged islands that serve as grand campsites. Craig Lake also supports an abundance of wildlife, including icons of the north like black bears, moose, and loons. Yet despite the park's physical beauty, it remains lightly visited thanks to its dearth of creature comforts and a wonderfully nasty entrance road that effectively turns away behemoth RVs. These factors have done much to preserve the park's peaceful and unspoiled character over the years. One can only hope that the road will be allowed to stay in its current bad-tempered state so that future generations of paddlers will be able to enjoy this wilderness gem.

Back in the early 1950s, the land that now comprises the state park was privately owned by Fred Miller of the Miller Brewing Company. An avid sportsman, he built two cabins on the land and gave names to three area lakes. One of these lakes—Clair—he named after his daughter. The other two—Craig and Teddy—are commonly believed to have been named for his sons, but in actuality they were named for two friends whose identities have become obscured over time. Today, those two cabins remain intact and are available for rent. In 1954 Miller died in an airplane crash and the land was sold to a U.P. timber company. In 1966 the tract was acquired by the state, and one year later, it was made into a state park. It has been a favorite destination for Michigan anglers, paddlers, and hikers ever since (a portion of the North Country Trail runs through the heart of the park).

Craig Lake State Park

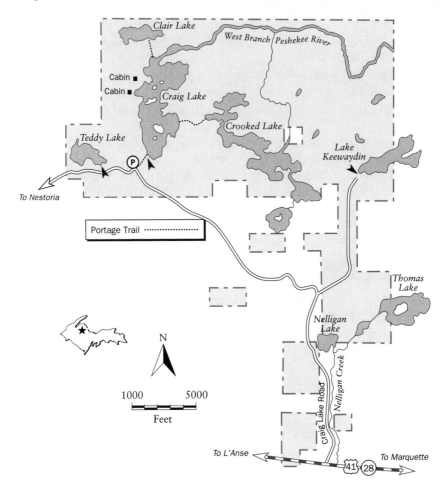

Clair Lake

West Branch Peshekee River

Cabin ■
Cabin ■

Craig Lake

Crooked Lake

Teddy Lake

Lake Keewaydin

To Nestoria

Portage Trail ·······················

N

Thomas Lake

Nelligan Lake

Nelligan Creek

Craig Lake Road

1000   5000

Feet

To L'Anse

To Marquette

41 28

The main parking lot in the state park is located at the southern end of Craig Lake itself. No vehicles are permitted beyond this point; canoeists and other visitors must haul all boats and gear from the lot to the first access point on Craig Lake, about 0.2 mile away. The cabins are located about 1.5 miles north of the parking lot along Craig Lake's western shoreline.

Once you have put in on the southern end of Craig Lake, you have several different exploration options. One alternative is to explore Craig Lake itself. The lake is big (374 acres) and scenic, with several craggy islands, picturesque northwoods shorelines, and looming granite cliffs that gird sections of its northern reaches. In addition, the West Branch of the Peshekee River originates out of the lake's upper northeastern corner. Another option for paddlers is to make the 0.5 mile portage from Craig Lake to Crooked

Lake, a lovely conglomeration of sheltered bays. At the southern base of Crooked Lake, meanwhile, are two unnamed lakes that reportedly are great for fishing (how do 12-inch perch sound?). These lakes are separated from Crooked Lake by a beaver dam.

Smallmouth bass anglers, meanwhile, often head for the loon-haunted waters of Clair Lake. This smaller body of water is connected to Craig Lake's northern end via a difficult 0.3-mile portage trail. You can investigate all three of these lakes over the course of a weekend if you wish, but many visitors set aside a week or so to enjoy the park's spectacular setting and peaceful atmosphere.

Other lakes contained within Craig Lake State Park are not as attractive for paddlers but still receive some attention, especially from canoeists who also fish. These include Teddy Lake, which is situated next to the North Country Trail, and Lake Keewaydin. Both of these lakes have separate parking areas located nearby. Canoeists and kayakers interested in checking out Lake Keewaydin should keep in mind that motorboats are permitted on its waters.

Access: The road leading to **Craig Lake State Park** is located approximately 7 miles west of Van Riper State Park on U.S. Highway 41/M–28. Take Craig Lake Road north from the highway for about 6 miles to the Craig Lake parking area. This is an exceedingly rough and rocky road that passes through actively logged sections of Copper Country State Forest; allow for a half hour or better to reach the parking lot. If you do not have a four-wheel-drive truck or other vehicle with high road clearance, do not attempt to negotiate this road.

Additional Help

MA & G grid: 111, D7.

Camping: Two backcountry cabins are maintained at Craig Lake State Park and can be reserved in advance. Both are located at the northwest end of Craig Lake and afford nice views of the lake. The smaller cabin includes four rooms, a wood stove, and accommodations for six people; the larger building sleeps up to fourteen and has six rooms and a big fireplace. Electricity is not available in either cabin.

Dispersed backcountry camping is allowed anywhere in the park, except near the two cabins and on a privately owned island on Clair Lake. In addition, designated camping facilities are located on the east shore of Craig Lake, south of the portage trail to Crooked Lake (three tent pads), and on Crooked Lake, near the east end of the portage trail (two tent pads).

Food, gas, and lodging: Imperial Heights, Ishpeming, L'Anse.

For more information: Van Riper State Park.

Rentals/guided trips: None.

Drummond Island

Character: A paddler's paradise of sheltered bays, forested islands, and limestone-studded shorelines in northern Lake Huron.

Location: Eastern Chippewa County, directly east of the Upper Peninsula mainland in Lake Huron.

Size: Group of fifty-six islands, of which Drummond Island is the largest (87,000 acres and approximately 80 miles of shoreline).

Skill level: Intermediate/advanced.

Hazards: Significant stretches of exposed and rocky shoreline; submerged boulders and shoals far offshore; windy conditions/inclement weather can create very rough seas; motorboat and freighter traffic on western side of island in De Tour Passage.

Maps: USGS 1:25,000 - Lime Island-MI, De Tour Village-MI, Burnt Island-MI, Whitney Bay-MI, Drummond-MI, Meade Island-MI, Drummond SE-MI, Marble Head-MI; 1:100,000 - Drummond-MI, De Tour Village-MI; 1:250,000 - Blind River-MI, Alpena-MI. NOAA charts 14882, 14880.

The paddling: Drummond Island and its many satellite islands combine to form a marvelous playground for seasoned kayakers. Of course, Drummond's quiet bays and forested shoreline also can be explored and enjoyed by less experienced paddlers on day trips and overnighters, provided they select sensible destinations and take heed of the various hazards of the area. But the Drummond archipelago is particularly suited to veteran kayakers. Drummond features long sections of exposed shoreline, and exploration of some of the outer islands in Potagannissing Bay requires open crossings of a mile or more. In addition, limited access points restrict long-distance paddles to strong kayakers who can handle rough seas, especially along Drummond's rugged eastern ramparts.

But if you are a veteran paddler armed with an appropriate respect for Great Lakes weather, Drummond offers many rewards. Its major bays—Potagannissing and Whitney—are dotted with unspoiled islands, and Drummond's wooded shores are home to healthy populations of loons, herons, and other waterfowl. Drummond even boasts spectacular geologic forms at Marble Head, an expanse of 100-foot-high limestone cliffs that tower over the island's North Channel waters. Best of all, the Drummond Island region sees remarkably light motorboat traffic, even on summer weekends. This factor, combined with the area's considerable natural beauty, makes Drummond Island one of the premier kayaking destinations in the state.

Drummond Island is one of three islands that form the heart of the Manitoulin chain in northern Lake Huron. The other two islands—Manitoulin and Cockburn—are part of Canada, but quirky cartography made Drummond part of the United States back in the early nineteenth century. Prior to that time, the island's history was shaped by its proximity to the St. Mary's River, a major travel route for Ojibwa Indians, early fur traders, and missionaries.

Today, Drummond and its outer islands offer plenty of exciting paddling options for modern-day explorers. Top-flight attractions on the island's remote east side, for example,

Wild sunflowers pop through the rocks along the shore of Drummond Island.

include peaceful Glen Cove and imposing Marble Head. These limestone palisades lie about 4 miles to the south of Glen Cove, which can be reached by putting in at the end of Glen Cove Road.

Another great day-trip option is Whitney Bay, on Drummond's southwest side. This beautiful area is largely undeveloped and supports loons, cormorants, minks, otters, and other wildlife. The forest-fringed bay features several picturesque islands and crystal-clear waters that allow you to scan the rocky bottom on calm days. A trio of islands—Garden, Bellevue, and Arnold—guard the entrance to Whitney Bay. Paddlers who move beyond these islands will be rewarded with fine views of the De Tour Reef Light to the west and the seemingly endless expanse of Lake Huron to the south. A tiny spit of state-owned land known as No Name Island is also part of the Whitney Bay mix. Located just north of Garden Island, this island is a viable picnicking and overnight camping destination for paddlers.

Another excellent area to explore is Potagannissing Bay, a large area of water that contains many of Drummond's outer islands. Most of these islands are privately owned and thus off-limits to curious kayakers. But the bay does hold two islands that can be used for leg-stretching and picnicking. The first of these—Bow Island—is located 1 mile northeast of Drummond Island's Dix Point and 3 miles northwest of the launch site at Drummond Township Park. Situated squarely between Little Trout Island and Surveyors Island, this state-owned island can be used for overnight camping excursions.

Drummond Island

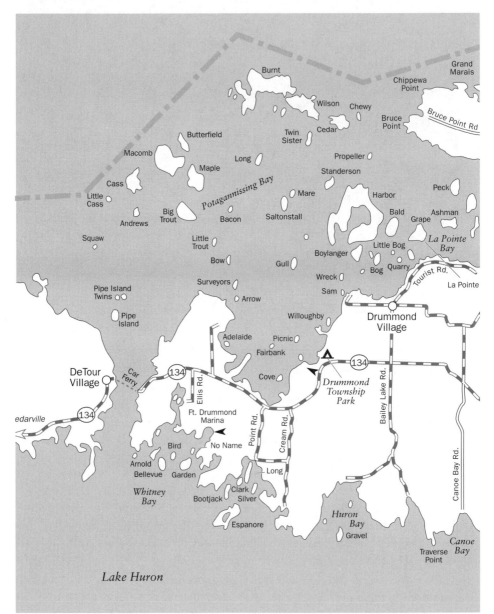

Burnt

Wilson Chewy

Chippewa
Point

Grand
Marais

Twin Cedar
Sister

Bruce
Point

Bruce Point Rd

Butterfield

Macomb

Long

Propeller

Maple

Standerson

Peck

Cass

Mare

Harbor

Little
Cass

Potagannissing Bay

Bald

Ashman

Big Bacon Saltonstall
Trout

Grape

Andrews

La Pointe
Bay

Squaw

Little
Trout

Little Bog

Boylanger

Bow

Gull

Bog Quarry

La Pointe

Wreck

Tourist Rd.

Surveyors

Sam

Pipe Island
Twins

Arrow

Willoughby

Drummond
Village

Pipe
Island

Adelaide

Picnic

Fairbank

DeTour
Village

Car
Ferry

134

Cove

Drummond
Township
Park

134

Bailey Lake Rd.

edarville

134

Ellis Rd.

Ft. Drummond
Marina

Point Rd.

Cream Rd.

Canoe Bay Rd.

Bird

No Name

Arnold
Bellevue Garden

Long

Whitney
Bay

Clark
Bootjack Silver

Huron
Bay

Espanore

Gravel

Canoe
Bay

Traverse
Point

Lake Huron

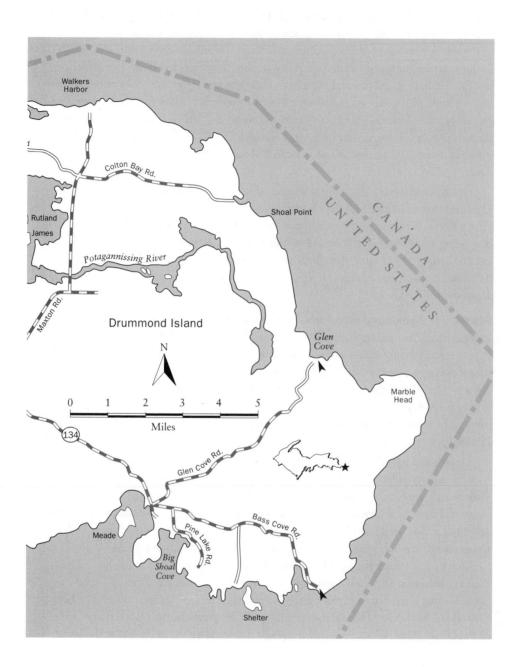

Walkers
Harbor

Colton Bay Rd.

Shoal Point

Rutland

James

Potagannissing River

Maxton Rd.

Drummond Island

N

Glen
Cove

Marble
Head

0   1   2   3   4   5

Miles

134

Glen Cove Rd.

Bass Cove Rd.

Meade

Pine Lake Rd.

*Big
Shoal
Cove*

Shelter

CANADA

UNITED STATES

The second Potagannissing Bay destination worthy of mention is Harbor Island, a horseshoe-shaped island located in the heart of the bay. This gorgeous 700-acre island is a USFS nature preserve of notable richness and variety. It provides important nesting habitat for shoreline birds and has become a key stopover for migratory birds. In addition, its woods contain lynx, red fox, and black bear. Camping on Harbor Island is not permitted, but a hillside picnic area on the island's western shoreline overlooks the cove, providing great views of its stunning turquoise waters and wooded shoreline. This picnic area is particularly popular during midsummer, when its fields of milkweed nourish large colonies of monarch butterflies. Harbor Island is located about 3.5 miles northeast of Drummond Township Park.

Finally, Drummond Island attracts seasoned kayakers who want to see it all, from the gleaming walls of Marble Head to the tranquil waters of the island's numerous rocky bays. Expert kayakers looking to circumnavigate the island can count on a trip of 80 miles or so, depending on how closely they follow the shoreline. If you are considering such an extended trip, keep in mind that you'll need to make camp on undeveloped public land on at least one or two occasions. Keep a clean camp when doing so, as black bears roam across the entire island.

Access: The Drummond Island ferry runs on a regular schedule throughout the year, transporting island residents and visitors across the St. Mary's River, a waterway that is heavily used by freighters and recreational boats alike. During the summer season, the ferry makes two regularly scheduled runs per hour (at ten and forty minutes after) and sometimes runs continuously during heavy traffic periods. During the winter months (January 2 through March 31) the ferry runs once an hour and does not operate from late night until early morning. Fare payments are collected on the De Tour side. Call (906) 297–8851 for more information.

Drummond has relatively few launch sites that can be easily utilized by kayakers. Perhaps the most popular launching spot on the island is the beach at **Drummond Township Park**, which lies 6 miles inland from the ferry off M–134 (Channel Road). This launch site provides paddlers with access to Potagannissing Bay and its many islands. Whitney Bay and other sections of the southwestern shoreline, meanwhile, can be accessed from the **Fort Drummond Marina**, which lies on Whitney Bay Road. The marina charges a small fee for launching. To reach the launch site, take M–134 (Channel Road) 1 mile inland from the ferry, then take Ellis Road south for a mile or so to Whitney Bay Road and follow the signs. Visitors interested in exploring the island's east side can put in at the end of **Glen Cove Road**, a 20-mile trek from the ferry facilities. Kayakers can also launch from the end of **Bass Cove Road**, which lies 6 miles east of Johnswood on the south end of the island.

Additional Help

MA & G grid: 116, A2–A4 and B2–B4; 117, B5.

Camping: The only established campground on the island is Drummond Township Park, a rustic 40-site facility which sees heavy use. In addition, large swaths of the Drummond Island coastline (and interior) are part of Lake Superior State Forest and thus open to wilderness trippers looking for a place to bed down for the night. Finally, both Bow Island (in Potaginnissing Bay) and No Name Island (located just north of Garden Island in Whitney Bay) are state-owned islands that can be used by kayakers for camping. Notable nearby camping areas on the mainland, meanwhile, include Detour State Forest Campground (25 rustic sites).

Food, gas, and lodging: Drummond, De Tour.

For more information: Lake Superior State Forest, Drummond Island Tourism Association.

Rentals/guided trips: Great Northern Adventures.

Escanaba River

Character: This swift and strong river flows through some of the Upper Peninsula's most spectacular country.

Location: Southern Marquette County and western Delta County.

Length: 118 miles (Middle Branch and mainstream).

Run: 47 miles, from Gwinn to County Road 420.

Average run time: 15–20 hours.

Class: I–II, with occasional class II–III rapids.

Skill level: Intermediate.

Optimal flow: May–June, September–October.

Average gradient: 8 feet per mile (12 feet per mile below Boney Falls Dam).

Hazards: Fast current can create dangerous conditions, especially during springtime and other high-water periods; discharges from Boney Falls Dam can change river conditions quickly; rocky ledges and boulders present throughout much of river corridor.

Fishing: Prized trout-fishing river, both in upper branches and mainstream; waters below Boney Falls are "quality trout waters" with special fishing regulations.

Maps: USGS 1:25,000 - Gwinn-MI, Anderson Lake-MI, Swimming Hole Creek-MI, Woodland-MI, Cornell-MI, Perkins-MI, Gladstone-MI; 1:100,000 - Gwinn-MI, Escanaba-MI; 1:250,000 - Marquette-MI, Escanaba-MI.

The paddling: The Escanaba River sweeps through some of the Upper Peninsula's most attractive and remote woodlands, making it an appealing option for paddlers with a taste for extended wilderness trips. But while the river has many charms—its waters are clear and strong and its scenic shoreline supports a rich variety of wildlife, including mink, otter, coyote, deer, and black bear—the Escanaba's vulnerability to water-level fluctuations make timing an important factor when planning paddling expeditions on its waters. Canoeists who put in during the spring and other high-water periods, for example, should be seasoned whitewater paddlers. Wilderness trippers, meanwhile, may want to avoid putting in during the height of summer, when very shallow conditions prevail along much of the river.

The Escanaba River and its branches combine to form one of the Upper Peninsula's largest river systems. Its tributaries extend deep into the central Upper Peninsula, draining a watershed of more than 900 square miles. Many of these tributaries, including the Escanaba's East, Middle, and West Branches, are popular with anglers, but none of these streams offer good canoeing conditions. Quality paddling water does not present itself until Gwinn, where the river's middle and east branches converge.

Paddlers looking to begin their trip in Gwinn have a couple of different put-in options. Popular launching spots include a community park that offers access to the East Branch just above its confluence with the Middle Branch, and the M–35 Bridge, which offers

Escanaba River

Middle Branch Escanaba River

East Branch Escanaba River

To Negaunee

35

Gwinn

Iron Pin Trail

557

Sawmill Creek

West Branch Escanaba R.

Escanaba River Rd.

W. Maple Ridge Rd.

529

Rock

426

Boney Falls Basin

430

St. Nicholas Road

523

519

35

Burnt Camp Access

To Manistique

426

Gladstone

420

35

41

2

Green Bay

N

0 1 2 3 4 5
Miles

Escanaba

To Iron Mountain

2

41

35

To Menominee

access to the Middle Branch about 1 mile upstream of its juncture with the East Branch. Another put-in spot is located a few miles downstream, off Iron Pin Trail.

The mainstream below Gwinn is 50 to 60 feet wide with a rocky bottom and depths of 2 to 3 feet. The river passes through rolling forests of pine and hardwoods at a generally brisk pace for the next several miles, churning up class II rapids immediately below Gwinn and above its junction with the West Branch, a dozen miles downstream. This section of the Escanaba winds through state forest land and includes numerous fine shoreline camping sites.

The Sawmill Creek access site is located about 2 miles downstream from the mainstream's confluence with the West Branch (about 14 miles downstream from Gwinn). Sawmill Creek boosts the Escanaba's water volume once again, but shallower conditions prevail for the next several miles, as the mainstream channel widens significantly. The section of the river from Sawmill Creek to Boney Falls Basin is not particularly vexing to paddle during springtime or other high-water periods, but midsummer paddlers can count on real bump-and-grind conditions along extended portions of this segment, especially if they're traveling with loaded canoes (water levels are alleged to be higher in the morning, when a power plant located upstream at Princeton discharges water).

As you approach Boney Falls Basin, the river banks continue to widen (to 200 feet or more) and the shoreline begins to sprout cottages. Occasional riffles and light rapids pop up as well, created by the river's trademark river bottom of bedrock and stony ledges. This is a particularly beautiful segment of the Escanaba, marked by natural stone terraces that display a pleasing blend of northwoods forest scenery. Paddlers concluding (or beginning) their trip at Boney Falls Basin can use the launch site midway down its western shoreline, off County Road 523. The dam itself can be portaged on the left.

The Escanaba River's most spectacular—and hazardous—stretch of water is a 3-mile run immediately below Boney Falls Dam. Here the river spans more than 200 feet across as it rumbles like a freight train through a canyon-like corridor of forest-topped limestone. Paddlers who traverse this open gorge are rewarded with great views of open sky, sheer rock walls that rise 20 feet or more out of the water, sparkling waterfalls, and high ramparts of unspoiled forest that gird the river corridor all the way to the horizon.

The gorge below Boney Falls Dam is an undeniably breathtaking section of river, and much of it is a straightforward run. But paddlers unfamiliar with fast, pushy water should not attempt it. Sudden discharges from the dam (preceded by a warning horn) can reportedly overtake and swamp open canoes. Moreover, the uppermost reaches of the gorge feature boulders and rocky ledges that churn up dangerous class II–III rapids, and occasional boulders and ledges farther downstream can upend unwary paddlers. And make no mistake, this can be a scary section to dump in. Much of the river is only 3 to 4 feet deep, but the current is very swift, the river bottom of boulders and bedrock is unforgiving, and the high limestone walls that guard its banks are formidable.

The gorge ends a mile or so downstream from the CR–430 Bridge, which spans the river but provides no access due to high and rocky banks. As the canyon's rocky walls give way to lower banks of woodlands, the river continues to widen and increased development

The powerful Escanaba River carves a rocky canyon on its way to Lake Michigan.

appears in the form of homes and cottages. The Escanaba itself, meanwhile, intersperses shallow riffles with sections of big, swift water. Good access spots along this section of the river include CR–519 (6 miles downstream from the dam) and the Burnt Camp access site (7 miles downstream). Access is also possible at the bridge off St. Nicholas Road, about 3 miles downstream from the dam.

As you approach Escanaba, the river runs through a mix of woods and farmlands. It also assumes a pool-and-riffle temperament for a time before slowing down as it enters the first of three dam-created impoundments that offer little in the way of paddling pleasure. You can take out at the public access site near the CR–420 Bridge, located on the west side of the first impoundment.

Access: The Middle Branch of the Escanaba is accessible from the **M–35 Bridge** in Gwinn. The East Branch is also accessible in Gwinn, at **Gwinn Community Park**. Another Gwinn-area access site is located off the **Iron Pin Trail**. To reach it from Gwinn, take Johnson Lake Road south from M–35 for 0.7 mile to Iron Pin Trail (also called High-banks Road on some maps), then continue south on Iron Pin Trail for about 3 miles to a large parking area near a power line. A short trail delivers visitors to the river's edge.

The **Sawmill Creek** access site is located on Escanaba River Road. Take CR–529 (West Maple Ridge Road) west from M–35 at the town of Rock for 9 miles, then turn north on Escanaba River Road for 5 miles to reach the launch. To reach the **Boney Falls Basin** access site, take CR–426 north out of Escanaba for 10 miles, then go north on CR–523 for 4 miles. To access the river at **County Road 519**, take CR–426 to CR–523, proceed north on CR–523 for 1 mile, then east on CR–519 for 0.5 mile. The **Burnt Camp** access site is located off CR–426, approximately 9 miles northwest of Escanaba and 1 mile east of Cornell. The **County Road 420 Bridge** lies 3 miles west of Gladstone and 6 miles north of Escanaba.

Additional Help

MA & G grid: 89, A6–A7, B8; 101, B5, C6, D6.

Camping: A small (six-site) county campground is located 9 miles west of Rock on CR–529, then 1 mile north on Escanaba River Road. Shoreline camping also is available above Boney Falls Dam in Escanaba River State Forest. In addition, a township campground (8 sites) is maintained at Boney Falls Basin, and Pioneer Trail Park (56 sites) provides modern amenities near the rivermouth. This latter park is located on U.S. 2/U.S. 41 on the northern bank of the river midway between the towns of Gladstone and Escanaba.

Food, gas, and lodging: Escanaba, Gladstone, Gwinn.

For more information: Escanaba River State Forest.

Canoe liveries: None.

Access Point	Float Distance To Next Access Point
M–35 Bridge at Gwinn	5 miles
or	
Gwinn Community Park	5 miles
Iron Pin Trail Access Area	10 miles
Sawmill Creek	15 miles
Boney Falls Basin	7 miles
CR–519	1 mile
Burnt Camp	14 miles
CR–420	Take Out

Fayette State Park

Character: A picturesque historic park that provides access to the best paddling waters in Big Bay de Noc.

Location: Delta County at the southern end of the Garden Peninsula.

Size: 711 acres, with 3 miles of shoreline along Big Bay de Noc.

Skill level: Beginner/advanced (depending on areas explored).

Hazards: Exposure to southwest winds, reflective waves off limestone cliffs, infrequent landing sites from Sand Bay to Sac Bay.

Maps: USGS 1:25,000 Fayette-MI, Nahma-MI; 1:100,000 Manistique-MI; 1:250,000 Escanaba-MI. NOAA chart 14908.

The paddling: Fayette State Park is a great launching point for paddlers interested in exploring the eastern shoreline of Michigan's picturesque Garden Peninsula. The shoreline of the park itself includes 3 miles of sandy beaches, sheltered bays, and high limestone bluffs. In addition, visiting kayakers often stray beyond the park's boundaries to explore the rugged islands, limestone cliffs, and cobblestone beaches that also grace the peninsula shoreline.

Fayette State Park is one of the more unusual facilities in Michigan's state park system. Its centerpiece is the celebrated ghost town of Fayette, a village that grew up around a nineteenth-century iron-smelting operation. Founded in 1866 by Fayette Brown of the Jackson Iron Company, the company town thrived for two decades before declining profits forced the closure of the smelting operation in 1891. The closure devastated the village, but it managed to maintain a pulse for the next several decades as a backwater resort. Finally, however, the village's last residents drifted away. The township and its surrounding land were subsequently purchased by the state in 1959, and an effort was undertaken to preserve the village's twenty-some buildings and its stone furnace complex. Today, the townsite is an attractive and interesting reminder of a bygone era in Michigan's history, and an enjoyable place to check out when the day's paddling is done.

The kayaking around Fayette is suitable for novice paddlers, provided they limit their exploration to the park shoreline and immediate environs. The township sits on a curling spit of land between Sand Bay, which has a pleasant beach area backed by cedar, pine, and hardwood forest, and Snail Shell Harbor, a tranquil little cove guarded by tremendous limestone bluffs. You can check out both areas—and receive fine views of the village itself to boot—in a single leisurely afternoon of paddling.

Kayakers can also venture northward to Snake Island, a low island of cobblestone that is prime nesting habitat for cormorants and gulls. Visitors should not land on the island for this reason, but a circuit around the island affords plenty of bird-watching opportunities anyway. This island is located about 1.5 miles north of the entrance to Snail Shell Harbor and lies about 0.5 mile off the mainland. In addition, a state access site is located on

Fayette State Park

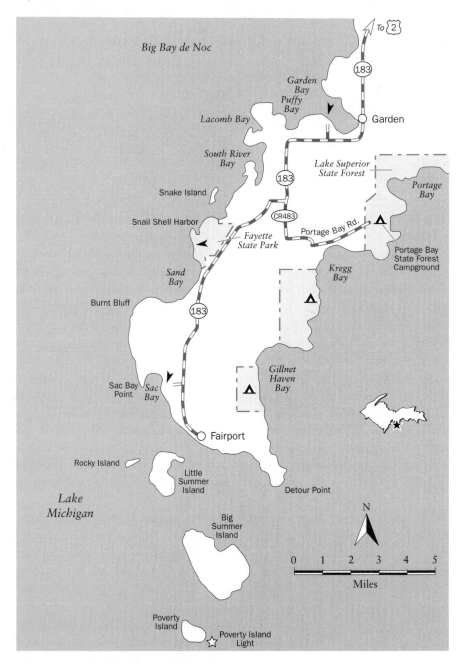

the southern shoreline of Garden Bay, about 7 miles north of the park. This scenic stretch of the peninsula is highlighted by two pretty bays (South River and Lacomb) that can be explored along the way.

The waters south of Fayette also will please kayakers. The 8-mile stretch from Snail Shell Harbor down to Sac Bay includes both sandy beaches (at Sand Bay) and craggy cobblestone shorelines that are protected from all but southerly and southwesterly winds. But the most impressive segment of this paddle is a 2-mile stretch of beautiful limestone cliffs that stretch 100 feet and more above the water's surface. These towering formations, located two-thirds of the way down to Sac Bay, are particularly captivating on evening paddles, when the sun casts its dying light on the massive stone walls. You can then move on to Sac Bay, which features a shoreline park with parking and limited facilities. If you do decide to investigate these cliffs, however, take heed of weather conditions. Southerly winds can create rough seas from here down to Sac Bay, and landing spots are few. In fact, much of the strand south of Sand Bay consists of rocky shoreline that make landings difficult. Given these factors and the mileage involved (16 miles round-trip), kayakers with little experience on big water should not attempt this section of the peninsula.

Experienced expedition kayakers, on the other hand, have an array of exciting options to choose from once they reach the southern tip of the Garden Peninsula. One alternative is to venture out to a handful of islands that jut down into Lake Michigan. But even the nearest of these islands—the Summer islands and Poverty Island—require significant open crossings. Only paddlers with advanced skills should consider investigating these islands, and then only when the weather cooperates.

Another option is to push on around DeTour Point and explore the bays that line the eastern shoreline of the Garden Peninsula. Both Gillnet Haven Bay and Kregg Bay offer primitive camping on national forest land along here, and they are ideally situated for paddlers wishing to make multi-day treks from Fayette State Park to Portage Bay State Forest Campground or vice versa (approximately 30 miles one way). This route, however, is very exposed to winds out of the east, and should only be attempted by experienced kayakers.

Access: To reach **Fayette State Park**, take U.S. 2 to Garden Corners, then drive south on M–183 for 17 miles. The park's boat ramp and its beach are located at the south end of the park. **Sac Bay County Park** lies on County Road 438, 4 miles south of Fayette State Park off M–183. The access site on **Garden Bay** is about 2 miles west of Garden, directly off M–183.

Additional Help

MA & G grid: 90, C3.

Camping: Fayette State Park maintains 80 semi-modern sites (electricity, vault toilets, no showers) in a wooded setting. Other nearby camping options include Portage Bay State Forest Campground (18 rustic sites) on the east side of the Garden Peninsula, about 5 miles from Fayette. This campground is located 10 miles south of Garden via CR–483 and Portage Bay Road, and looks out on a sandy cove that is ideal for early morning paddles. In addition, paddlers making overnight treks can camp on national forestland in Gillnet Haven Bay and Kregg Bay.

Food, gas, and lodging: Garden, Fairport.

For more information: Fayette State Park.

Rentals/guided trips: Great Northern Adventures.

Ford River

Character: This lively U.P. river is an ideal springtime destination for winter-weary canoeists with an itch to scratch.

Location: Delta County.

Length: 90 miles.

Run: 16 miles, from County Road 414 to M–35.

Average run time: 6–7 hours.

Class: I–III.

Skill level: Intermediate.

Optimal flow: April–May; October.

Average gradient: 9 feet per mile.

Hazards: Occasional rapids that rate class II–III; fallen trees and other blowdown.

Fishing: Smallmouth bass, walleye, and northern pike.

Maps: USGS 1:25,000 - Schaeffer-MI, Chandler-MI, Ford River-MI; 1:100,000 - Escanaba-MI; 1:250,000 - Escanaba-MI.

The paddling: The Ford River is a relatively unheralded but nonetheless delightful Upper Peninsula river that offers fine day-trip opportunities from late April through early June. During those few weeks, spring runoff swells the Ford's volume to levels that make it a swift and spirited river. As summer approaches, though, the stream's water level drops significantly and the river becomes a much less enjoyable river to float. Indeed, bump-and-scrape conditions typically prevail through significant sections of the stream by early summer. Explore the Ford in springtime, then, when its cold, clear waters are still foaming and jumping.

The Ford actually runs through four U.P. counties (Dickinson, Marquette, Menominee, and Delta) before emptying into Lake Michigan at the northern entrance to Green Bay. But much of the river is unrunnable because of blowdowns, beaver dams, and narrow, brushy banks. Decent canoeing opportunities do not present themselves until the stream's final miles or so, when the Ford opens up sufficiently to provide openings past fallen trees and other deadfall.

Most canoeists put in at CR–414, where the Ford runs fast and clear. Another option is to put in at CR–537, about 3.5 miles farther downstream. The current slows around here and maintains its languid pace for the next several miles. The shoreline, meanwhile, ranges in width from 50 to 80 feet as it passes by pretty woodlands and occasional homes.

Access and parking are problematic at CR–533—located about 5 miles downstream from CR–414—because of private property. Once you pass below this bridge, the Ford's pace picks up again and the riverbed changes from sand to mixed gravel and bedrock. Rocky ledges also appear more frequently in this section. These rugged limestone formations line the river corridor off and on all the way to the rivermouth.

Ford River

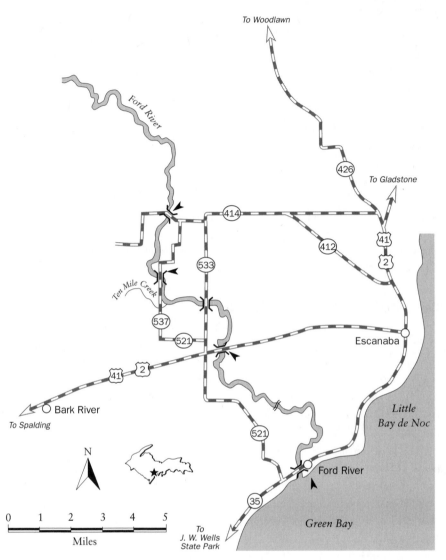

The river's most challenging sections appear below U.S. 2/U.S. 41, so this bridge can be used as a take-out by inexperienced paddlers. From U.S. 2 to M–35, another 7 miles downstream, you can count on long stretches of fun riffles and light (class I) rapids through rock gardens and sections of broken bedrock. But this section also includes slow spots that provide you with ample opportunity to ponder the Ford's woodsy shoreline and stony ledges.

The most challenging rapids on the Ford can be found midway between U.S. 2/U.S. 41 and the rivermouth, shortly after the stream divides and then reunites around a big island. Created by a narrowing of the river's ledges, this class II–III run churns up standing waves capable of swamping an open canoe in early spring. Paddlers should scout this piece of whitewater in advance and portage (on either bank) if uncertain of their ability to successfully negotiate it.

From here, you can count on another few miles of light rapids (class I–II) created by small boulders and exposed bedrock. As you approach M–35, however, the Ford takes on a more relaxed demeanor. Its current slackens and its depth increases significantly. Homes and cottages also pop up with more frequency as you enter the outskirts of the small town of Ford River. The boat launch at M–35, which is popular with Lake Michigan anglers, appears on the left bank just above the rivermouth.

Access: The bridge at **County Road 414** lies 7 miles west of CR–414's juncture with CR–426, just north of Escanaba. The **County Road 537** bridge is 4 miles south of CR–414. The bridge on **U.S. 2/U.S. 41** is 6 miles west of Escanaba. The **M–35** access site is just below the bridge in Ford River.

Additional Help

MA & G grid: 89, C7.

Camping: Private property lines both sides of the river in its lower reaches, effectively eliminating streamside camping as an option. **J.W. Wells State Park** (155 sites) lies about 23 miles south of the Ford's rivermouth on M–35. In addition, a local public campground called **Pioneer Trail Park** (50 sites) is located on U.S. 2/U.S. 41 between Escanaba and Gladstone.

Food, gas, and lodging: Escanaba, Gladstone.

For more information: Escanaba River State Forest.

Canoe liveries: None.

Access Point	Float Distance To Next Access Point
CR–414	3 miles
CR–537	6 miles
U.S. 2/U.S. 41	7 miles
M–35	Take Out

Fox River

Character: A picturesque but deadfall-strewn U.P. stream that offers tremendous trout fishing.
Location: Runs through Schoolcraft County before joining the Manistique River near Germfask.
Length: 35 miles.
Run: 24 miles, from Fox River State Forest Campground to Manistique River take-out in Germfask.
Average run time: 12–16 hours.
Class: I.
Skill level: Intermediate.
Optimal flow: May–September.
Average gradient: 5 feet per mile.
Hazards: Numerous deadfalls, dam remnants, overhanging tree limbs, and other navigational challenges; "spreads" area below M–77.
Fishing: Excellent brook trout-fishing stream (18 miles above Seney are designated as a Blue Ribbon trout stream).
Maps: USGS 1:25,000 - Sunken Lake-MI, Seney NW-MI, Seney-MI, Germfask-MI; 1:100,000 - Two Hearted River-MI, Manistique Lake-MI; 1:250,000 - Sault Ste. Marie-MI.

The paddling: The Fox River has been a favored U.P. trout-fishing destination ever since Ernest Hemingway haunted these northwoods (the author's "Big Two Hearted River" story was actually based on his experiences along the banks of the Fox). But it receives only light pressure from paddlers, due to the logjams and other navigational hazards that periodically appear as you make your way down the river corridor. These obstacles won't faze experienced wilderness canoeists. But they make the Fox a poor choice if you're looking to introduce someone to the joys of canoeing. The narrow river requires carryovers or portages at multiple points, and the latter can be an epic hassle, due to the overgrown banks and absence of trails. Moreover, the Fox is infamous for housing summertime mosquito populations that can drive even the hardiest visitors batty.

In other respects, though, the Fox is a paddler-friendly river. It flows at a relaxed gait throughout its length, is free of rapids, and remains floatable throughout most summers. The stream also runs through attractive northwoods country, passing through lowland swamps, open plains, and forests of spruce, pine, and balsam along its southeasterly course. Finally, the wild country through which it runs is host to a wide variety of creatures great (moose and black bear) and small (otter and waterfowl). Despite these appealing aspects, however, you and your paddling partner should undertake an honest self-appraisal of your canoeing skills and capacity for enduring discomfort before tackling this stream.

Few paddlers put in above the Fox River State Forest Campground, as the river is choked with deadfalls at numerous points above here. Passage is clearer below the campground, although logjams and windfalls remain a factor all the way down to the stream's union with the Manistique, 24 miles downstream. From the campground down to Seney, the sand-bottomed river runs 30 to 40 feet wide, though overgrown banks of tag alders can

Fox River

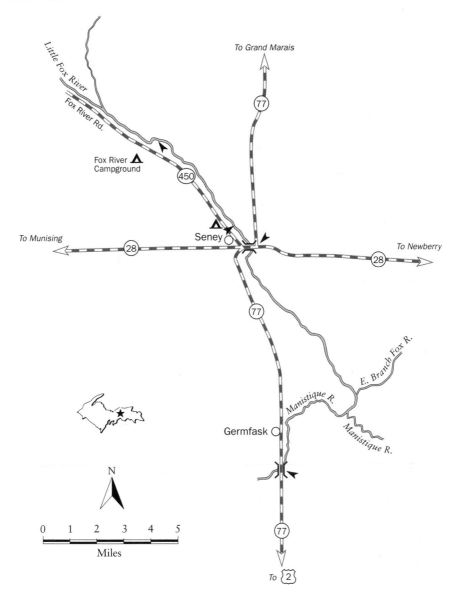

To Grand Marais

Little Fox River

Fox River Rd.

Fox River Campground

450

77

To Munising

28

Seney

To Newberry

28

77

Manistique R.

E. Branch Fox R.

Manistique R.

Germfask

N

0 1 2 3 4 5
Miles

77

To ② 2

make the corridor feel tighter than that. Water depth averages 2 to 4 feet, with deeper holes at the outer bends.

Primary access sites to the river in Seney are the municipal park, located just north of town, and the M–28 Bridge. As you make your way downstream from Seney, you skirt the Seney National Wildlife Refuge and enter an extended stretch of marshland "spreads" in which the river braids up. This maze of channels is fairly easy to negotiate, however, and peters out after a couple of miles. Below the "spreads," the river widens to 40 to 50 feet and deepens to 2 to 6 feet as it twists through peaceful and remote forestland. Occasional shoreline campsites can be found in this marshy lowland terrain, but they're not a dime a dozen.

The East Branch of the Fox joins with the mainstream about a dozen miles south of Seney, adding significantly to the river's volume. Less than a mile farther down, the Fox enters the Manistique River, which is in essence a bigger and clearer version of the Fox. From here you have a 3-mile float to the M–77 Bridge take-out just south of Germfask (if you are interested in exploring more of the Manistique, check out our entry on that stream).

Access: The **Fox River State Forest Campground** is 5 miles northwest of Seney, just off County Road 450 (Fox River Road). The **Seney Municipal Campground** also lies off CR–450, about a mile north of Seney. In addition, several unmarked two-tracks branch off from Fox River Road between these two campgrounds. These two-tracks wind eastward down to the river's edge, providing additional access. The last take-out spot before you enter the Manistique River is the **M–28 Bridge** in Seney. The first access site on the Manistique after it joins with the Fox is in Germfast at the **M–77 Bridge**.

Additional Help

MA & G grid: 103, A8; 104, A1–B1.

Camping: Decent camping spots are interspersed along the river corridor. Other camping alternatives include the Fox River State Forest Campground (6 rustic sites) and a state forest campground on the East Branch of the Fox (16 rustic sites). The Fox River facility is located 5 miles northwest of Seney via CR–450 (Fox River Road). The East Branch campground is right off M–77, 8 miles north of Seney. Finally, Seney maintains a municipal campground located 0.5 mile northeast of Seney on CR–450 (Fox River Road).

Food, gas, and lodging: Germfask, Seney.

For more information: Lake Superior State Forest.

Canoe liveries: Northland Outfitters, Big Cedar Campground and Canoe Livery.

Access Point	Float Distance To Next Access Point
Fox River State Forest Campground	7 miles
Seney Municipal Campground	1 mile
M–28 Bridge	16 miles
M–77 Bridge	Take Out

Grand Island

Character: A wonderful kayaking alternative to Pictured Rocks, Grand Island offers sandy beaches, protected bays, historic lighthouses, and breathtaking sandstone palisades.

Location: One mile north of Munising in Lake Superior.

Size: 13,500-acre island featuring 30 miles of shoreline.

Skill level: Intermediate/advanced (depending on conditions).

Hazards: Rough seas, very cold water temperature (high 30s/low 40s Fahrenheit in midsummer), rapidly changing weather, limited landing options along some stretches of shoreline.

Maps: USGS 1:25,000 - Wood Island-MI, Wood Island SE-MI, Munising-MI, Indian Town-MI; 1:100,000 - Au Sable Point-MI, Munising-MI; 1:250,000 - Marquette-MI. NOAA charts 14963, 14969.

The paddling: Grand Island is one of Michigan's top sea-kayaking destinations. Formerly the home of Ojibwa Indians and French trappers, the island rivals nearby Pictured Rocks National Lakeshore in the beauty and grandeur of its rugged shoreline. Its forested interior, meanwhile, supports black bear, deer, grouse, and a wide range of waterfowl, and features miles of hiking/biking trails that attract visitors from all around the state.

Situated less than a mile off the shoreline of the Upper Peninsula in Lake Superior, Grand Island has many scenic attractions that are easily accessible and can occupy paddlers for days. Moreover, its geography offers protection from northerly and westerly winds, making the island an appealing alternative when choppy seas scuttle plans to tour Pictured Rocks. On those occasions, you can light out for the southern end of the island and explore Murray Bay, a well-protected cove of sandy beaches and low-lying woodlands. Murray Bay boasts a day-use area with picnic tables and pit toilets and three lakeshore camping sites (reservations required for the single group site), as well as a shipwreck that is visible from the surface on calm days. The *Bermuda*, a 145-foot wooden schooner that perished in the late 1800s, is located a few hundred feet northwest of Muskrat Point. Just east of Murray Bay, meanwhile, is the picturesque Grand Island Harbor Light, which guided ships into Munising Harbor from the late 1860s until the early 1900s. This historic lighthouse, also known as the East Channel Light, is one of the region's best-known landmarks.

Grand Island's other major bay is Trout Bay, located on the island's eastern side. Easily accessible if you launch from Sand Point on the mainland, it features four beach-front campsites (first come, first served) and another shipwreck—the *Herman H. Hettler*, a 210-foot steamer that sank in 1926—that can be seen from the surface when Superior is calm. The wreck of the *Hettler* is located just outside of the bay at the island's easternmost point. Other characteristics of the island's eastern shoreline include sandstone cliffs and small sea caves.

Grand Island's eastern ramparts are great fun to explore, and the distant lights of Munising, shining across Superior's waters, will enchant kayakers overnighting on Murray Bay. But the island's most spectacular shoreline is located on the north end, where tower-

Grand Island

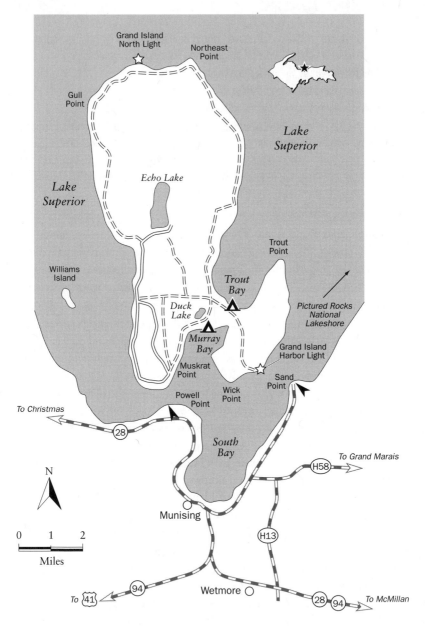

ing 200-foot cliffs look out on the lake's vast expanses. Colorful sandstone walls and sea caves mark the island's northwest corner, and as you paddle to the east you will find the North Beach, an oasis of sandy beach nestled between twin fortresses of rock. At night the waters off the island's northern shores shine with the reflection from the Grand Island North Light, a nineteenth-century lighthouse perched atop the cliffs that continues to guide Great Lakes freighters traversing Superior's icy waters. Take heed of changing weather conditions on this side of the island, though, for the rocky shoreline limits landing options to the aforementioned beach area.

The island's western shoreline is also great to explore, although paddlers should again exercise caution. Sandstone cliffs tower over the water along much of this stretch, severely limiting landing options and creating the capacity for dangerous reflective waves (the main resting spot along this shoreline is a sand beach located in a small bay midway up the island). On calm evenings, however, these walls give off a beautiful sunlit glow that is well worth observing firsthand.

Grand Island's charms are many, and kayakers visiting its shores often set aside three or four days to check it out. But you need to exercise caution when navigating its waters. The island's west, north, and northeast shorelines are wholly unprotected from inclement weather, which can develop very quickly on Lake Superior. Moreover, the water is extremely cold; sea kayakers who tackle Grand Island without appropriate gear and skills are courting disaster.

Access: Many kayakers launch from the National Lakeshore headquarters at **Sand Point** in Grand Island Harbor, located 4 miles northeast of Munising at the end of Sand Point Road. Another popular launch spot is **Powell Point**, located 2 miles west of Munising off M–28 at the Grand Island ferry dock facility; the southernmost tip of Grand Island, Williams Landing, lies just 0.5 mile north of Powell Point. A third mainland launching spot is the Hiawatha National Forest **Bay Furnace** campground, located 5 miles west of Munising off M–28.

Additional Help

MA & G grid: 102, A3–A4; 114, D3.

Camping: On Grand Island, Trout Bay (4 sites) and Murray Bay (3 sites); on mainland, Pictured Rocks National Lakeshore (see entry on Pictured Rocks) and Bay Furnace (50 sites), 5 miles west of Munising off M–28 on the shores of Lake Superior.

Food, gas, and lodging: Munising.

For more information: Hiawatha National Forest.

Kayak Rentals/guided trips: Great Northern Adventures, Northern Waters.

The historic Grand Island East Channel Light began guiding boats into Munising Harbor in 1868.
Photo by Deb Hausler.

Horseshoe Bay Wilderness Area

Character: A lovely stretch of wild coastline just a few minutes' drive from the Mackinac Bridge.
Location: The north shore of Lake Huron in the eastern Upper Peninsula, near St. Ignace.
Size: 7 miles of coastline along Horseshoe Bay and St. Martin Bay.
Skill level: Intermediate.
Hazards: Deep, cold water on Lake Huron; winds out of the east or north can create high waves.
Maps: USGS 1:25,000 - Evergreen Shores-MI, Charles-MI; 1:100,000 - Cheboygan-MI, Sault Sainte Marie South-MI; 1:250,000 - Cheboygan-MI, Sault Ste. Marie-MI. NOAA chart 14880.

The paddling: The Horseshoe Bay Wilderness Area features 7 miles of pristine sand beach and wild, rocky coastline at the northern end of Lake Huron. Once a prime Native American hunting and fishing grounds, it is home to a wide variety of wildlife, including black bear, deer, coyote, beaver, otter, mink, eagles, and osprey. Although the wilderness lies just a few miles north of the Mackinac Bridge and the tourist town of St. Ignace, it remains relatively unknown and undisturbed—a perfect place to explore by kayak.

Paddlers can put in at the National Forest Service boat launch at the mouth of the Carp River in St. Martin Bay, less than 2 miles north of the wilderness area boundary. The shoreline along this stretch consists of rocky points alternating with lowland marshes. Inland, you will pass by forested ridges with stands of balsam and cedar, as well as shallow swamps. It is another 2 miles around Grosse Point into Horseshoe Bay. Keep in mind that there are two parcels of private property on the south side of this point.

From Grosse Point, it is about a 6-mile paddle southward around Horseshoe Bay to Rabbit Back Point. The southern part of the shoreline is an expanse of sand beach. The only developed trail in the wilderness area leads 1.5 miles east and south from the beach to the Foley Creek Campground. There is another potential launch site at the southern end of Horseshoe Bay Wilderness, where a gravel road leads to the shoreline, but parking is limited.

Access: To reach the Forest Service boat launch at the **mouth of the Carp River**, take Interstate 75 north 14 miles from St. Ignace and exit at M–134. Cross back over the highway on M–134 west, then turn south on Mackinac Trail (H–63). Follow Mackinac Trail 3 miles, past the Carp River Campground, until it crosses under Interstate 75. Then turn left on the Forest Service road and follow the signs to the boat launch. To reach the put-in at the **south end of the Horseshoe Bay Wilderness**, take I–75 north about 3 miles from St. Ignace and exit at Castle Rock Road/Mackinac Trail (H–63). Follow H–63 north about 2 miles, past the casino, then turn right. This unnamed road ends at the Lake Huron shore along the southern edge of the wilderness area.

Horseshoe Bay Wilderness Area

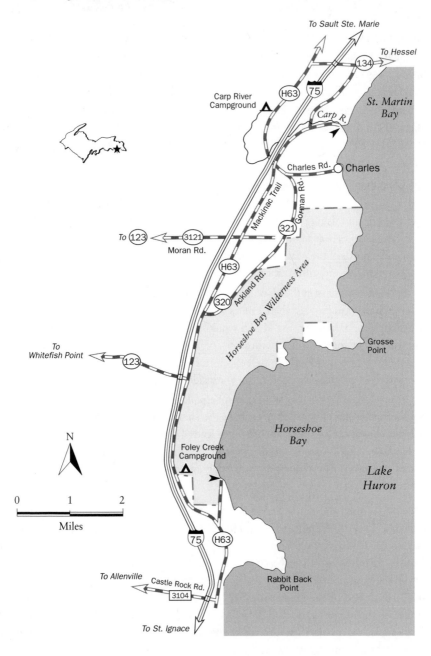

Additional Help

MA & G grid: 94, A3; 106, D3.

Camping: Foley Creek National Forest Campground, 6 miles north of St. Ignace off H–63; Carp River National Forest Campground, 8 miles north of St. Ignace off H–63.

Food, gas, and lodging: St. Ignace.

For more information: Hiawatha National Forest, St. Ignace Ranger District.

Indian River

Character: A mellow river with a wilderness feel, the Indian flows through the forested hills and lowland marshes of Hiawatha National Forest.

Location: Alger and Schoolcraft Counties in the central Upper Peninsula.

Length: 41 miles.

Run: 36 miles, from Fish Lake to Indian Lake.

Average run time: 16–18 hours.

Class: Flatwater.

Skill level: Beginner/intermediate.

Optimal flow: May–September.

Average gradient: 2 feet per mile.

Hazards: Occasional logjams that may require portaging between Thunder Lake Road and Indian River Campground; shallow channels that may require dragging in the spreads below Eight Mile Bridge; possible high winds and waves on Indian Lake.

Fishing: Brook and brown trout above Eight Mile Bridge; northern pike, bass, and walleye below Eight Mile Bridge; spring sturgeon runs from Indian Lake.

Maps: USGS 1:25,000 - Corner Lake-MI, Steuben-MI, Thunder Lake-MI, Hiawath-MI; 1:100,000 - Munising-MI; 1:250,000 - Marquette-MI.

The paddling: The Indian River offers paddlers a number of options for day or overnight trips through the varied terrain of Hiawatha National Forest. The shoreline scenery ranges from rolling hills topped with mixed hardwood and conifer forests to lowland marshes teeming with wildlife. Moreover, unlike many Upper Peninsula rivers, the Indian generally maintains sufficient water levels for paddling into the summer and fall.

The U.S. Forest Service has established a canoe trail covering 36 miles of this designated Wild and Scenic River, from Fish Lake (near Munising) to Indian Lake (near Manistique). The character of the river varies from one section to the next, allowing paddlers to choose a specific section to suit their interests and abilities or tackle a longer stretch and enjoy the variety. Throughout the canoe trail, the Indian averages 30 to 50 feet wide and 1 to 3 feet deep with a moderate current.

The canoe trail begins at the Fish Lake public access, about 15 miles south of Munising. At this point, the Indian consists of a series of small lakes. It is less than a mile to Widewaters Campground, a Forest Service unit that offers another access site. From here, the river narrows and picks up speed, flowing over a sandy bottom and between low, wooded hills. Paddlers will encounter light riffles over the next mile or so, before crossing under the H–13 bridge.

Downstream from H–13 the Indian gradually slows and widens to between 40 and 50 feet. It is another 3.5 miles to Ten Mile Bridge (Forest Road 2258). Shortly before the bridge, a small channel to the right provides access to a chain of small lakes. Most of the

Indian River

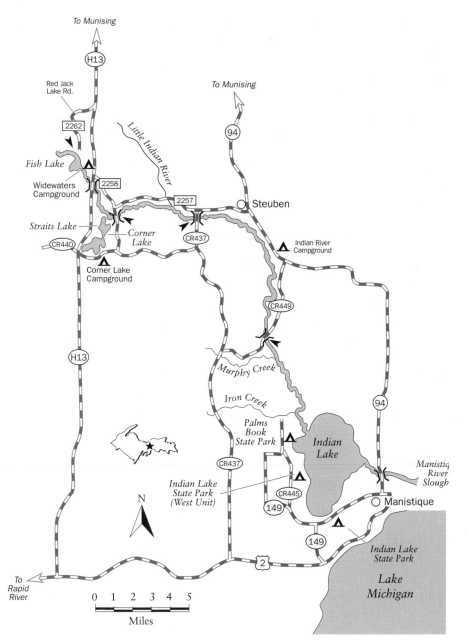

To Munising

H13

Red Jack
Lake Rd.

2262

To Munising

94

Little Indian River

Fish Lake

Widewaters
Campground

2258

2257

Steuben

Straits Lake

Corner
Lake

CR437

Indian River
Campground

CR440

Corner Lake
Campground

CR449

H13

Murphy Creek

Iron Creek

Palms
Book
State Park

Indian
Lake

94

CR437

Indian Lake
State Park
(West Unit)

CR445

149

Manistiq
River
Slough

Manistique

N

149

Indian Lake
State Park

To
Rapid
River

2

Lake
Michigan

0 1 2 3 4 5

Miles

property along the shores of these lakes is private, but it is possible to work your way southward into Corner Lake, which features a USFS campground on its south shore.

There are also plenty of good riverside camping options on national forest land below the Ten Mile Bridge. Along the 7-mile stretch to Thunder Lake Road Bridge (County Road 437), the banks gradually rise to 30 feet above the river. The Forest Service requests that paddlers refrain from climbing the steep and sandy banks in this area due to erosion problems that have damaged the fishery.

From Thunder Lake Road, it is 3 miles to the town of Steuben. The stretch of river immediately above and below the town can be troublesome, with logjams and sweepers that may require portaging. Access is poor at the FR–2213 bridge just south of town. The next suitable access spot is 5 miles downstream at the Indian River Picnic Area and Campground, maintained by the USFS. Use the wooden steps near the footbridge for put-ins and take-outs.

Downstream from the campground, the Indian narrows and flows a bit faster between steep banks. Occasional logjams combine with tight bends to test the maneuvering skills— and tempers—of beginners through this stretch. Fittingly, it is 8 miles to Eight Mile Bridge (CR–449). Over the last few miles above the bridge, the river slows and widens as it enters a marshy area.

Paddlers who are not fond of marsh and lake canoeing may want to take out at Eight Mile Bridge. From there, the Indian continues to spread into a network of shallow, braided channels that wind their way between the reeds and tall grasses of a lowland marsh. Those who paddle the remaining 8 miles to Indian Lake are likely to encounter a variety of wildlife.

The river enters Indian Lake—the fourth-largest lake in the U.P. at 8,650 acres—in its northwest corner. Paddlers can follow the shoreline southwest about 2 miles to the public boat launch at Palms Book State Park, home of the lovely Kitch-Iti-Kipi Spring. It is another 4 miles to the West Shore Campground at Indian Lake State Park. Indian Lake is fairly shallow, and thus tends to be warmer than many other U.P. lakes. Still, paddlers should use caution on the popular lake due to the potential for high winds and waves, as well as motorboat traffic.

Access: To reach the **Fish Lake public access**, take H–13 south from Munising for 13 miles, then go west 1 mile on FR–2262 (Red Jack Lake Road). The **Widewaters Campground** is located 0.5 mile west of H–13 off FR–2262. **H–13** crosses over the Indian River about 14 miles south of Munising. To reach the **Ten Mile Bridge**, take H–13 south 14 miles from Munising, then go east about 3 miles on FR–2258. The **Thunder Lake Road Bridge** is located 2 miles west of Steuben, or 20 miles north of U.S. Highway 2, on CR–437. The **Indian River Campground** is located 20 miles north of Manistique on M–94. To reach the **Eight Mile Bridge**, take M–94 north 19 miles from Manistique, then go southwest about 5 miles on CR–449. Alternately, take CR–437 north 13 miles from U.S. 2, then proceed northeast 4 miles on CR–449. The take-out at **Indian Lake** is located in Palms Book State Park, which is 8 miles north of U.S. 2 on M–149. Access the improved boat launch from the north entrance.

Additional Help

MA & G grid: 102, C3–C4; 103, C5 and D6.

Camping: There are a number of campgrounds near the Indian River in Hiawatha National Forest. Widewaters Campground (34 large, secluded sites in a wooded area along the river) and Indian River Campground (5 large, wooded sites on a bluff overlooking the river) provide direct access to the Indian. Indian Lake State Park, located 5 miles west of Manistique on CR–442, features two modern campgrounds with a total of 302 sites. The South Shore Campground, with 158 sites in a grassy area on the shore of Indian Lake, is the more popular of the two units, thanks to its flush toilets and showers. The West Shore Campground, located 2 miles north of CR–442 off CR–455, offers 144 sites in a wooded area 0.5 mile from the lake.

Food, gas, and lodging: Manistique, Munising.

For more information: Hiawatha National Forest, Rapid River/Manistique Ranger District.

Canoe liveries: Hiawatha Resort and Campground.

Access Point	Float Distance To Next Access Point
Fish Lake Public Access	0.5 mile
Widewaters Campground	1.5 miles
H–13 Bridge	3.5 miles
Ten Mile Bridge (FR–2258)	7 miles
Thunder Lake Road Bridge (CR–437)	8 miles
Indian River Campground	8 miles
Eight Mile Bridge (CR–449)	8 miles
Indian Lake	Take Out

49 ![wave icon] Isle Royale National Park, Inland Lakes

Character: A network of pristine lakes cradled in the heart of rugged and remote Isle Royale National Park.

Location: Isle Royale is located in the northwest corner of Lake Superior, almost 60 miles from the northern tip of Michigan's Upper Peninsula, 35 miles from Thunder Bay, Ontario, and 17 miles southeast of Grand Portage, Minnesota.

Size: The island is 45 miles long and 9 miles wide. The nine-lake chain favored by canoeists includes both small lakes (Wood Lake, Lake Livermore) and larger lakes (7-mile-long Siskiwit Lake).

Skill level: Intermediate.

Hazards: Deep water; potential for rough seas on outer shores.

Fishing: Inland lakes contain walleye, northern pike, yellow perch, and lake, rainbow, and brook trout. A Michigan fishing license is required to fish in Lake Superior. No license is needed to fish in the inland lakes and streams, but state size and possession limits apply.

Maps: USGS 1:25,000 Little Todd Harbor-MI, Point Houghton-MI, Todd Harbor-MI, Malone Bay-MI, McCargoe Cove-MI, Lake Richie-MI, Belle Harbor-MI, Mott Island-MI, Rock Harbor-MI; 1:100,000 Siskiwit Bay-MI, Todd Harbor-MI; 1:250,000 Hancock-MI, Thunder Bay-MI.

The paddling: Isle Royale National Park is one of Michigan's greatest natural treasures. A rough-hewn wilderness paradise that juts out of the northern reaches of icy Lake Superior, the park features both unspoiled lakes and coves and deep swamps and forestlands, all laid over a rocky foundation of rugged ridges and valleys. The island also nurtures a wonderfully diverse array of wildlife, including eagles, peregrine falcons, loons, hooded mergansers, great blue herons, otters, beavers, red foxes, and snowshoe hares. Isle Royale's most famous inhabitants, however, are its moose and wolf populations. The fortunes of these two species have been closely intertwined ever since the winter of 1948–1949, when timber wolves first wandered across the frozen ice of Lake Superior to make the island their home. A half-century later, ongoing scientific studies of the predator-prey relationship between these two majestic creatures continue to provide valuable insights into each species' behavioral patterns and way of life.

Given Isle Royale's scenic splendor and untamed character, it has naturally emerged as a favorite destination for wilderness campers. More than 160 miles of trails criss-cross the island, making it a mecca for hardy backpackers, and sea kayakers ply its outer shores and satellite islands (see our entry on Isle Royale's outer shores for more information on kayaking in the national park). But another great way to explore the island is via extended canoe expeditions on a chain of sparkling lakes that run across its eastern flank. These lakes, connected by portage trails to each other and to bays on the island's northern and southern shores, offer a week or more of fine paddling in a truly wondrous wilderness setting.

Paddlers have the option of using island ferries or water-taxi services to begin their journeys at various points along the shoreline, including Chippewa Harbor, Malone Bay,

Canoeists on one of the sheltered bays of Isle Royale.

or McCargoe Cove. Many canoeing parties, however, paddle right out of Rock Harbor, which is lined with forested islands that provide protection from Lake Superior proper. Nonetheless, people planning to paddle Rock Harbor need to exercise appropriate caution. If storms move in, take shelter at one of the harbor's shoreline campgrounds or quiet coves until good conditions return.

At the western end of Rock Harbor is Moskey Basin, a prime gateway to Isle Royale's inland lakes. Many folks look to Moskey Basin Campground as their first camp, not only because of its lovely surroundings, but also because it enables them to delay the 2.2-mile portage to Lake Richie that awaits them until morning. The long haul is worth the effort, though. Paddlers who hump their gear to Lake Richie's shores are rewarded with unspoiled woodlands of sugar maple, spruce, cedar, and pine and beautiful cobalt waters that teem with northern pike.

Once you reach Lake Richie, you have a variety of options from which to choose. Some paddlers look southward to Lake Whittlesey and Wood Lake, a lightly visited pair of lakes that offer tranquil paddling and excellent pike and walleye fishing (Chippewa Harbor also is often used by canoeists interested in checking out these lakes). Other paddlers continue westward to Intermediate Lake and Siskiwit Lake. The latter lake is the largest body of water on the island (7 miles long and more than 140 feet deep). It features a rugged, forested shoreline, several wild and picturesque islands, and many coves to explore. Windy conditions capable of kicking up sizeable waves of 2 feet or more sometimes descend on this lake, however, so exercise appropriate caution when navigating its waters.

Isle Royale National Park, Inland Lakes

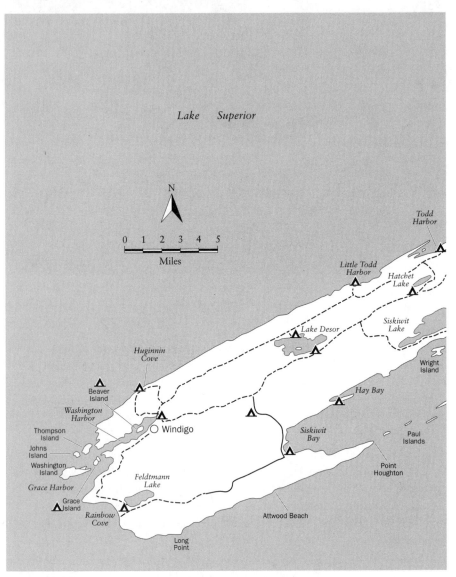

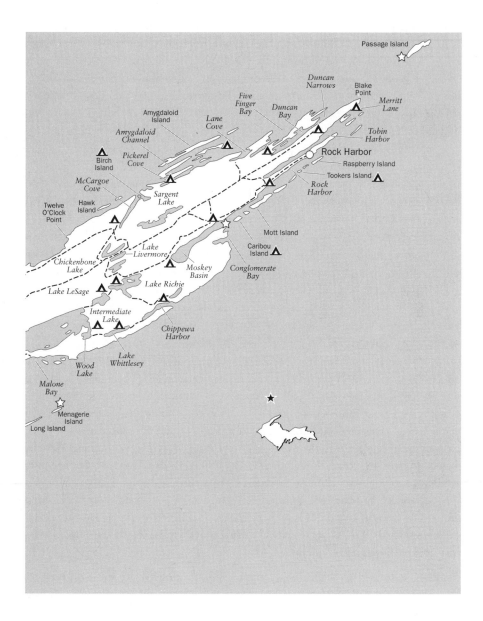

Passage Island

Duncan
Narrows

Blake
Point

Merritt
Lane

Five
Finger
Bay

Duncan
Bay

Amygdaloid
Island

Lane
Cove

Tobin
Harbor

Amygdaloid
Channel

Pickerel
Cove

Rock Harbor

Birch
Island

Raspberry Island

Tookers Island

McCargoe
Cove

Rock
Harbor

Sargent
Lake

Twelve
O'Clock
Point

Hawk
Island

Mott Island

Lake
Livermore

Caribou
Island

Chickenbone
Lake

Moskey
Basin

Conglomerate
Bay

Lake LeSage

Lake Richie

Intermediate
Lake

Chippewa
Harbor

Wood
Lake

Lake
Whittlesey

Malone
Bay

Menagerie
Island

Long Island

Another option for paddlers who reach Lake Richie is to set their sights northward to Lake LeSage and beyond. Lake LeSage and its neighbor to the north, Lake Livermore, are both pretty waterways. Visitors to Chickenbone Lake, meanwhile, will find a scenic, boomerang-shaped lake that attracts a lot of wildlife. The northern arm of Chickenbone extends toward McCargoe Cove, a beautiful bay of high forested bluffs and peaceful waters. Pretty Birch Island, featuring one of the nicest little campgrounds in the entire park, guards the northern entrance to the cove; beyond lies open Lake Superior water, with no protecting islands until Pickerel Cove.

One of the positive things about planning a canoe trip on Isle Royale's inland waters is that you can customize any trip to your own party's preferences and paddling pace. The paddling itself is easy and can be undertaken by beginners in the company of more experienced campers. Indeed, some of the park's most enthusiastic canoeists are kids. But the impact of extended portages and the general wilderness conditions that prevail in Isle Royale's interior should be weighed if you are planning a trip that includes novice canoeists.

Whatever itinerary you decide on, be assured that all of Isle Royale's inland lakes are worthy of exploration. Each of the lakes shimmers with the possibility of moose and other wildlife sightings, and all of them are fringed with scenic forestlands and good campgrounds. And no matter which lakeshore you choose to camp on, you'll always turn in wondering if you might later be awakened by the piercing midnight howl of distant wolves on the prowl. You can't ask much more than that out of a wilderness camping trip.

Note: Visitors should contact Isle Royale before finalizing any paddling plans in or around the park. In 1999 the park approved a new general management plan that dictates several significant changes in park offerings and visitor management. Many of these changes, such as establishment of no-wake zones in park harbors and restrictions on generator use at designated dock facilities, are expected to be introduced quickly. Other changes will take place over the course of several years, depending on funding and other factors. These changes include removal of docks at Duncan Bay, Threemile Bay, and Siskiwit Bay; relocation of the dock at McCargoe Cove so that the existing campground can be used exclusively by hikers and paddlers; and creation of new, paddler-accessible campgrounds on six outer islands. Most of these changes will have a greater impact on kayakers camping along the Lake Superior shoreline than canoeists exploring the park's interior, but they are nonetheless worth noting.

Access: Isle Royale National Park, which is open from April 16 to October 31, is accessible only by boat or floatplane. Seaplane service from Houghton to the designated floatplane landing area at Tobin Harbor on the southeast end of the island is available from Isle Royale Seaplane Service, P. O. Box 371, Houghton, Michigan 49931; (906) 482–8850. These planes can accommodate up to five passengers, but will not transport canoes or kayaks.

Mainland ferry services run from both Houghton and Copper Harbor on Michigan's Keweenaw Peninsula. Both of these ferries transport canoes and kayaks for an additional fee. The trip from Copper Harbor to Isle Royale's Rock Harbor is four and a half hours one-way on the 81-foot, 100-passenger *Island Queen III* (heads up to travelers prone to seasickness: Lake Superior swells can make passage on this vessel seem like an exceptionally long and arduous one). Call (906) 289–4437 for reservations. The voyage from Houghton to Rock Harbor is six hours one-way on the *Ranger III*, a 165-foot vessel that can accommodate up to 125 passengers. Reservations on the *Ranger III* are accepted by fax or mail only: Isle Royale National Park, 800 East Lakeshore Drive, Houghton, Michigan 49931; fax (906) 482–8753. In addition, a ferry service operating out of Grand Portage, Minnesota, offers transportation to Isle Royale, making stops at several spots around the island; call (715) 392–2100 for more information.

Finally, water-taxi services to various points along the island's outer shores are available, providing paddlers with additional drop-off and pick-up options. Contact Rock Harbor Lodge (906) 337-4993 for more information.

Additional Help

MA & G grid: 114, 115.

Camping: Camping is available at designated sites throughout Isle Royale National Park, but all of them place limits on consecutive night stays (one to three days, depending on the campground). Some of the campgrounds feature three-sided shelters that can house up to six people.

Food, gas, and lodging: Rock Harbor (on Isle Royale); Houghton and Copper Harbor, Michigan, and Grand Portage, Minnesota (on mainland).

For more information: Isle Royale National Park.

Canoe rentals: Concession operators at Rock Harbor or Windigo.

Portage Distances

Chippewa Harbor to Lake Whittlesey	0.6 mile
Chippewa Harbor to Lake Richie	1.2 miles
Lake Whittlesey to Wood Lake	0.6 mile
Siskiwit Lake to Malone Bay	0.2 mile
Siskiwit Lake to Intermediate Lake	0.4 mile
Intermediate Lake to Lake Richie	0.6 mile
Lake Richie to Moskey Basin	2.2 miles
Lake Richie to Lake LeSage	0.6 mile
Lake LeSage to Lake Livermore	0.6 mile
Lake Livermore to Chickenbone Lake	0.2 mile
Chickenbone Lake to McCargoe Cove	0.7 mile

50 Isle Royale National Park, Shoreline and Outer Islands

Character: A beautiful wilderness paradise of clear bays, rocky shores, and windswept islands.

Location: Isle Royale is located in the northwest corner of Lake Superior, approximately 60 miles from Michigan's Keweenaw Peninsula, 35 miles from Thunder Bay, Ontario, and 17 miles from Grand Portage, Minnesota.

Size: The Isle Royale archipelago consists of one large island (Isle Royale) and approximately 400 satellite islands. The main island is 45 miles long and 9 miles wide, making for a circumnavigation of approximately 110 miles.

Skill level: Intermediate (for Rock Harbor, Five Fingers, Siskiwit Bay, and other protected areas); expert (for routes along exposed shoreline and/or circumnavigation of island).

Hazards: Icy Lake Superior waters; motorboat traffic; long sections of exposed shoreline with no landings; famously unpredictable weather.

Fishing: A Michigan fishing license is required to fish in Lake Superior. No license is needed to fish in the inland lakes and streams, but state size and possession limits apply.

Maps: USGS 1:25,000 Feldtmann Lake-MI, Windigo-MI, Feldtmann Ridge-MI, Sugar Mountain-MI, Little Todd Harbor-MI, Point Houghton-MI, Todd Harbor-MI, Malone Bay-MI, McCargoe Cove-MI, Lake Richie-MI, Belle Harbor-MI, Mott Island-MI, Rock Harbor-MI; 1:100,000 Siskiwit Bay-MI, Todd Harbor-MI; 1:250,000 Hancock-MI, Thunder Bay-MI. NOAA charts 14968, 14976.

The paddling: Isle Royale National Park is one of Michigan's premier wilderness kayaking destinations. The park, which includes the main island of Isle Royale as well as hundreds of satellite islands, is an oasis of rock and forest in the most remote sector of mighty Lake Superior. Its main island, riddled with long ridges and valleys from stem to stern, wears a pelt of marshland and deep forest that supports wolf, moose, red fox, snowshoe hare, beaver, mink, and other animals (see our entry on Isle Royale's inland lakes for more information on the park's interior and its animal population). Its many coves and outlying islands, meanwhile, are girded with rocky outcroppings and northern boreal spruce-fir forests that echo with the aching cry of loons and the rustle of northern winds. This scenic and evocative beauty, coupled with Superior's dangerous allure, draws sea kayakers to Isle Royale in ever greater numbers.

Extended sections of the Isle Royale coastline can be explored by intermediate paddlers who are proficient in rougher seas, possessed of self- and assisted-rescue skills, and knowledgeable about the many potential hazards of paddling on Lake Superior. Sections such as Rock Harbor and the Five Fingers, for instance, offer miles of paddling along protected or semi-protected areas of the park. But Isle Royale features miles of shoreline that are exposed and/or inaccessible by boat, and Lake Superior's icy waters have a well-deserved reputation as an incubator for sudden and powerful storms. Given these factors, only expert kayakers should attempt to paddle the island from tip (Blake Point) to tail (Washington Island). Circumnavigation of the island (an 110-mile enterprise) should only be attempted by the most seasoned and accomplished of kayakers.

Sunset over the picturesque coastline of Isle Royale National Park. Photo by Deb Hausler.

Paddlers can use island ferries or water-taxi services to begin their journeys at various points along the shoreline, including Chippewa Harbor, Malone Bay, McCargoe Cove, or Washington Harbor. Most kayakers, however, paddle out of Rock Harbor, which features facilities for folks who arrive on the island via the mainland ferry services that operate out of Copper Harbor and Houghton. If you point your kayak westward from here, you will find a coastline that stretches along the southeastern side of Isle Royale from the facilities at Rock Harbor to the campground at Moskey Basin. A chain of forested islands runs parallel to the harbor on its southern flank, shielding kayakers from Lake Superior proper. These islands include Tooker's Island and Caribou Island, both of which have campgrounds that can be used by paddlers, and Mott Island, home of the national park headquarters. The entrance to Moskey Basin, meanwhile, is guarded by the Rock Harbor Lighthouse at its southern end.

Paddlers continuing westward from the waters of Rock Harbor on to Chippewa Harbor should only proceed in good conditions; this 6-mile run features only one area of shelter (Conglomerate Bay) along an otherwise exposed shoreline that is particularly vulnerable to southerly and easterly winds. Malone Bay is the next major destination for kayakers working their way clockwise around the island. Located about 9 miles west of Chippewa Harbor, Malone Bay includes a shoreline campground, a smattering of picturesque islands, and towering stands of northcountry forest that march away into the island's interior. The approach to Malone Bay, however, is vulnerable to southerly winds and has poor landing options.

Isle Royale National Park, Shoreline and Outer Islands

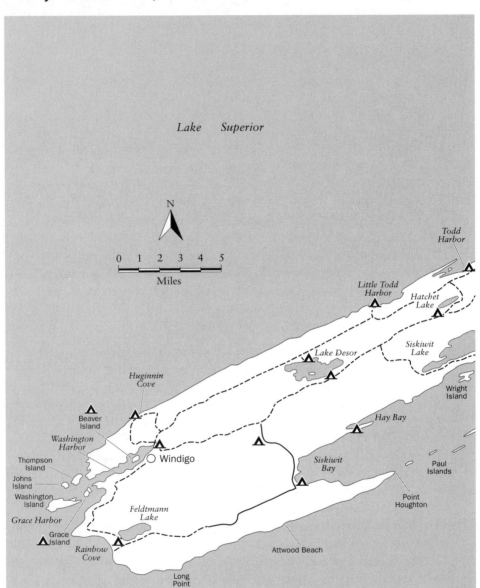

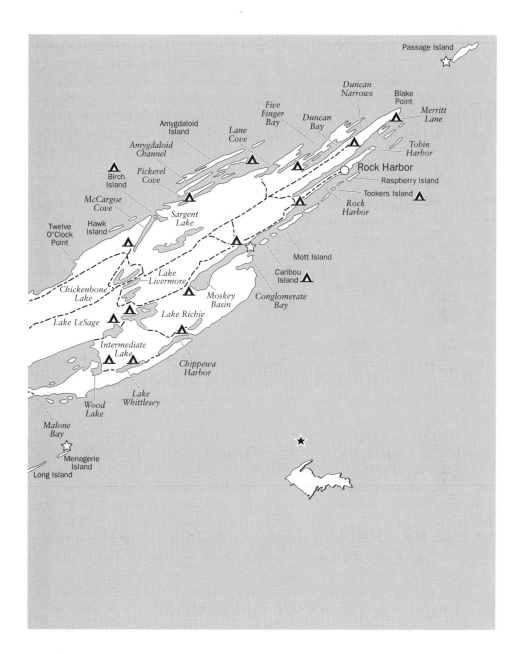

As you continue westward along Isle Royale's southern shoreline, you enter Siskiwit Bay, a large body of water that is separated from Lake Superior by a thin line of reefs that trail away from Point Houghton, the bay's southern arm. Nonetheless, Superior often kicks up rough seas in Siskiwit, so consult the marine forecast before setting out. This bay includes a couple of nice campgrounds, most notably at Hay Bay, a small cove at the eastern edge of Siskiwit Bay on the mainland. Another notable attraction in Siskiwit Bay is the Menagerie Island Lighthouse, a weathered nineteenth-century tower perched on an island of low cliffs in the far southeastern corner of the bay. This handsome lighthouse, which continues to guide boaters via an automated light system, should only be approached under calm weather conditions due to its exposed location.

The 25-mile paddle from Siskiwit Bay Campground to Grace Island in Washington Harbor is a lovely one, with cobblestone beaches and nodding forests adorning the shoreline and all of Lake Superior sprawling out to the west and south. This segment is remote and vulnerable to southerly winds, however, so proceed with caution. If you have to camp overnight along this leg, Long Point and Attwood Beach offer good camping opportunities in peaceful surroundings. Contact the park for information on camping in undesignated areas.

Washington Harbor is a little bastion of civilization on the island's western end. Windigo—the primary destination for ferries running from Minnesota—lies at the eastern end of the harbor. It includes a ferry dock, ranger station, store, laundromat, and showers. The harbor includes a couple of campgrounds (at Windigo and on Grace Island), but these are also popular with powerboaters. Proposed campgrounds on Johns Island and Washington Island should help relieve the crowded conditions that currently prevail in this area.

The 20-mile paddle from Washington Harbor to Little Todd Harbor is the most dangerous stretch of shoreline in the park. Rock walls rise out of the water along much of this section, creating reflective waves and making landings impossible. These short cliffs give way periodically (every mile or two) to small and rocky beaches, but these beaches are exceptionally difficult to land on except in calm conditions. The best refuge from bad weather along this section can be found at Huginnin Cove, about 5 miles northeast of Washington Harbor. Needless to say, this section should only be attempted by top-notch kayakers in good weather. The shoreline from Little Todd Harbor to Todd Harbor is similarly bereft of good landing spots.

The bay at Todd Harbor is a handsome one, speckled with islands and alive with wildlife. But the campground is immensely popular with backpackers, so arrive early if you hope to nab a site there. McCargoe Cove lies another 4 miles east of Todd Harbor. This quiet cove is one of the most attractive in the entire park. It lies in a corridor of deep forest that looms high above the water, and features several scenic little coves and inlets that attract anglers. Campgrounds can be found on Birch Island, which sits at the bay's northern entrance, and at the cove's southern end.

The 1-mile crossing from McCargoe Cove to Amygdaloid Channel is an exposed one that should not be attempted except in calm conditions. The Channel, however, marks the western entrance to Isle Royale's famed Five Fingers area, a delightful maze of wild islands and sheltered bays that hold many kayakers spellbound for two or three days. Most of the region can be traversed entirely by boat (though short portages connect Lane Cove to Stockly Bay and Five Finger Bay to Duncan Bay). Indeed, a good part of the Five Fingers area's charm is that paddlers can pick their way through its fjord-like channels in whatever fashion they please, secure in the knowledge that whether they choose to roam through the island-studded waters of Five Finger Bay or the quiet confines of Pickerel Cove (which features a canoe/kayak-only campground and healthy populations of waterfowl), they will find miles of beautiful scenery. Campgrounds in the Five Fingers area can also be found at Duncan Bay, Duncan Narrows, Lane Cove, and Belle Isle, but paddlers should note that these sites are also popular with other park visitors. Isle Royale's recent decision to institute no-wake regulations in the Five Fingers area will further enhance paddler enjoyment of this wonderful region.

Paddlers kayaking eastward from the Five Fingers out of Duncan Bay Narrows face about 1.5 miles of water vulnerable to northerly winds before reaching Blake Point, the exposed eastern tip of the island. The waters around Blake Point are potentially treacherous, so navigate through this area with care. Another option is to bypass Blake Point entirely by using an 0.8-mile portage trail that connects Duncan Bay to Tobin Harbor. Be forewarned, though: This portage is an unpleasant one that includes steep sections with switchbacks. Kayakers working their way westward from Blake Point to Rock Harbor, meanwhile, can explore the rugged islands and shorelines of Merritt Lane and Tobin Harbor (both of which have campsites) before moseying back to civilization for a hot shower.

Note: Visitors should contact Isle Royale before finalizing any paddling plans in or around the park. In 1999 the park approved a new general management plan that dictates several significant changes in park offerings and visitor management. Many of these changes, such as establishment of no-wake zones in park harbors and restrictions on generator use at designated dock facilities, are expected to be implemented quickly and will undoubtedly please paddlers plying the park's outer shores. Other changes—many of which will have a direct impact on kayaking in the park—will take place over the course of several years. These changes include removal of docks at Duncan Bay, Threemile Bay, and Siskiwit Bay (thus making these sites more attractive to wilderness paddlers who prefer the sounds of loons to those of powerboat generators and radios); relocation of the dock at McCargoe Cove so that the existing campground can be used exclusively by hikers and paddlers; creation of new campgrounds at Crystal Cove, Fishermans Home, Johns Island, McCargoe Cove, Washington Island, and Wright Island; and elimination of some facilities at Rock Harbor.

Access: Isle Royale National Park, which is open from April 16 to October 31, is accessible only by boat or floatplane. Seaplane service from Houghton to the designated floatplane landing area at Tobin Harbor on the southeast end of the island is available from Isle Royale Seaplane Service, P. O. Box 371, Houghton, Michigan 49931; (906) 482–8850. These planes can accommodate up to five passengers, but will not transport canoes or kayaks.

Mainland ferry services run from both Houghton and Copper Harbor on Michigan's Keweenaw Peninsula. Both of these ferries transport canoes and kayaks for an additional fee. The trip from Copper Harbor to Isle Royale's Rock Harbor is four and a half hours one-way on the 81-foot, 100-passenger *Island Queen III* (heads up to travelers prone to seasickness: Lake Superior swells can make passage on this vessel seem like an exceptionally long and arduous one). Call (906) 289–4437 for reservations. The voyage from Houghton to Rock Harbor is six hours one-way on the *Ranger III*, a 165-foot vessel that can accommodate up to 125 passengers. Reservations on the *Ranger III* are accepted by fax or mail only: Isle Royale National Park, 800 East Lakeshore Drive, Houghton, Michigan 49931; fax (906) 482–8753. In addition, a ferry service operating out of Grand Portage, Minnesota, offers transportation to Isle Royale, making stops at several spots around the island; call (715) 392–2100 for more information.

Finally, water-taxi services to various points along the island's outer shores are available, providing paddlers with additional drop-off and pick-up options. Contact Rock Harbor Lodge at (906) 337–4993 for more information.

Additional Help

MA & G grid: 114, 115.

Camping: Camping is available at designated sites throughout Isle Royale National Park, but all of them place limits on consecutive night stays (one to three days, depending on the campground). Some of the campgrounds feature three-sided shelters that can house up to six people. Keep in mind that the campgrounds located on the outlying islands are popular with motorboaters, while many of the sites on Isle Royale itself are heavily used by backpackers. Given this reality, kayakers should try to reach desired camping spots by early afternoon, when sites are more likely to be available.

Food, gas, and lodging: Rock Harbor (on Isle Royale); Houghton and Copper Harbor, Michigan, and Grand Portage, Minnesota (on mainland).

For more information: Isle Royale National Park.

Canoe rentals: Concession operators at Rock Harbor and Windigo.

Guided trips: Great Northern Adventures.

Paddling Distances

Rock Harbor to Moskey Basin	8 miles
Rock Harbor Lighthouse to Chippewa Harbor	6 miles
Chippewa Harbor to Malone Bay	10 miles
Malone Bay to Hay Bay	6 miles
Hay Bay to Siskiwit Bay Campground	5 miles
Siskiwit Bay Campground to Grace Island	25 miles
Grace Island to Hugginin Cove	5 miles
Huginnin Cove to Little Todd Harbor	15 miles
Little Todd Harbor to Birch Island (McCargoe Cove)	12 miles
Birch Island to Belle Isle	5 miles
Belle Isle to Blake Point	10 miles
Blake Point to Rock Harbor	4 miles

51 Keweenaw Water Trail–Portage Waterway

Character: A protected waterway that slices through the heart of the Keweenaw Peninsula, offering up views of woodlands and the twin cities of Houghton and Hancock.
Location: Central Houghton County.
Size: 47 miles.
Skill level: Intermediate.
Hazards: Heavy winds, rebounding waves along breakwall areas.
Maps: USGS 1:25,000 Oskar-MI, Hancock-MI, Chassell-MI, Point Mills-MI, Laurium-MI, Portage Entry-MI; 1:100,000 Hancock-MI; 1:250,000 Hancock-MI. NOAA charts 14971, 14972.

The paddling: This 47-mile-long flatwater pathway bisects the Upper Peninsula's storied Copper Country. Commonly known as the Portage Waterway, it marks the southern end of the Keweenaw Water Trail, which encompasses the northern half of the Keweenaw Peninsula. It is also Michigan's first operational segment of a proposed Lake Superior Water Trail network meant to ultimately circle the entire lake. Unlike other Keweenaw-area kayaking destinations, the Portage Waterway does not include dramatic shorelines of craggy rock or remote forestlands. In fact, shoreline development and ruins from the region's copper-mining past typify significant stretches of the waterway. Nonetheless, pockets of wilderness wetlands do exist in the trail's southern reaches, and the waterway provides kayakers with a fascinating perspective on the twin cities of Houghton and Hancock. These towns, links to a bygone era in Michigan history, developed on opposite sides of the Portage River. Today, they continue to face one another, their shopfronts and church steeples poking out from the high, forested bluffs that guard the waterway.

The southernmost section of the Keweenaw Water Trail contains the most remote-feeling stretches of paddling. This 8-mile segment, from sandy Keweenaw Bay to the small village of Chassell, features grassy marshes and streams that can be explored, as well as a couple of rustic camping alternatives. This segment also includes a number of other notable sites, including a Corps of Engineeers access site along the west shore near channel marker 9; a parcel of state land approximately 1 mile north of the Corps of Engineers site on the eastern shore that can be used for camping (look for channel marker 15); and a Sturgeon River Sloughs access site approximately 1 mile west of the main channel (the entrance to the sloughs lies opposite channel marker 20).

Paddlers continuing north into Portage Lake will find pretty big water that can kick up sizeable waves on windy days. This factor, coupled with the increased presence of motorboats, encourages many paddlers to stick close to the lake's heavily developed western shoreline. At channel marker 31 you can either veer northeast into Dollar Bay—which has an access site on the south side of the channel—or follow the Portage River westward to Houghton-Hancock. The length of this segment from Chassell to Houghton-Hancock is about 11 miles.

Keweenaw Water Trail–Portage Waterway

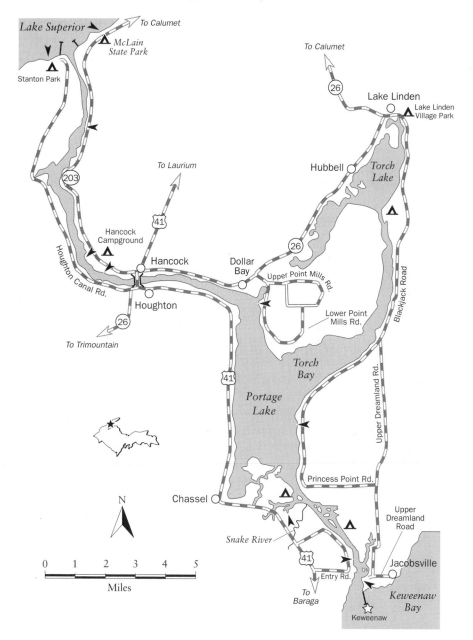

Kayaking between the towering bluffs housing Houghton and Hancock is a wonderful way to check out these bustling towns. Remnants of the region's copper mining and smelting industries still stand sentinel over the waterway here, along with the abandoned hulks of old fishing boats. But the shorelines of both towns buzz with activity during the summer, as does the double-deck vertical lift bridge that spans the waterway, connecting the two downtown areas. As you pass under the cavernous bridge, traffic thundering above your head, it is best to use one of the side channels rather than the heavily used center channel. Several access sites in the immediate area make this section of the water trail one of the easiest to explore.

Moving westward from Houghton-Hancock, you enter the formal shipping channel, where occasional big freighters roam. You may even see the *Ranger II*, the Park Service ship that regularly delivers hikers and paddlers to Isle Royale National Park. Notable shoreline sites along this segment of the waterway include the Hancock Campground (near channel marker 42) and two access points. The first of these lies just north of the Hancock Campground, near channel marker 46; the second one is located at the north end of the Lily Pond Harbor of Refuge, on the eastern shoreline. Keep in mind that the two northernmost miles of this segment of the water trail feature steel breakwalls that can create significant reflective waves. The mouth of the waterway, meanwhile, is home to campgrounds at Stanton Township Park (on the west shore) and McLain State Park (on the east shore). McLain State Park also maintains a preferred harbor inside the Lake Superior breakwall. The entire length of this segment from Houghton-Hancock to the waterway's north entrance is approximately 10 miles.

A final option for paddlers looking to explore the Keweenaw Water Trail is to check out its Torch Lake segment. This section of the water trail extends northeast out of Portage Lake through Torch Bay and all the way to Lake Linden, on Torch Lake's northern shoreline. As you progress up Torch Bay the passage gradually narrows and the shoreline bristles with cottages and cabins. The Torch Lake "Cuts"—a dredged canal that connects Torch Bay to Torch Lake—runs through several parcels of state land that provide limited backcountry camping opportunities. The best remote camping destination on this segment lies on the eastern shoreline of Torch Lake, about 0.25 mile north of the end of the "Cuts." Inaccessible by land, this spot offers high ground and nice views of the peninsula's interior. In addition, Torch Lake can be directly accessed via boat launching facilities in Hubbell and Lake Linden. Unfortunately, this lake's attractiveness is marred somewhat by stamp sand piles, abandoned machinery, and other remains of the copper-mining industry scattered along its western shoreline. This section of the water trail, from Houghton-Hancock to Lake Linden, tallies about 18 miles one-way.

Access: Access sites are scattered all along the length of the Keweenaw Water Trail. Sites near the entrance to Keweenaw Bay include a launching ramp off **Upper Dreamland Road**, about 1 mile west of Jacobsville, and a ramp on **Portage Entry Road**, approximately 5 miles south of Chassell and 2 miles east of U.S. Highway 41. Another good access point in this area is the **Sturgeon River Sloughs**. This site is located directly off U.S. 41, about

2 miles south of Chassell. Other put-in alternatives for paddlers include a ramp in **Chassell** and a ramp 1 mile south of **Dollar Bay**, on Lower Point Mills Road.

An excellent access site in the Houghton-Hancock area is the **Houghton Waterfront Park**, which can be reached by taking M–26 south from its juncture with U.S. 41 for 0.5 mile, then going right onto Houghton Canal Road for about 0.25 mile. Other put-in options here include the **Houghton & Hancock Marina**, located on the Hancock side of the waterway on M–26, and the **Hancock Campground**, located 2 miles west of the bridge off M–203 (Canal Road). Finally, the state maintains a small launch site just north of the Hancock Campground that is accessible from M–203.

Up in the northern reaches of the waterway, **Stanton Township Park** and **McLain State Park** offer access and camping facilities to kayakers. Stanton Township Park is located on Houghton Canal Road, about 10 miles northwest of Houghton. McLain State Park lies off M–203, approximately 8 miles north of Hancock. Both of these sites also offer easy access to Lake Superior. Another put-in option for paddlers is **Lily Pond**, located about 5 miles north of Hancock off M–203.

Paddlers interested in exploring the Torch Lake arm of the waterway have a few options as well. One small ramp near the mouth of Torch Bay lies off **Princess Point Road**, approximately a dozen miles south of Lake Linden. Five miles farther north, on **Bootjack Road**, a local restaurant makes its dock facilities available to visiting kayakers. Finally, the village of **Lake Linden** maintains a launch site on the north end of Torch Lake off M–26.

Additional Help

MA & G grid: 118, C3, C4, and D4; 119, C5 and D5; 111, A5.

Camping: McLain State Park is located at the western entrance to the Portage Waterway along Lake Superior; accommodations include 103 modern sites, 6 small cabins equipped with electricity and other modern amenities, and one rustic cabin. Other camping options include the City of Hancock Campground (51 sites), located just west of Hancock; the Stanton Township Park, located on the west end of the waterway south of McLain State Park; and Lake Linden Village Park, on the north end of Torch Lake. A few canoe-only camping sites are also scattered along the Water Trail, on the southeastern shore of Torch Lake and on the eastern shore of the Portage River, south of where the dredged channel begins.

Food, gas, and lodging: Houghton, Hancock, Baraga.

For more information: Keweenaw Tourism Council, McLain State Park.

Rentals/guided trips: Keweenaw Adventure Company.

A kayaker passing through the Keweenaw Water Trail near Houghton.

52 Les Cheneaux Islands

Character: This venerable resort area in northern Lake Huron boasts a maze of forested islands, sheltered channels, and limestone-girded coves that are ideal for exploration by kayak.

Location: Mackinac County along the shores of northern Lake Huron, about 2 dozen miles northeast of the Mackinac Bridge.

Size: Thirty-six islands along a dozen miles of Lake Huron shoreline.

Skill level: Beginner/intermediate.

Hazards: Heavy boat traffic on summer weekends; potential exposure to rough seas along southern edge of islands.

Maps: USGS 1:25,000 - Goose Island-MI, Cedarville-MI, Prentiss Bay-MI; 1:100,000 Saulte Ste. Marie South-MI, Cheboygan-MI; 1:250,000 - Sault Ste. Marie-MI, Cheboygan-MI. NOAA chart 14885.

The paddling: A longtime playground for sailboats, cabin cruisers, and mahogany runabouts, the sheltered bays and channels of Les Cheneaux Islands—known as "the Snows" in local parlance—have attracted growing numbers of kayakers in recent years. Granted, the region is hardly a wilderness paddling destination. The mainland and several of the larger islands are lined with summer homes and boathouses, some of the smaller islands are similarly adorned with rustic private retreats, and the major channels buzz with motorboat activity on summer weekends. In addition, private ownership of most of the islands severely limits launch, picnicking, and camping alternatives. Nonetheless, Les Cheneaux Islands offer plentiful pockets of tranquility and quiet amid the resort community trappings. Many of the islands still feature quiet marshes, crystal-clear bays, and pristine shorelines of cedar and hardwood forest, and the Snows' numerous antique summer houses and classic boathouses conjure up visions of an earlier, sepia-hued era in Michigan history. These qualities make the region an underrated gem for sea-kayaking enthusiasts.

The eastern end of Les Cheneaux Islands is dominated by several midsized islands. The largest of these is Hill Island, which bristles with cottages and docks. Its neighbor to the immediate south is Island No. 8, which mixes summer homes with long stretches of woodsy shoreline. Coryell and Boot Islands, meanwhile, offer some of the best paddling in all the Snows. Largely undeveloped, these islands treat visitors to unspoiled vistas of poplar, birch, cedar, and spruce woodlands that march to the edge of white cobblestone beaches. Much of the water around Coryell Island—including the 0.5-mile channel between it and the mainland—is relatively well protected, but Boot Island is part of an outer ring of islands that are more vulnerable to southern and southeasterly winds. The south end of Boot Island opens out into Lake Huron proper, making it an unwise destination for inexperienced kayakers or those venturing out in rough weather.

Immediately to the west of Boot Island is Government Island, the sole camping alternative for kayakers exploring the eastern end of the Snows. Many kayakers use the island,

Les Cheneaux Islands

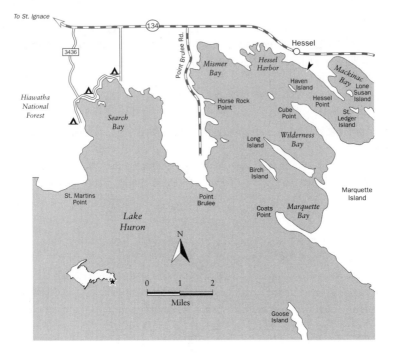

which is managed by Hiawatha National Forest, as a base for day trips to all corners of Les Cheneaux Islands. But while the island features an attractive blend of cedar and hardwood forest and boulder-strewn beaches, years of indifferent (or downright abusive) treatment by campers and picnickers have taken some of the luster off of this jewel. You'll also want to avoid the island's southern reaches in inclement weather, when extensive shoals and strong winds can combine to create treacherous conditions. To explore Government Island and other destinations on the east side of the Les Cheneaux archipelago, launch from the Lakeside Road boat launch, located a few miles east of Cedarville south of M–134.

To the west of Government Island and in the middle of the Snows archipelago is picturesque La Salle Island, a big island that extends northward nearly all the way to Cedarville before finally petering out 0.25 mile short of the mainland. The island's central location, coupled with its proximity to the mainland and major cruising areas like Muscallonge Bay, Les Cheneaux Channel, and Cedarville Bay, make it a less than peaceful paddling destination on summer weekends. The most notable feature of the island's quieter southern reaches, meanwhile, is a shallow waterway that appears only during high-water periods at the southern end of Government Bay on the island's east side. When it appears, this channel will provide you with passage between Government Island and La Salle Island.

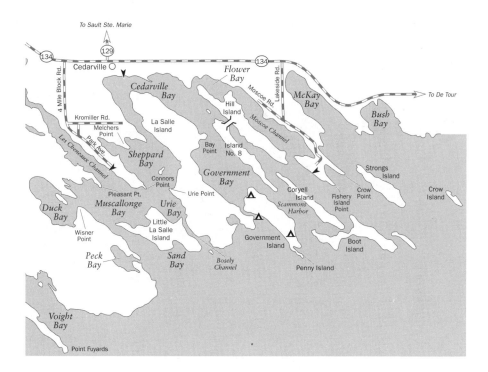

During normal water levels, however, you'll either have to portage this stretch or paddle around Government Island to reach the southern shore of La Salle.

The western end of Les Cheneaux Islands is dominated by Marquette Island, by far the largest of the islands in this Lake Huron archipelago. Highlights of Marquette Island's eastern shoreline include Duck Bay and Peck Bay, shallow and marshy coves that offer refuge from the motorboat traffic of Les Cheneaux Channel (Duck Bay is a Nature Conservancy project area). These peaceful bays are home to a wide array of waterfowl, including ducks, herons, and cormorants. If you're of a mind to investigate these spots, you can launch just west of Connors Point at the end of Park Avenue. This launch site is located midway between Hessel and Cedarville right on Les Cheneaux Channel, so keep an eye out for motorboat traffic.

The waters off the northern and western shores of Marquette Island are popular with kayakers and boaters alike (the major western entrance into Les Cheneaux Islands passes between the mainland and the west side of Marquette Island, connecting Hessel with the endless blue expanses of Lake Huron). This section of the Snows is less protected than the cluster of islands to the east, and motorboat traffic often contributes to choppy conditions. But the area's many picturesque bays and tiny, cedar-studded islands make this an attractive destination for experienced paddlers (novice paddlers should stick to the more pro-

Kayakers approaching one of the quaint islands in the "Snows."

tected island clusters to the east). Wilderness Bay, Mismer Bay, and Marquette Bay are all worth checking out, and Voight Bay—located at the far southern end of Marquette Island, on the outer perimeter of the Snows—is a lovely, unspoiled cove. Day-trippers plying these waters often put in at the public dock in Hessel. If you're a strong paddler interested in building a campfire at the end of the day, however, you may want to consider launching from Search Bay, a tract of national forest land west of Point Brulee. The distance from Point Brulee to Hessel Harbor is significant—about 6 miles one-way—but a number of quality camp sites are strung along the sandy shores of the bay.

Access: Since most of the property on the mainland and in Les Cheneaux Islands is in private ownership, access to the region's waterways is limited. Public docks in both **Hessel** and **Cedarville** are launch options, though heavy boater use, parking fees, and restrictions on overnight parking have to be weighed. These facilities are located in the hearts of the two towns and are easily reached by following street signs.

Most kayakers, however, launch from one of the following two sites, depending on their itinerary. The main launch site on the eastern end of the Snows lies at the end of **Lakeside Road**. To reach this access site, take M–134 east out of Cedarville for approximately 5 miles, then follow Lakeside Road south for about 3 miles. Another heavily used launch site is located midway between Hessel and Cedarville off M–134. Take Four-Mile Block Road (1 mile west of Cedarville and 5 miles east of Hessel) south for 1.5 miles to **Park Avenue**, then go southeast for 1 mile to the put-in.

Additional Help

MA & G grid: 107, D5; 95, A5–A6.

Camping: The only camping available on the islands is at Government Island. Primitive camping is permitted anywhere on the island. In addition, several designated sites equipped with picnic tables, fire rings, trash cans, and outhouses are scattered along the shoreline, but these first come, first served sites are popular with area boaters and bear many telltale signs of overuse. No permits are required to camp on Government Island. Primitive camping is also available at Search Bay, a lovely and secluded cove located 6 miles west of the Snows. This bay is part of Hiawatha National Forest and features eight to ten sites along Lake Huron. Popular with locals, these sites can be reached by taking M–134 west from Hessel 4.5 miles to Forest Road 3436. Take FR–3436 south for about 1.5 miles until it ends at a two-track. Sites can be found in either direction along this rough two-track, which hugs the shoreline.

Food, gas, and lodging: Hessel, Cedarville.

For more information: Les Cheneaux Island Area Tourist Association, Hiawatha National Forest.

Rentals/guided trips: Great Northern Adventures.

53 Lime Island

Character: A unique vacation spot nestled in the heart of the lower St. Mary's River.

Location: Nominally part of Chippewa County, the island lies approximately 7 miles northwest of De Tour Village in the middle of the St. Mary's River, between the eastern U.P. mainland and Canada's St. Joseph Island.

Size: Approximately 2.5 miles long and 1 mile wide; 6.5 miles of shoreline.

Skill level: Advanced (for those attempting 3-mile crossing to and from the mainland); intermediate (waters around Lime Island).

Hazards: Heavy boat traffic, including massive freighters that create formidable wakes; strong river currents.

Maps: USGS 1:25,000 - Goetzville-MI, Lime Island-MI; 1:100,000 - Sault Ste. Marie South-MI; 1:250,000 - Sault Ste. Marie-MI. NOAA chart 14882.

The paddling: Lime Island has only recently emerged as a popular destination for Great Lakes kayakers. For many years, the island was known primarily as a fueling station for Great Lakes freighters. In the mid-1980s, however, its corporate owners donated it to the state. DNR officials subsequently devised a management plan that successfully transformed the island and its fading facilities into an unassuming but relaxing getaway spot. Today, Lime Island offers an appealing cocktail of wilderness and rustic comfort for experienced paddlers.

Lime Island's central hub of activity is its protected harbor. This facility, which also is popular with pleasure boaters, sits on the northwest side of the island, directly across from the small mainland town of Raber. The harbor's perimeter is garnished with six rustic cabins and eight tent-camping platforms, all of which look out on the St. Mary's shipping channel. These accommodations make great bases from which to explore the entire island, and their placement provides visitors with both stunning sunsets and front-row seats to the endless parade of freighter traffic that marches up and down the St. Mary's. The harbor area also features a restored schoolhouse and other facilities, a picnic area, and easy access to the island's network of trails. The trail system is a good one, but hikers should properly secure snacks and other food (black bears roam the island) and beware of the island's plague of poison ivy.

The island itself can be easily explored by kayakers with intermediate abilities, provided they keep an eye on motorboat traffic. But actually getting to the island from the mainland by kayak is tricky business. The crossing is 3.3 miles long and takes paddlers across a major shipping channel. The potential for mishap is considerable. For this reason, only highly skilled and experienced paddlers should even consider making this crossing; all other kayakers interested in exploring Lime should arrange for motorized boat transportation to the island.

The island itself includes more than 6 miles of wild and woodsy shoreline that can easily be explored in an afternoon. Possible picnic stops are especially numerous on Lime's

Lime Island

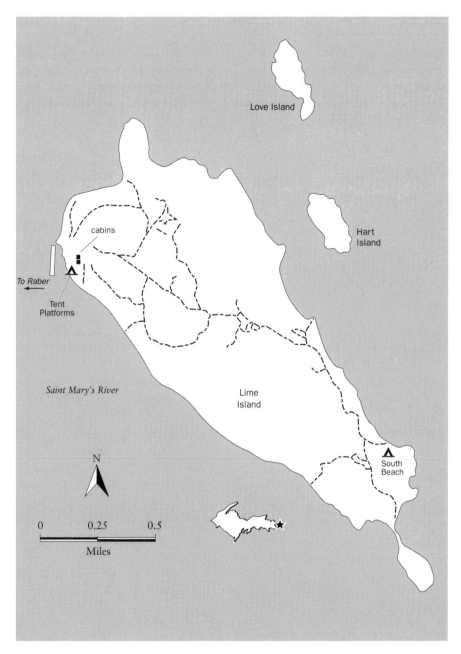

Love Island

Hart Island

cabins

To Raber

Tent Platforms

Saint Mary's River

Lime Island

N

South Beach

0   0.25   0.5

Miles

sandy eastern and southern reaches, where you may be treated to aerial acrobatics from representatives of the island's osprey population. You can also extend your day by swinging past two islands—Hart and Love—that lie less than 0.5 mile off Lime's northeast shore. The waters surrounding these undeveloped isles are also popular with motorboats, though, so keep your eyes peeled.

Access: Boat launch and parking facilities are located in **Raber**, directly across the St. Mary's River from Lime Island. Raber lies off M–48, about 10 miles north of the juncture of M–48 and M–134.

Additional Help

MA & G grid: 107, D8; 116, A1.

Camping: Eight tent-camping platforms run along Lime Island's western flank. These look directly out over the Lime Island harbor to the main shipping lane, providing campers with a great view of the freighters that rumble up and down the St. Mary's on their way to distant ports all around the world. The platforms are connected to the dock facilities and the mainland by a long boardwalk. They are available on a first come, first served basis for a small fee. Just north of the platforms are six rustic cabins that also look out over the shipping channel from atop a bluff. These solar-powered cottages can accommodate up to eight people and must be reserved in advance. Both the cottages and the tent platforms are available from Memorial Day Weekend through mid-September. Limited tent camping is also available in a designated area at South Beach Campground, on the island's southeast side.

Food, gas, and lodging: Raber, De Tour Village.

For more information: Lake Superior State Forest; DNR Area Office, Sault Ste. Marie.

54 Manistique River

Character: A sleepy, family-friendly river that flows through Seney National Wildlife Refuge and Lake Superior State Forest.

Location: Schoolcraft County in the central Upper Peninsula.

Length: Approximately 70 miles, from Manistique Lake to the city of Manistique on Lake Michigan.

Run: 43 miles, from County Road 498 east of Germfask to Merwin Creek State Forest Campground.

Average run time: 12–16 hours.

Class: Flatwater.

Skill level: Beginner/intermediate.

Optimal flow: April–October.

Average gradient: Less than 2 feet per mile.

Hazards: Occasional submerged logs and deep holes.

Fishing: Bass, northern pike, walleye.

Maps: USGS 1:25,000 - Seney-MI, Germfask-MI, Marsh Creek Pool-MI, Merwin Lake-MI; 1:100,000 - Manistique Lake-MI, Munising-MI, Manistique-MI; 1:250,000 - Marquette-MI, Sault Ste. Marie-MI.

The paddling: The highlight of a trip on the mellow Manistique is passing through Seney National Wildlife Refuge. The 95,000-acre refuge is home to some 200 species of birds—including bald eagles, osprey, loons, trumpeter swans, mergansers, and ring-necked ducks—as well as wolves and moose. Slipping quietly through the refuge in a canoe provides great opportunities for viewing this assortment of wildlife. But the Manistique is popular with both canoeists and anglers during the summer months, so if animal sightings are your goal, early morning or evening hours may be the best time to be on the river. There is no camping in Seney National Wildlife Refuge, although canoeists are allowed to stop along the river for picnics (pack out all trash, of course).

The Manistique flows southwest from Manistique Lake to the city of Manistique on Lake Michigan. Its moderate current, remote feel, and lack of tricky obstacles make it an ideal river for families. The first put-in is a public access site on CR–498, about 3 miles east of M–77. A lowhead dam located a short distance downstream can be portaged on the right.

At this point, the smallish river has just emerged from Manistique Lake. Less than a mile downstream, however, it joins forces with the Fox River and widens to between 60 and 80 feet. The water is brownish-red in color but relatively clear. Depths range from 2 to 10 feet over a mostly sandy bottom.

About 7 miles downstream, the river crosses under M–77 south of the small town of Germfask. There is a roadside park and picnic area that offers access down a steep bank. Shortly after the M–77 Bridge, the Manistique enters Seney National Wildlife Refuge. For the next 10 miles, it winds through low, forested hills that are home to abundant wildlife.

Manistique River

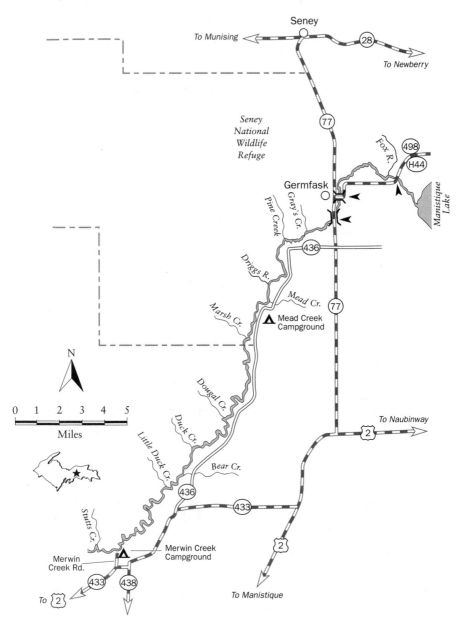

The only thing that will distract your attention away from game-spotting is the need to steer around an occasional submerged log or overhanging branch.

The appearance of Mead Creek State Forest Campground marks the end of the wildlife refuge on the left bank, but the Seney Refuge extends another couple miles on the right bank. The campground features a concrete boat ramp just inside the mouth of Mead Creek. After leaving Seney altogether, the Manistique meanders through Lake Superior State Forest to the take-out at Merwin Creek Campground. It gradually widens to between 80 and 120 feet but maintains its remote feel and moderate current. There are numerous possible campsites along the banks on state land. About 2 miles below the take-out, the Manistique enters a series of marshy sloughs that characterize the remaining 20 miles to Lake Michigan.

Access: The public access site on **CR–498** (also known as Forest Highway 44) is located about 3 miles east of Germfask. Another possible put-in is the roadside park at the **M–77 Bridge** about 1 mile south of Germfask. To reach the access site at **Mead Creek**, take M–77 south from Germfask about 2 miles (or north from U.S. Highway 2 about 8 miles) and turn west on CR–436. Follow 436 west and south about 4 miles to the campground. To reach the take-out at **Merwin Creek**, take U.S. 2 east 2 miles from Manistique and turn north on CR–433. Follow 433 northeast about 5 miles to Merwin Creek Road. Proceed north about 1 mile to the campground.

Additional Help

MA & G grid: 104, C1; 103, C8–D8.

Camping: The two Germfask liveries that service the Manistique also host private camp-grounds. Camping is also available along the river in Lake Superior State Forest. There are rustic state forest campgrounds at Mead Creek (ten sites on a bluff above the river) and Merwin Creek (eleven sites along the river). There is no camping within Seney National Wildlife Refuge.

Food, gas, and lodging: Seney, Germfask, Manistique.

For more information: Seney National Wildlife Refuge, Lake Superior State Forest.

Canoe livery: Northland Outfitters, Big Cedar Campground and Canoe.

Access Point	Float Distance To Next Access Point
CR–498 (H-44)	7 miles
M–77 Bridge	9 miles
Mead Creek Campground	27 miles
Merwin Creek Campground	Take Out

Marquette

Character: Sandy beaches, imposing cliffs, historic lighthouses, and scenic harbors all adorn the shoreline of the Upper Peninsula's largest city.

Location: Central Marquette County, on the Lake Superior coastline.

Size: 10 miles of coastline, from Little Presque Isle to South Beach Park.

Skill level: Intermediate.

Hazards: Sections of rocky and exposed shoreline; extremely cold water; motorized traffic on the water, from pleasure boats to freighters.

Maps: USGS 1:25,000 - Marquette-MI, Marquette NW-MI; 1:100,000 - Marquette-MI; 1:250,000 - Marquette-MI. NOAA chart 14970.

The paddling: Marquette is our kind of town. Attractive and robust in a distinctly "north-country" sort of way, the city perches on a scenic stretch of Lake Superior shoreline that is replete with attractive sea-kayaking spots. Moreover, the bustling town is situated within a few hours' drive of many of the Upper Peninsula's finest canoeing rivers and inland lakes. Little wonder, then, that the rooftops of many of the vehicles that line Marquette's neighborhood streets bristle with strapped-down kayaks and canoes.

But while canoeists and river-kayakers have to stray outside the city limits to sate their paddling appetites, Marquette-area sea-kayakers merely have to walk out their front doors. Indeed, the waters that guard this handsome city's eastern flanks include a wide array of attractions, from rugged Lake Superior coastline to harbors that provide refuge to massive Great Lakes freighters. And the city itself is pleasing to observe from the water, for much of its downtown district sits atop high bluffs that look out over the lake.

Paddling opportunities along the Marquette-area shoreline can easily be divided into two sections, north and south of Presque Isle Park. The park itself is a 328-acre beauty situated at the north end of Marquette on a craggy peninsula. It features agate beaches, forests of windswept pines, and high cliffs that plunge directly into Lake Superior's frigid waters. It also has good launch points that can deliver you in either direction along the coastline.

If you are interested in exploring the coastline south of Presque Isle Park, you can launch from the sand beach that lies at the peninsula's southern base, next to Presque Isle Marina. This puts you right in Presque Isle Harbor, which is sheltered from the lake by a long breakwater. From here you can work your way southward past the ore docks and freighters to Picnic Rocks and Shiras Park, which has a nice beach. Another mile down the coastline stands Marquette Harbor Light, one of Michigan's most famous and evocative lighthouses. This red lighthouse, which sits atop a rocky bluff overlooking Superior's pewter seas, remains part of an active Coast Guard station. Just north of this lighthouse is McCarty's Cove, a swimming beach that can also be used as a launch.

South of Lighthouse Point is Marquette Bay, a second harbor that is also augmented by a breakwater that juts out into the lake. Marquette Bay provides kayakers with great views of the city's striking skyline. Marquette's waterfront is lined with century-old stone

Marquette

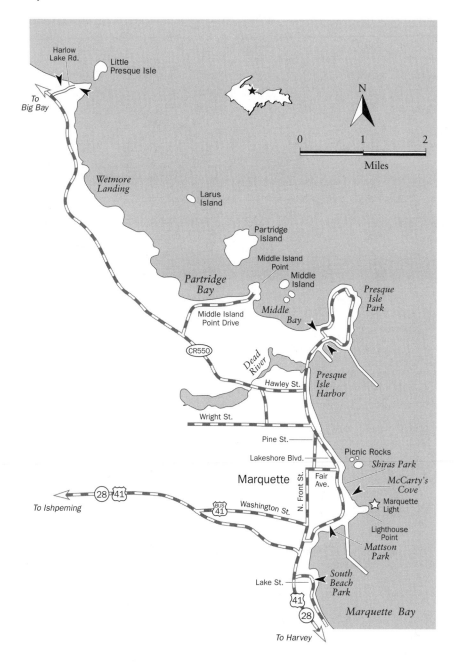

The Marquette Harbor Light stands on a rocky point overlooking Lake Superior.

buildings made from granite and red sandstone. Many of these buildings—such as the twin-towered Catholic cathedral that watches over the town's southern reaches—boast dramatic architecture of a bygone era. This cityscape is particularly beautiful to observe on morning paddles in the harbor, when its stony spires and sandstone walls shine with the day's first light.

Potential put-in/take-out points within Marquette Bay include Mattson Park at the base of the breakwater and sandy South Beach Park, which lies just south of a large power plant along the shoreline. South Beach Park is located a mile or so south of Mattson Park, past extensive dock facilities.

The shoreline north of Presque Isle Park offers a far different sort of paddling experience. Here the ore docks, freighters, and distant traffic noise that mark Marquette's southern reaches are absent. Instead, kayakers who make the 6-mile jaunt from Presque Isle Park northward to Little Presque Isle are treated to a tapestry of sandstone cliffs, rocky islands, and storm-hardened evergreen forests.

A sandy beach at the northern base of the Presque Isle peninsula makes a dandy launching site for exploring this area. From here you can easily explore the peninsula itself, which features high cliffs, gravelly beaches, and wind-whipped pines. You can then push westward up the coastline through Middle Bay, which houses Middle Island, Middle Island Point, and Partridge Island. The latter island, located 2 miles northwest of the Presque Isle Park launch site, is a particularly picturesque landmark. The island, which is home to bald eagles and other birds, features cliffs that rise far above Superior's frigid waters. These islands provide some shelter from rough seas. The remainder of the trip to Little Presque Isle is more exposed, however, and features stretches of coastline composed of low cliff walls and boulders that offer few landing options. When the barometer drops and the wind rises, this unforgiving shoreline can also kick up dangerous reflective waves.

About 4 miles north of Presque Isle Park, Sugarloaf Mountain rises out of the high hills that flank the shoreline. Wetmore Landing, a big sandy beach available for day use, appears shortly thereafter (the parking lot for the beach is 0.25 mile away, though, making this a poor choice for launching). After leaving Wetmore Landing, low sandstone cliffs return. These walls prevail along the shoreline until the approach to Little Presque Isle, a small knob-like peninsula that juts out into the lake (at normal water levels, a channel of waist-high water actually separates this wooded peninsula from the mainland). Sandy beaches are present on both sides of the peninsula where it meets the mainland, but beware of rocks and small boulders when paddling in. Hidden boulders and shoals also skirt the island's outer edges. These can create lumpy water when the weather turns sour.

Looking north from Little Presque Isle, the shoreline remains a ruggedly scenic one all the way up to Big Bay, 20 plus miles distant. Expert kayakers occasionally explore this beautiful but challenging nugget of Lake Superior shoreline, but all others should look elsewhere for their paddling pleasure.

Note: Marquette is currently envisioned as the centerpiece of a proposed Lake Superior Water Trail segment that will someday extend all the way from Big Bay to Grand Marais along Superior's southern shores. Sea-kayaking enthusiasts hope to eventually create a water trail that encompasses all of Lake Superior (established sections have been put together in Wisconsin, Minnesota, and Michigan's own Keweenaw Peninsula).

Access: Presque Isle Park is at the end of Lakeshore Boulevard, 3 miles from downtown. The **sand beach** at the north end of Presque Isle Harbor is next to Presque Isle Marina, also off Lakeshore Boulevard. **Shiras Park** lies at the southern end of Presque Isle Harbor, off Lakeshore Boulevard. **McCarty's Cove** is located next to the Coast Guard station off Lakeshore Boulevard, between Hewitt and Ohio Streets. **Mattson Park** is also on Lakeshore Boulevard, at the southern end of town where Washington Street enters the business district. To reach **South Beach Park**, take U.S. 41 south out of downtown for about a mile, then travel east on Lake Street for 0.25 mile. To reach **Little Presque Isle**, take County Road 550 (Big Bay Road) north out of Marquette for about 6 miles to Harlow Lake Road. This dirt road, which leads directly to Little Presque Isle, is the second one on the right after the parking lot for Sugarloaf Mountain.

Additional Help

MA & G grid: 113, D5.

Camping: Marquette Tourist Park is a modern facility with 100 campsites. It is on the northern outskirts of town, directly off CR–550 (Big Bay Road) on the Dead River.

Food, gas, and lodging: Marquette.

For more information: Marquette Convention and Visitors' Bureau, Hiawatha Water Trail Association.

Rentals/guided trips: Great Northern Adventures.

56 Menominee River

Character: A short, scenic stretch of river that features one of the most challenging whitewater runs in the Midwest.

Location: Along the Wisconsin border near Iron Mountain in the southwestern Upper Peninsula.

Length: Approximately 90 miles, from the intersection of the Brule, Paint, and Michigamme Rivers in Iron County to the city of Menominee on Green Bay.

Run: 4 miles, from Little Quinnesec Falls Dam through Piers Gorge to U.S. Highway 8.

Average run time: 2–4 hours.

Class: II–V.

Skill level: Advanced.

Optimal flow: May–September.

Hazards: Large, unpredictable water volume; powerful rapids with huge boulders, standing waves, souse holes, and other dangerous obstacles; 8- to 10-foot drop at Missicot Falls.

Maps: USGS 1:25,000 - Norway-MI; 1:100,000 - Escanaba-MI; 1:250,000 - Escanaba-MI.

The paddling: For a brief but memorable 4-mile stretch, the Menominee River offers expert paddlers a challenging, class II–V whitewater run that ranks among the best in the Midwest. In fact, the sheer volume of water tumbling through the scenic, forested cliffs of Piers Gorge invites comparisons to major Western rivers. This stretch attracts skilled whitewater kayakers from throughout the region and also plays host to guided whitewater rafting trips.

The Menominee begins in Iron County, at the point where the Michigamme River joins the Brule and Paint Rivers. It typically runs wide, slow, and deep as it delineates the Wisconsin border all the way to Green Bay. But about 25 miles from its source—just downstream from Iron Mountain—the Menominee abruptly changes character. As it approaches Piers Gorge, the river constricts from its usual width of 300 feet to less than 100 feet and plummets through a series of intense rapids and waterfalls.

The run begins just downstream from Little Quinnesec Dam in the city of Niagara, Wisconsin. The first 1.5 miles are mostly flatwater with a fast current. As you approach Piers Gorge, you'll notice rocky cliffs beginning to rise on the left bank. Then the Menominee divides in two around a midstream island, with the heaviest flow going toward the right. This is Sand Portage Falls, a class II–III drop that is a popular surfing spot.

After negotiating Sand Portage Falls, paddlers can catch their breath over nearly a mile of flatwater. But then the Menominee begins its rapid descent through Piers Gorge (named for the structures lumbermen built in the 1800s to help them guide logs down the river). Shortly before the water drops off the horizon at the beginning of the run, you'll see a landing on the left bank. This sandy spot provides access to a foot trail on the Michigan side that can be used to scout or portage the next 0.5 mile of nearly continuous rapids.

First up is Missicot Falls, which features an 8- to 10-foot drop and rates class IV–V. Paddlers should be aware of a large boulder at the bottom that can be hidden in high water.

Menominee River

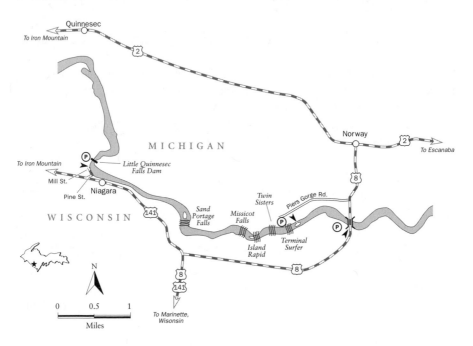

Next, the river splits around a small island. The main current flows toward the left, creating large standing waves. The fun continues 200 yards later at the Twin Sisters, an irregular series of class II–III drops. After a short stretch of class I water, paddlers reach Terminal Surfer, a class III ledge drop that spans most of the width of the river and is usually run on the far right.

There is a gravel landing on the left about 0.25 mile below this last major rapid. A trail leads up to the parking lot off Piers Gorge Road. This parking lot also provides access to the network of foot trails that follow the Michigan side of the Menominee through Piers Gorge. Or you can proceed another 0.75 mile on relatively quiet water to take out on the Wisconsin side just upstream from the U.S. 8 Bridge.

The water level on the Menominee is inconsistent due to releases from the Little Quinnesec Dam at Niagara. The normal flow ranges from 1,400 to 1,700 cubic feet per second, and rafting companies run the river up to 4,500 cfs. But flows sometimes reach dangerously high levels, as much as 16,000 cfs. The Menominee is big water and includes dangerous rapids. It should only be attempted by expert paddlers after careful scouting. You can scout over land by following the trails on the Michigan side, or on water by taking a guided whitewater rafting trip.

Access: To reach the put-in from Norway, take U.S. 8 south into Wisconsin and turn right onto U.S. 141. Follow 141 northwest 2 miles into Niagara, where it becomes River Street. Turn right on Pine Street, then left on Mill Street. Follow Mill Street to a small vacant lot just downstream from the **Little Quinnesec Dam**. To reach the **Piers Gorge Road** access, take U.S. 8 south from Norway about 1.5 miles and turn west on Piers Gorge Road. The parking lot is 0.5 mile ahead. The **U.S. 8 Bridge** is located 2 miles south of Norway. The take-out and parking lot are on the upstream Wisconsin side of the river.

Additional Help

MA & G grid: 88, B1.

Camping: Lake Antoine County Park (eighty modern sites), 3 miles northeast of Iron Mountain on Lake Antoine Road (County Road 396); Carney Lake State Forest Campground (fourteen rustic sites), 16 miles northeast of Iron Mountain via M–95 and the Merriman Truck Trail.

Food, gas, and lodging: Norway, Quinnesec, Iron Mountain.

For more information: Copper Country State Forest.

Guided trips: Argosy Adventures Rafting, Kosir's Rapid Rafts.

Access Point	Float Distance To Next Access Point
Niagara, Wisconsin	3.25 miles
Piers Gorge Road	0.75 mile
U.S. 8 Bridge	Take Out

The Menominee River races through Piers Gorge, creating some of the most intense whitewater in the Midwest.

Net River

Character: A rough gem that promises solitude in a wild northwoods setting.
Location: Central Iron County.
Length: 30 miles.
Run: 12 miles, from Old U.S. Highway 41 to Snake Rapids.
Average run time: 6–8 hours.
Class: Flatwater, with occasional class I rapids (class II–III water at Chipmunk Falls).
Skill level: Intermediate.
Optimal flow: April–May, October.
Average gradient: 4 feet per mile.
Hazards: Whitewater at Chipmunk Falls and Snake Rapids; periodic deep holes.
Fishing: Despite its reputation as a fine smallmouth bass stream, the Net receives little fishing pressure.
Maps: USGS 1:25,000 - Tunis-MI, Porter Lake-MI, Sunset Lake-MI; 1:100,000 - Iron River-MI; 1:250,000 - Iron River-MI.

The paddling: Remote and wild, the Net River is one of those underpublicized Upper Peninsula streams that is ideal for paddlers looking to disappear for a springtime afternoon or weekend. Unlike the nearby Paint River (of which the Net is a tributary), the Net is both highly seasonal and difficult to access. Summertime water levels are generally too low to support paddling, and put-in spots are limited to a handful of secluded sites. These factors have kept the Net far beneath the radar of most canoeists and anglers over the years. But if you're willing to brave the stream's rugged access roads and are capable of grappling with the obstacles inevitably conjured up by a true wilderness river, the Net is an engaging early-season alternative.

The mainstream of the Net River originates about 1 mile west of U.S. 141, where its eastern and western branches meet. To explore this upper portion of the river, put in at the bridge on Old U.S. 141. This access site will put you on the Net's East Branch, about 0.75 mile upstream from its confluence with the West Branch. Once the two branches join, the Net settles into a sleepy gait as it twists through a mix of deep forest and marshland. But while the river's upper section offers peaceful paddling conditions, it is likely to be punctuated by occasional beaver dams that will require portaging.

The Wide Waters impoundment lies about 5 miles downstream from where the Net's main branch begins. Bordered by picturesque stands of pines and hardwoods, this natural impoundment holds a tantalizing variety of fish, including northern pike, yellow perch, and smallmouth bass. From Wide Waters to the Snake Rapids access site, the river settles into a rhythm in which long pools of nearly currentless water alternate with short spurts of rapids. The most challenging of these rapids is Chipmunk Falls, located about 5 miles below Wide Waters. This run offers a couple hundred yards of class II–III whitewater when the river is high, but subsides to bottom scraping and class I water during summer and

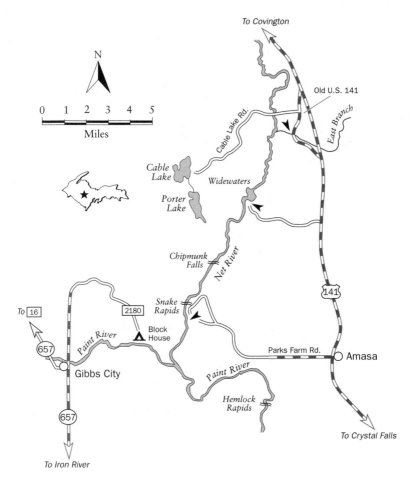

other low-water periods. Chipmunk Falls is located at one of the most inaccessible sections of the entire river, so if you have any doubts about your ability to make this run, make sure you portage.

The Net's second significant stretch of whitewater can be found about 2 miles downstream from Chipmunk Falls. This section, known as Snake Rapids, offers several hundred yards of straightforward class I–II whitewater in high water. During periods of low water, however, you may be reduced to walking your boat through this section. Portaging is also an option, albeit an unattractive one given the overgrown shoreline. The public access site is located on the left bank at the end of these rapids.

The Net is a pretty and remote river that is perfect for spring excursions.

The Snake Rapids access site is your last take-out option before the Net joins the Paint River another 3 miles downstream. Canoeists who reach this confluence and choose to float the Paint downstream will have to grapple with Upper and Lower Hemlock Rapids before reaching their first take-out option, at the bridge on County Road 643 (Bates-Amasa Road). See our entry on the Paint River for more information on these dangerous rapids.

Access: The put-in at **Old U.S. 141 Bridge** lies on Old U.S. 141, which curls to connect to U.S. 141 at two different junctures, 8 and 11 miles north of Amasa. Either route will take you to the bridge in 2 or 3 miles. **Wide Waters** is accessible via a 4-mile-long gravel road that is located approximately 6 miles north of Amasa on U.S. 141. To reach the access site at **Snake Rapids**, take Parks Farm Road west from its juncture with U.S. 141. Follow the signs for 9 miles to the put-in. Keep in mind, though, that this backcountry road disintegrates into very rough gravel in its latter stages. To reach the **Block House** USFS Campground on the Paint River, take CR–657 north from U.S. 2 for approximately 13 miles, then go east on Forest Road 2180 (FR–347 on many maps) for 4 miles.

Additional Help

MA & G grid: 98, A4 and B4.

Camping: Occasional streamside camping possibilities materialize from Wide Waters on down, as the Net spends much of its time winding through Copper Country State Forest. Ottawa National Forest's Block House campground offers two secluded sites (no water) on the Paint River.

Food, gas, and lodging: Crystal Falls, Amasa.

For more information: Copper Country State Forest.

Canoe liveries: None.

Access Point	Float Distance To Next Access Point
Old U.S. 41 Bridge	5 miles
Wide Waters	7 miles
Snake Rapids	Take Out

58 Ontonagon River, East Branch

Character: Runnable for only a few weeks of the year, this river offers continuous whitewater thrills in a wild setting.

Location: Eastern Ontonagon County.

Length: 60 miles.

Run: 7.5 miles, from Forest Road 208 to U.S. Highway 45.

Average run time: 3–4 hours.

Class: II–III.

Skill level: Advanced.

Optimal flow: Mid-April–May.

Average gradient: 25 feet per mile.

Hazards: Nearly continuous class II–III rapids through steep and rocky terrain; fallen trees and other deadfall; remote setting far from medical help.

Fishing: None on this section of the river.

Maps: USGS 1:25,000 - McKeever-MI, Rockland-MI; 1:100,000 - Ontonagon-MI; 1:250,000 - Iron River-MI.

The paddling: The East Branch of the Ontonagon River is home to one of the most intense, sustained whitewater runs in all of Michigan. Most of this stream's 60-mile length is impassable at any time of year, due to massive deadfalls, beaver dams, and narrow, rocky stretches. But as it surges northward from its origins in Iron County to join the Middle Branch, its last few miles open up sufficiently to create an exciting and dramatic whitewater run through a strikingly rugged piece of northern wilderness.

This stream is best paddled in springtime. Indeed, negotiating the East Branch's rock-strewn corridor can turn into a tiresome exercise in portaging and bottom-scraping at the lower water levels that often prevail from early summer onward. During springtime, however, when snowmelt pumps up the volume, this river offers 7.5 miles of nearly continuous class II–III water that will delight accomplished whitewater paddlers. On the other hand, the East Branch's steep gradient, its numerous jagged rocks and boulders, and its relentless nature make it a poor—and potentially dangerous—choice for canoeists and kayakers without whitewater experience.

The run begins at a washed-out bridge at the end of East Branch Road about 7 miles south of the juncture of M–38 and M–26. (See the Access section below for more information on using this put-in site, which is privately owned.) The river here features creamy brown water (which makes reading the river more difficult throughout) and a moderate current that gives paddlers a little time to get dialed in. The current picks up speed quickly, however, as it passes through increasingly steep terrain marked by crumbling clay bluffs and thick forests of pine, hemlock, cedar, and hardwoods.

From the put-in to the take-out 7.5 miles downstream, the East Branch churns up an extended chain of class II–III rapids that charge through banks that range from 45 to 75

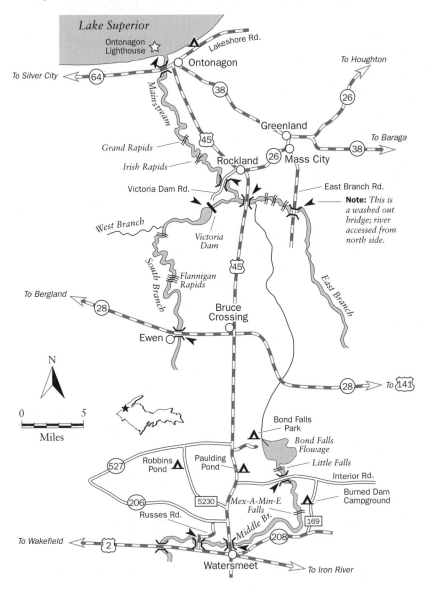

feet wide. The main obstacles in this whitewater are the constellations of sharp rocks and boulders that line the riverbed, but you also need to keep your eyes peeled for occasional fallen trees that may block channels that were clear the previous spring. High standing waves and boulder-framed chutes proliferate throughout, adding to the general uproar.

Eddies, meanwhile, serve as the primary rest stops, for the tributary offers little in the way of slow water for you to catch your breath.

The action on the East Branch subsides as it approaches its juncture with the Ontonagon's Middle Branch. The take-out is just upstream from U.S. 45 on the right, a short distance downstream from the merger of the two tributaries. This access site also serves as the primary put-in point for the Ontonagon's mild-tempered mainstream, which winds northward for 24 miles before emptying into Lake Superior.

Access: The primary put-in for this whitewater run is at a washed-out bridge 5.5 miles south of Mass City, at the end of **East Branch Road**. Access is on private property, however, so you must secure permission before you unload your boats and put in (the landowner lives at the end of the road). The take-out is at the **Military Bridge** landing on U.S. 45.

According to Ottawa National Forest literature, paddlers can also put in 8 miles farther upstream at the bridge on Gardner Road, located about 1 mile southwest of Forest Road 1180 and 8 miles south of Mass City. But the stretch from Gardner to East Branch Road is a portage-intensive affair due to deadfalls, etc., and few paddlers find these extra miles of slower water to be worth the hassle.

Additional Help

MA & G grid: 109, C7–C8.

Camping: Twin Lakes State Park (sixty-two sites) is located on Lake Roland, 23 miles southwest of Houghton on M–26. Other nearby camping options include rustic facilities in state and national forest land. To reach the Copper Country State Forest campground at **Emily Lake** (nine sites), take Emily Lake Road south from M–26 at Twin Lakes State Park for 2 miles, then go east (follow the signs) for 0.5 mile. The Ottawa National Forest campground at **Courtney Lake** (twenty-one sites) is 7 miles east of Mass City on M–38, then 1 mile south on FR–1960 (Courtney Lake Road). The national forest also maintains the **Sparrow Rapids** campground (6 sites) on the East Branch's upper reaches; it is 0.25 mile north of Kenton on FH–16, then 4 miles northwest on FR–1100.

Food, gas, and lodging: Rockland, Greenland, Ontonagon.

For more information: Ottawa National Forest.

Canoe liveries: None.

Access Point	Float Distance To Next Access Point
East Branch Road	7.5 miles
Military Bridge (U.S. 45)	Take Out

59 Ontonagon River, Mainstream

Character: A big, sleepy river that winds through scenic woodlands before emptying into Lake Superior.

> see map on page 250

Location: Northern Ontonagon County.

Length: 24 miles.

Run: 24 miles, from U.S. Highway 45 to Ontonagon.

Average run time: 7–10 hours.

Class: Flatwater/class I.

Skill level: Beginner/intermediate.

Optimal flow: May–October.

Average gradient: Less than 3 feet per mile.

Hazards: Two brief stretches of light class I–II whitewater; deeper water, powerboats, and vulnerability to winds in final few miles.

Fishing: Productive fishery includes trout, salmon, northern pike, and walleye.

Maps: USGS 1:25,000 - Ontonagon North-MI, Ontonagon South-MI, Firesteel-MI; 1:100,000 - Ontonagon-MI; 1:250,000 - Iron River-MI.

The paddling: Unlike its rambunctious tributaries, which twist and shout as they rush through Michigan's craggy northern parts, the mainstream of the Ontonagon River sighs and gurgles contentedly for most of its 24-mile length. The mainstream is formed by the juncture of the East and Middle Branches just upstream of the access site at U.S. 45, and it gets another injection of volume from the West Branch about 1 mile below the put-in. These tributaries combine with other feeder streams to broaden the Ontonagon to 150 feet or more in its upper reaches, a size that it maintains for most of its length before it empties into Lake Superior. But the mainstream's inconsequential gradient serves to keep rough water to a minimum throughout. Indeed, long stretches of the Ontonagon are so slow that the current is nearly imperceptible. This mild temperament, coupled with the numerous camping and picnicking spots that line its banks, make the mainstream the most family-friendly river in the Ontonagon system.

Paddlers looking to explore the entire mainstream can put in at a roadside park on the upstream side of the U.S. 45 bridge (also known as Military Bridge). This is also a popular access site for anglers. Another option is to put in 3 miles farther downstream at Victoria Road Bridge. No other access spots exist between this bridge and the rivermouth, so day-trippers are encouraged to get an early start.

For the next several miles, the Ontonagon features a slow-to-moderate current as it glides through deep valleys of birch, spruce, hemlock, aspen, and hardwoods over a river bottom of sand and red clay. At some points, the banks rise 200 feet or more above the river corridor. The woods that adorn the tops of these ridges, meanwhile, are a patchwork of private timber land and National Forest land. Sandbars, meanwhile, pop up around many bends, providing paddlers with good options for leg-stretching and picnicking.

The only rapids of any significance on the mainstream appears midway through the trip. Irish Rapids (class I–II during normal water levels) appear about 5 miles below Victoria Bridge, at an island that divides the Ontonagon in two. Paddlers should take the right channel, which funnels the bulk of the river's volume. Experienced canoeists should have no difficulty with the ensuing run, which lasts for a couple hundred feet. Others may want to portage, especially during spring runoff, after storms, or during other high-water periods.

Three miles below Irish Rapids is Grand Rapids (class I–II), a succession of rocky ledges that get scrapy at low water levels. During high water, however, the ledges churn up significant standing waves. Below Grand Rapids, the river slows to a creep once again as it passes through sections of Copper Country State Forest. The Ontonagon remains wide (200 feet or better), deep, and slow for the remainder of its length. As it meanders northward, it also exits the hill country that marked its upper reaches and enters thickly wooded lowlands. The final few miles above Ontonagon, meanwhile, see a fair amount of motorboat traffic, especially on summer weekends. By the time the Ontonagon reaches the rivermouth at Lake Superior, it spans several hundred feet from bank to bank. The public access site in Ontonagon Harbor is located on the left side of the river, a short distance downstream from a railroad trestle.

Access: The access site at **Military Bridge** is located just south of U.S. 45 where it passes over the river. **Victoria Road Bridge** lies 2 miles southwest of Rockland on Victoria Dam Road. The take-out at **Ontonagon Harbor** is at the public marina in the center of town.

Additional Help

MA & G grid: 109, B6, C7.

Camping: Ontonagon maintains a township park with camping facilities 1 mile northeast of town near Lake Superior, on Lakeshore Road. In addition, Porcupine Mountains Wilderness State Park is a half-hour drive to the west. This vast and beautiful park provides visitors with a wide array of camping options, including nearly 200 sites at modern facilities. Rustic campsites, frontier-style cabins, and at-large backcountry camping options are available to hardier souls.

Food, gas, and lodging: Ontonagon, Rockland.

For more information: Ottawa National Forest.

Canoe liveries: None.

Access Point	Float Distance To Next Access Point
Military Bridge (U.S. 45)	3 miles
Victoria Road Bridge	21 miles
Ontonagon	Take Out

60 Ontonagon River, Middle Branch

Character: Canoeable throughout the summer, this river offers a mix of placid water and light rapids as it carries paddlers through scenic U.P. lowlands.

see map on page 250

Location: Originates in eastern Gogebic County and winds into eastern Ontonagon County, where it joins the mainstream.

Length: 60 miles.

Run: 23 miles, from Watersmeet to Bond Falls Flowage.

Average run time: 8 hours.

Class: I–II.

Skill level: Intermediate.

Optimal flow: May–October.

Average gradient: 5 feet per mile.

Hazards: Light rapids interspersed throughout the run; two sets of rapids (Mex-I-Min-E Falls, Little Falls) that should be portaged by all but advanced paddlers.

Fishing: Healthy populations of brook, brown, and rainbow trout; Bonds Fall Flowage also supports walleye, smallmouth bass, and northern pike.

Maps: USGS 1:25,000 - Fuller-MI, Trout Creek-MI, Paulding-MI; 1:100,000 - Wakefield-MI, Ontonagon-MI; 1:250,000 - Iron River-MI.

The paddling: The Middle Branch of the Ontonagon River is a pleasant stream that is popular with both canoeists and anglers. Its popularity among paddlers is due in part to the fact that it is the only tributary of the Ontonagon—and one of the few rivers in the western U.P.—that has regular livery service. Anglers, meanwhile, roam the river in search of the trout that haunt its murky waters. But the Middle Branch still sees far less traffic than Lower Peninsula streams, and peaceful stretches of river are always plentiful.

Good canoeing on the Middle Branch begins around Watersmeet. From here to Burned Dam Campground, the river is suitable for paddlers with basic skills. You can put in either at Russes Road Bridge (Forest Road 6110) or at the U.S. Highway 45 access site, both of which are in the immediate Watersmeet vicinity. The river is quite narrow (10 to 30 feet) in this upper section due to the dense alders that crowd the corridor. The current is slow, the water dark, and biting flies can be truly heinous in this upper section during midsummer floats.

Below U.S. 45 the river gradually opens up as it twists and turns though thick stands of alder and cedar that provide little in the way of rest stop options. About a half-hour downstream from the U.S. 45 Bridge, you'll encounter two sets of granite pillars planted in the stream. These pillars can wreak havoc on novice canoeists because of the quick current on the approach, but experienced paddlers should be able to negotiate their way past these obstacles without incident.

As you approach the bridge at Buck Lake Road, the banks of the Middle Branch continue to slowly widen as the river passes through marshly lowland. The current remains mellow for the most part, though patches of faster water do begin to appear. About a half-hour below Buck Lake Bridge, you'll find an extended stretch of fast water through tight banks (10 to 20 feet) that can create light rapids at higher volumes. A railroad trestle spans the bridge another ten minutes downstream; stay to the right to pass through here.

The float from the trestle to Burned Dam Campground is about a two-hour trip. The river widens steadily through here, reaching widths of 60 feet or more as it enters a pretty valley in which low, wooded banks give way to towering forests in the distance. The open nature of the river corridor in this section exposes paddlers to stiff headwinds from the north, but it's a small price to pay for the scenery. The current remains slow to moderate through here as well. The only exception is a stretch of light rapids located about a half-hour above the campground. You'll find this water midway between two small bridges that span the river (the bridges are part of a local off-road vehicle trail network).

You will be able to hear Mex-I-Min-E Falls long before you see them. Take out on the right bank just above the falls. From here, you can either portage your boat and return to the river (the portage is about 300 feet long) or roll out your sleeping bag at Burned Dam Campground, which borders the falls.

Below Burned Dam the river serves up spicier fare for paddlers. The 6.5-mile run from Burned Dam to Interior Bridge features several challenging runs through hardy class I–II rapids garnished with sweepers and sharp turns. The most significant whitewater in this section is a 100-yard dash through class I–II water about 3 miles above Interior Bridge. These rapids, though, are interspersed with long stretches of slower water that provide plenty of time for chatter, fishing, or quiet reflection, whatever your taste.

Below Interior Bridge the Middle Branch's current slackens again as it passes over a river bottom of mixed sand, gravel, and rock. Fallen trees and other deadfall remain common through here, and occasional portages will likely be necessary. A final series of rapids is located about 2 miles downstream from Interior Bridge, just before the stream enters Bond Falls Flowage. These class II–III rapids, collectively known as Little Falls, consist of a pair of rocky rapids stacked right on top of one another. This is a technically challenging run that features lots of exposed rock at lower water levels. It should only be considered by advanced paddlers who scout carefully beforehand. All others should portage.

Below Little Falls the river enters the backwaters of Bond Falls Flowage. A county park and campground (Bond Falls Park) sits on the northwest shore of the reservoir, just west of the dam facility. The crossing is better than 2 miles long and can be tough sledding on windy days. If blustery conditions prevail here, you may want to consider hugging the lee shoreline and committing to some extra paddle strokes to reach the take-out.

Paddlers are discouraged from venturing below Bond Falls. Logjams clog the narrow river corridor in this lower section, and water levels are generally too low for enjoyable floating (much of the tributary's volume is diverted at the Flowage to the Ontonagon's South Branch).

Access: The put-in at **Russes Road** (FR–6110) is located 3 miles west of Watersmeet, about 0.5 mile north of U.S. 2 (some maps we consulted list this road as FR–378). The public site at the **U.S. 45 bridge** is located in Watersmeet. The bridge at **Buck Lake Road** is 3 miles northeast of Watersmeet, just north of County Road 208 (also known as Old U.S. 2). **Burned Dam Campground** can be accessed by car by taking CR–208 (Old U.S. 2) northeast out of Watersmeet for 7 miles to FR–169; the campground lies less than 2 miles north on FR–169. The bridge on **Interior Road** lies about 5 miles east of the road's juncture with U.S. 45, 8 miles north of Watersmeet. The park at **Bond Falls** is located on Bond Falls Road, 3 miles east of U.S. 45.

Additional Help

MA & G grid: 97, B6–B8.

Camping: Much of the stream passes through Ottawa National Forest, but good campsites along the river corridor are infrequent above Mex-I-Min-E Falls. The lone rustic campground on the Middle Branch is **Burned Dam Campground**, located off FR–169 at Mex-I-Min-E Falls. Located 10 miles east of Watersmeet, it includes five camping sites. Another option for paddlers intent on investigating Bond Falls Flowage is the thirty-site **Bond Falls** county campground (also known as Paulding Campground), located on the northwest end of the basin next to Bond Falls Dam.

Food, gas, and lodging: Watersmeet, Rockland, Ontonagon.

For more information: Ottawa National Forest.

Canoe liveries: Sylvania Outfitters.

Access Point	Float Distance To Next Access Point
Russes Road (FR–6110)	3 miles
U.S. 45	4 miles
Buck Lake Road (Old U.S. 2)	5 miles
Burned Dam Campground	6.5 miles
Interior Road Bridge	4.5 miles
Bond Falls (Paulding) Park	Take Out

Mex-I-Min-E Falls on the Middle Branch of the Ontonagon River.

61 Ontonagon River, South Branch

Character: A rugged and scenic river that alternates between flatwater and rollicking class I–II rapids.

see map on page 250

Location: Central Ontonagon County.

Length: 60 miles.

Run: 25.5 miles, from Ewen to Victoria Dam.

Average run time: 7–10 hours.

Class: I–III.

Skill level: Intermediate.

Optimal flow: May–September.

Average gradient: 8 feet per mile.

Hazards: Rock gardens throughout middle section of run (class I–II); class III rapids above entrance to Victoria Dam reservoir; remote setting far from roadways.

Fishing: Smallmouth bass fishery, with healthy populations of northern pike, perch, and walleye in Victoria Dam backwaters.

Maps: USGS 1:25,000 - Ewen-MI, Oak Bluff-MI; 1:100,000 - Ontonagon-MI; 1:250,000 - Iron River-MI.

The paddling: On U.P. maps, the Ontonagon River's many tributaries sprawl across the peninsula's northwestern hinterlands, extending watery tendrils through some of the wildest country remaining in the Midwest. Of these branches, the South offers the most interesting variety of canoeing conditions, from peaceful flatwater to challenging whitewater. Moreover, it is a more reliable destination for summer paddling trips than the Ontonagon's other major tributaries, which are vulnerable to water level fluctuations. The South Branch receives much of the Middle Branch's flow via a flume located about 8 miles upstream of Ewen. But while this diversion helps the stream maintain adequate volume for summertime floats, its lack of intermediate access sites—canoe trips on the South Branch are a straight shot from Ewen to Victoria Dam, more than two dozen miles downstream—keep pressure light.

Good canoeing on the South Branch begins at Ewen, where a nice access site can be found on the upstream side of the M–28 bridge. For the next several miles, the murky river moves along at a drowsy pace through a terrain of low woodlands and scattered farmlands. The river in these first few miles is about 45 to 60 feet wide and 2 to 4 feet deep, with wooded banks that periodically present sites that are suitable for overnight excursions. Similar campsites can be found all along the river corridor down to Victoria Basin.

After 6 miles or so, the river bottom takes on a rockier appearance as the South Branch flows deeper into Ottawa National Forest. The current also quickens, and after about 10 miles, the first rapids of any real consequence begin to crop up. This light whitewater marks the entranceway to a long series of fun class I–II rapids that roil the river off and on for the next 10 miles or so. The primary challenge in these rapids—which are collectively

A trip on the South Branch of the Ontonagon offers good opportunities for viewing wildlife.

known as Flannigan Rapids—are ubiquitous rock gardens. These can be negotiated by intermediate paddlers at normal water levels, although low water levels can create real bump-and-grind scenarios on some of the runs.

The West Branch of the Ontonagon unites with the South Branch about 4.5 miles above the entrance to the Victoria Dam backwaters. The mouth of the West Branch marks the end of Flannigan Rapids and widens the river to 100 feet or more in places. From here, the river also retains the name of the West Branch, even though it is the smaller of the two tributaries.

Light rapids appear again about a mile downstream from the junction of the two branches and continue as you make your way to the entrance of the basin. This whitewater is class I–II for the most part, but the basin is guarded by two significant rapids on the final approach. The first of these rapids is a formidable class III run located about 1 mile above the entrance to the backwaters. This treacherous piece of whitewater has the capacity to bend, fold, and (possibly) mutilate paddlers without advanced skills and appropriate equipment. It features a 5-foot drop, major backrollers, dangerous boulders, and standing waves that can easily swamp an open canoe at higher water levels. All but expert paddlers should portage this rapids, which can be seen and heard in advance.

The second major rapids is located another 0.5 mile downstream, right at the entrance to the Victoria Dam reservoir. This is a challenging class II rapids that is capable of swamping open boats during high-water periods. Portage if you are uncertain of your ability to tackle the run. Once you reach the backwaters of Victoria Dam, you face a 2-mile paddle to the landing at the dam. The take-out site is located on the left (northern) side of the basin near the dam facility.

Access: The put-in site at **Ewen** is located on M–28 on the upstream side of the bridge, on the east bank. The take-out at **Victoria Dam** is on the northern (left) shore of the reservoir. It is 5 miles southwest of Rockland on Victoria Dam Road.

Additional Help

MA & G grid: 109, C6–D6.

Camping: Overnight paddlers can set up camp along most of the river corridor, which passes through Ottawa National Forest. In addition, the U.S. Forest Service maintains two campgrounds a few miles south of the put-in at Ewen. The **Paulding Pond Campground** (four rustic sites) is located 8 miles north of Watersmeet on U.S. Highway 45, and the **Robbins Pond Campground** (three rustic sites) is 5 miles north of Watersmeet on U.S. 45, then 3 miles northwest on Forest Road 5230. Finally, a local campground with thirty sites is located at **Bond Falls Flowage** on the Middle Branch of the Ontonagon. This park is located on Bond Falls Road, 3 miles east of Paulding off U.S. 45.

Food, gas, and lodging: Watersmeet, Rockland, Ontonagon.

For more information: Ottawa National Forest.

Canoe liveries: Sylvania Outfitters.

Access Point	Float Distance To Next Access Point
Ewen landing (M–28)	25.5 miles
Victoria Dam	Take Out

Paint River

Character: An easygoing, scenic alternative to the brawling waterways that rumble through other areas of the western U.P.

Location: Central Iron County.

Length: 45 miles.

Run: 30 miles, from Gibbs City to Crystal Falls Dam.

Average run time: 12–15 hours.

Class: Flatwater, except for class III rapids at Upper and Lower Hemlock Rapids.

Skill level: Beginner (except for Upper and Lower Hemlock Rapids, which should only be attempted by advanced whitewater paddlers).

Optimal flow: May–October.

Average gradient: 4 feet per mile.

Hazards: In addition to Upper and Lower Hemlock Rapids, the river features class I–II whitewater immediately below the junction with the Net River and significant stretches of deep water.

Fishing: Healthy populations of smallmouth bass and trout attract anglers; the 19 miles between Forest Road 149 and Gibbs City is a designated Blue Ribbon Trout Stream.

Maps: USGS 1:25,000 - Gibbs City-MI, Sunset Lake-MI, Amasa-MI, Kelso Junction-MI, Crystal Falls-MI; 1:100,000 - Iron River-MI; 1:250,000 - Iron River-MI.

The paddling: The Paint River ranks as one of the Upper Peninsula's most family-friendly rivers. An important tributary of the Menominee River, the Paint ambles through remote forestland for much of its length, passing through patches of both Ottawa National Forest and Copper Country State Forest. Wide and slow, it is primarily a float-type river best known for the rich variety of wildlife that roam its banks and skyways. Still, occasional flashes of faster water prevent you from sliding too deeply into a "drifting-and-dreaming" mode, and the river does bare its teeth at Hemlock Rapids, a double-barreled blast of class III whitewater that should be portaged by all but advanced whitewater paddlers.

Paddlers visiting the Paint during high-water periods have the option of beginning their journey above Gibbs City on the stream's South Branch. Navigable for better than 18 miles before it joins with the North Branch, this flatwater stream can be accessed from Forest Highway 16. Most canoeists and kayakers, however, choose to put in at the Paint River Forks USFS campground. This campground, located just upstream of the loose cluster of homes designated on maps as Gibbs City, marks the juncture of the river's southern and northern branches. Another nearby put-in option is the bridge on County Road 657 (Gibbs City Road).

From Gibbs City to the Blockhouse USFS campground 5 miles downstream, the waterway dawdles through a pretty mix of high-banked forest and swampy alders. Averaging about 60 feet wide with countless deep holes, this stretch of the river is popular with trout anglers. During midsummer, however, you may have to drag your boat in places until

Paint River

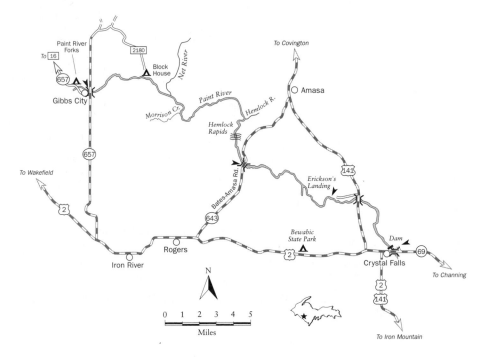

you reach the vicinity of Blockhouse. The Net River joins the Paint 1.5 miles below the Blockhouse campground.

A stretch of light whitewater greets paddlers immediately below the Paint's juncture with the Net, but after that the river slows to a crawl. As you glide across the next several miles of quiet water, the only sounds you are likely to hear are the rustle of wind through the woods and the dip of your paddle as you propel yourself forward. This peaceful stretch ends abruptly, however, at Upper and Lower Hemlock Rapids. These rapids, located about 12.5 miles below the Gibbs City Bridge, become audible before they come into view. The Upper Rapids are located just downstream from where the Hemlock River enters the mainstream from the east. This long and technically challenging stretch of whitewater requires tricky maneuvering and should only be considered by experienced whitewater paddlers, especially during high-water periods. The Lower Hemlock Rapids, located about 0.25 mile farther downstream, are equally challenging. They carry paddlers through a 2,000-foot-long gauntlet of rocks and boulders at speeds that leave no room for error. Miss one chute and you'll regret it. Given the fearsome reputation of the Upper and Lower Hemlock Rapids, most paddlers choose to sidestep them via the well-used portage trail that snakes along the left bank. If you do decide to run either of these rapids, scout carefully beforehand.

Below Lower Hemlock Rapids, the Paint resumes its placid demeanor, meandering through a corridor of lushly forested hillsides. Shoreline sites ideal for camping dot the riverbanks throughout this stretch. The bridge at Bates-Amasa Road (CR–643) lies 3.5 miles below the Lower Hemlock Rapids and is a popular put-in and take-out site.

From CR–643 to Crystal Falls, the Paint is wide and peaceful. You may scrape occasionally during low-water periods, but for the most part this 13-mile stretch takes you over slow and deep water. A popular public access site known as Erickson's Landing is located midway through this section of the river. As you approach the backwaters of Crystal Falls Dam, the river assumes pond-like characteristics. Take out on the left bank, where the town has carved out ample access and parking space.

Some folks continue paddling the Paint below the Crystal Falls Dam by resuming their journey at the M–69 Bridge. But this portage is a hassle, and much of the remaining river has been transformed into backwaters by the Little Bull Power Dam 9 miles farther downstream. Given these factors, we recommend taking out at Crystal Falls.

Access: To reach **Paint River Forks** Campground from Iron River, take U.S. 2 west for 2 miles, then follow CR–657 north for 10 miles. Another option is to put in at the **Gibbs City Bridge** on CR–657. To reach the **Block House** Campground, take CR–657 north from U.S. 2 for approximately 13 miles, then go east on FR–2180 (FR–347 on many maps) for 4 miles. The **Bates-Amasa Road Bridge** is located 5 miles north of U.S. 2 and 5 miles west of U.S. 141 on CR–643. The public access site at **Erickson's Landing** is located about 4 miles north of Crystal Falls off U.S. 141. The take-out spot for **Crystal Falls Dam** is located just north of M–69 on the east bank.

Additional Help

MA&G Grid: 98, C3 and C4; 99, C5 and D5.

Camping: Rustic camping at Paint River Forks National Forest Campground (4 sites, well and handpump) and Blockhouse National Forest Campground (2 sites, no water). Additional shoreline camping on public land. In addition, Bewabic State Park (144 modern sites) is located 5 miles west of Crystal Falls on U.S. 2.

Food, gas, and lodging: Crystal Falls, Iron River.

For more information: Ottawa National Forest.

Canoe liveries: None.

The peaceful Paint River is ideally suited for multi-day trips.

Access Point	Float Distance To Next Access Point
Paint River Forks Campground	1 mile
CR–657 (Gibbs City Road)	4 miles
Blockhouse Campground	12 miles
CR–643 (Bates-Amasa Road)	7 miles
Erickson's Landing	6 miles
Crystal Falls Dam	Take Out

![63] Pictured Rocks National Lakeshore

Character: A spectacular shoreline of rugged cliffs, remote beaches, and towering dunes that is best explored via sea kayak.

Location: Stretches along the southern shore of Lake Superior from Munising to Grand Marais.

Size: 42 miles of coastline.

Skill level: Intermediate/advanced.

Hazards: Lake Superior can become treacherous in a hurry, with strong winds, high waves, and icy water temperatures. To complicate matters, some areas of Pictured Rocks offer few landing options in case of emergency.

Maps: USGS 1:25,000 - Munising-MI, Indian Town-MI, Wood Island SE-MI, Grand Portal Point-MI, Trappers Lake-MI, Au Sable Point-MI, Grand Sable Lake-MI, Grand Marais-MI; 1:100,000 - Munising-MI, Au Sable Point-MI; 1:250,000 - Marquette-MI. NOAA charts 14963, 14969.

The paddling: Imagine dipping your paddle in clear, emerald-green water, and peering upward at the overhanging face of a 200-foot sandstone cliff. Mineral-laden water seeps from the rock, painting vertical stripes in every color of the rainbow. You cross through a shower of drips to enter a small cavern in the base of the rock, where you marvel at the play of light on the water and the smooth walls. The mechanical hum of a distant tour boat reminds you how lucky you are to be experiencing Pictured Rocks in the most intimate way possible—by sea kayak.

Pictured Rocks National Lakeshore may be the crown jewel among Michigan's many wonderful sea-kayaking destinations. The most famous part of the 42-mile protected shoreline lies at the west end of the park, where colorful sandstone cliffs tower above Lake Superior. The endless caress of wind and waves has carved the rocks into intricate formations—including arches, caves, and spires—that can best be explored by kayak. In the middle of the park is Twelvemile Beach, a remote stretch of white sand and pebbles rimmed by tall pines and white birches. Paddlers landing here will enjoy total solitude on one of the nation's great wild shores. The east end of the park is dominated by the Grand Sable Dunes, 300-foot-high mounds of shifting sand that offer intrepid climbers an outstanding panoramic view of the lake and surrounding wilderness.

Paddlers visiting Pictured Rocks should use extreme caution on Lake Superior. The water temperature of this lake is very cold, even in midsummer, and the big lake is notorious for its sudden changes in mood. Strong winds and high waves can arise with little warning, so it is important to obtain a good NOAA forecast on the radio before heading out and to remain alert for changing conditions. This advice is particularly vital when visiting the west end of the park. The namesake cliffs stretch over 15 miles and effectively limit the possible spots for emergency landings to a couple of rocky beaches. Of course, landing is less of a problem along the beaches and dunes of the eastern part of the park.

Several outfitters offer guided day trips and overnight excursions along the scenic coastline of Pictured Rocks National Lakeshore. We recommend hiring a guide if you are at all

Pictured Rocks National Lakeshore

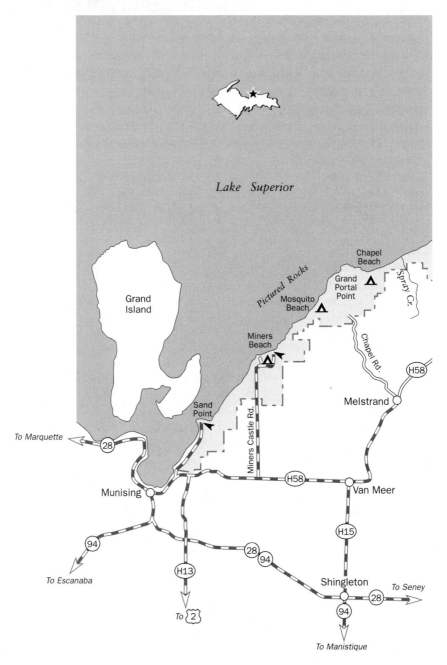

Lake Superior

Grand Island

Pictured Rocks

Chapel Beach

Grand Portal Point

Mosquito Beach

Spray Cr.

Miners Beach

Chapel Rd.

H58

Melstrand

Sand Point

Miners Castle Rd.

To Marquette

28

Munising

94

To Escanaba

H13

To 2

H58

Van Meer

H15

28 94

Shingleton

To Seney

28

94

To Manistique

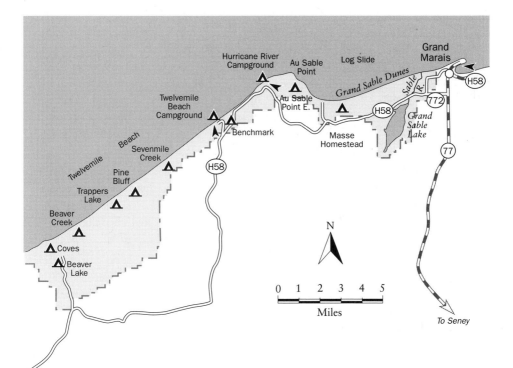

uncertain of your abilities or equipment. Although trips to view the Pictured Rocks themselves are highly weather dependent, the outfitters often use nearby Grand Island (see entry) as an alternative destination. The eastern shore of Grand Island is often calm when northwest winds make kayaking the national lakeshore too hazardous.

A 42-mile, end-to-end kayak excursion along Pictured Rocks National Lakeshore could begin at the Sand Point boat launch, near the headquarters at the west end of the park. The cliffs begin rising out of the lake a mile or so east of this put-in, and paddlers launching at Sand Point are treated to good views of Grand Island—less than a mile across Munising Bay—and its scenic lighthouse. From here to Miners Castle, the coastline is dominated by high, wooded hills with occasional outcroppings of exposed sandstone.

The 8-mile stretch of famous rocks begins at Miners Castle, a collection of oddly shaped spires jutting into Lake Superior. A 0.5 mile farther east is Miners Beach, a popular swimming location that also serves as a good launching spot for kayaks. From the parking lot, paddlers must carry their gear about 500 feet along a sandy trail, then down two flights of steep wooden stairs. From this point, it's a 15-mile round-trip paddle to see the highlights of the colorful sandstone formations.

The cliffs begin in earnest about 1 mile east of the launch site on Miners Beach. As you paddle along the sheer rock face, notice the large fragments that have "calved" from the wall above and dropped into the lake. Events of this magnitude don't happen often, but it is probably not a good idea to spend much time directly beneath the overhanging cliffs. In fact, we saw and heard bucket-sized loads of sand and pebbles tumble down from the top on several occasions.

The series of walls, ledges, and small caves continues for more than 2 miles until you reach a small beach at the mouth of the Mosquito River. This lovely area is popular with hikers and features one of the thirteen backcountry campgrounds along the coast.

Another 2 miles of paddling brings you to Grand Portal Point. Around the base of these imposing cliffs are half a dozen sea caves. A large sea arch once existed at this point, but it collapsed in the summer of 1999, providing further evidence of the ongoing battle between the rocks, wind, and waves. Just east of Grand Portal is Chapel Beach—another popular hiking and camping area that is a nice spot for lunch. The beach gets its name from Chapel Rock, a delicate, stand-alone formation connected to the cliff behind it by the ropelike root of a tall pine. Continuing east 0.5 mile from Chapel Rock, you'll come to another large sea cave—30 feet high, 30 feet wide, and 80 feet deep. It is another 1.5 miles to Spray Falls, where a small creek surges over the top of the cliff and plunges into Lake Superior.

From this point on, the rocky cliffs begin to recede inland. Paddlers interested in seeing the entire national lakeshore can continue eastward along Twelvemile Beach, an expanse of white sand and colorful pebbles against a backdrop of remote northwoods. As the name implies, it is 12 miles to Twelvemile Beach Campground, located in a birch forest on top of a high bluff. This campground is accessible by car, and it tends to be busy.

The dramatic cliffs of Pictured Rocks National Lakeshore are best appreciated from a kayak.

Paddlers interested in exploring the eastern end of Pictured Rocks may wish to begin their trip at the campground picnic area and work their way toward Grand Marais.

From Twelvemile Beach Campground, it is 3 miles to the other car-accessible campground along the shoreline, Hurricane River, which also offers access for paddlers. Look for the remains of a shipwreck just offshore from the mouth of the river. Another 1.5 miles of paddling takes you to Au Sable Point, which is topped by an 1874 lighthouse that continues to guide ships today. The reason for the light station becomes apparent just west of the point, where two more shipwrecks are visible in shallow water.

Continuing east, it is 2 miles to the Log Slide overlook, which marks the start of the Grand Sable Dunes. More than a century ago, loggers slid timber down the 300-foot bank via a wooden chute to be loaded into waiting schooners. Another 4 miles of paddling along the vast piles of sand and gravel brings you to the mouth of Sable Creek. A short walk upstream, Sable Creek tumbles through a narrow gorge and cascades over several rock terraces on its way to Lake Superior. Finally, 2 more miles of paddling brings you to Grand Marais Harbor, which has a public boat launch along its north side.

Access: The **Sand Point** boat launch, which is maintained by the park service, is located 4 miles northeast of Munising. Take H–58 east 1 mile from town, then turn north at the sign for Munising Falls and proceed 3 miles. To reach **Miners Beach**, take H–58 east 4 miles from Munising, and then go north 5 miles on H–13 (Miners Castle Road). Turn right at the sign for Miners Beach and continue 2 miles to the parking lot. **Twelvemile Beach Campground** is located 17 miles west of Grand Marais, or 33 miles east of Munising, off H–58. **Hurricane River Campground** is 12 miles west of Grand Marais off H–58. The public boat launch in **Grand Marais Harbor** is about a mile northeast of town on Grand Marais Avenue, between the city beach and the former U.S. Coast Guard station.

Additional Help

MA & G grid: 102, A3–A4; 114, D4; 115, D5, D6, C7, and C8; 116, C1.

Camping: The National Lakeshore maintains thirteen backcountry campgrounds along the coast. Permits are required for overnight stays in the backcountry. Reservations can be made in advance, by mail or fax, beginning January 15 of each year. Permits can also be acquired in person at the park visitor centers up to one day prior to the start of a trip. The cost is $15 for a party of up to six people. In addition, the Twelvemile Beach (thirty-seven sites) and Hurricane River (twenty-two sites) car campgrounds—which offer water and toilets—are accessible by kayak. Sites are allotted on a first come, first served basis for a $10 fee, and are usually full on summer weekends. There are also city campgrounds in both Munising and Grand Marais, as well as numerous small rustic campgrounds in nearby Hiawatha National Forest and Lake Superior State Forest.

Food, gas, and lodging: Munising, Grand Marais.

For more information: Pictured Rocks National Lakeshore.

Rentals/guided trips: Great Northern Adventures, Northern Waters.

A kayaker passes through the large sea arch that once traversed Grand Portal Point in Pictured Rocks National Lakeshore (the arch collapsed in 1999).

64 Presque Isle River

Character: An exciting whitewater river that runs through a gorgeous section of Michigan north-country.

Location: Gogebic and Ontonagon Counties in northwestern Upper Peninsula.

Length: 34 miles.

Run: 22 miles, from Marenisco to Steiger's Bridge.

Average run time: 15–18 hours.

Class: I–III.

Skill level: Advanced.

Optimal flow: May.

Average gradient: 13 feet per mile.

Hazards: Long sections of class I–III rapids in remote wilderness area; several unrunnable water-falls; extended class III–IV runs below Steiger's Bridge for experts only.

Fishing: Notable trout-fishing river in upper reaches and at mouth.

Maps: USGS 1:25,000 - Wakefield NE-MI, Thomaston-MI, Tiebel Creek-MI; 1:100,000 - Wakefield-MI, Ontonagon-MI; 1:250,000 - Iron River-MI.

The paddling: The Presque Isle is perhaps Michigan's best-known whitewater river. Its river corridor is a beautiful one, carved out of some of the state's wildest and most remote terrain. But it is the water itself that draws whitewater kayakers and canoeists from around the Midwest. As it rushes northward from its origins in rugged Michigan and Wisconsin forestlands to gush out into Lake Superior, the river packs extended runs of challenging whitewater together with thundering waterfalls to create an unforgettable paddling experience.

The 14-mile section of the Presque Isle from Marenisco's M–64 Bridge to the M–28 Bridge is a lovely one that will delight intermediate paddlers. It passes through lowlands of spruce, fir, aspen, and hardwoods, gathering strength from feeder streams as it moves northward. The river is fairly wide (50 to 60 feet) for much of this segment, with prevailing depths of 2 to 4 feet, but occasional logjams and fallen trees may require portages. Yondata Falls, located about 3 miles downstream from the put-in at M–64 Bridge, requires a long (0.25 mile) portage down a well-trodden trail. Bridges located above and below these falls also provide possible access. The section of the Presque Isle below Yondota Falls features a primarily slow-to-moderate current, but fun class I–II rapids do pop up from time to time to spice up the proceedings.

The river gets serious below M–28 Bridge. This change in temperament makes the bridge a popular launching point for veteran whitewater paddlers and a good take-out spot for less experienced folks. The first 2 miles downstream from the bridge are mellow and slow, but the current quickens considerably after you pass a washed-out bridge. From here down to Steiger's Bridge, strap yourself in for a ride that steadily increases in intensity and technical difficulty. Pool-and-riffle conditions prevail at first, but as you progress down the river these riffles grow into class II–III rapids, some of which culminate in foaming chutes

Presque Isle River

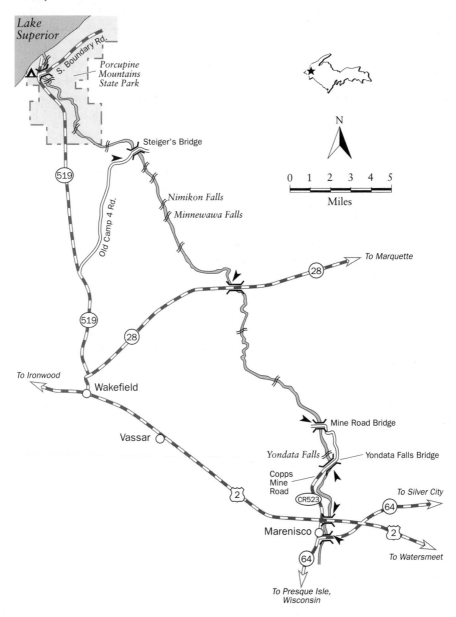

Lake Superior

S. Boundary Rd.

Porcupine Mountains State Park

Steiger's Bridge

519

Old Camp 4 Rd.

Nimikon Falls

Minnewawa Falls

N

0 1 2 3 4 5
Miles

To Marquette

28

519

28

To Ironwood

Wakefield

Vassar

Mine Road Bridge

Yondata Falls

Yondata Falls Bridge

Copps Mine Road

2

CR523

To Silver City

64

Marenisco

2

To Watersmeet

64

To Presque Isle, Wisconsin

and ledges of whitewater that drop as much as 4 feet. Formidable standing waves and back-rollers lurk at the base of many of these drops as well, poised to pounce on any mistake. Needless to say, paddlers are urged to scout these and other difficult sections of the river in advance.

Midway through the 8-mile run from M–28 to Steiger's Bridge are two waterfalls. The first of these, Minnewawa Falls, is a class III–IV run divided by a boulder-strewn island. This challenging stretch of chutes and ledges should only be run by highly skilled white-water paddlers, especially during high water levels. The second waterfall is Nimikon Falls, less than a mile downstream. Portage this falls—which features a 15-foot drop—on the right. Please exercise extreme caution on the approach to these dangerous falls.

From Nimikon Falls to Steiger's Bridge, the Presque Isle rambles along at a fast pace, furnishing long stretches of class I–III rapids along the way. This exhilarating run concludes at remote Steiger's Bridge, which is situated off an old logging road.

The Presque Isle River continues on below Steiger's Bridge, but it quickly becomes a potentially dangerous river that will challenge the abilities of even expert whitewater kayakers and canoeists. The section below Steiger's Bridge includes miles of continuous class II–IV rapids, with sustained runs that reach class V levels during springtime. The Presque Isle also passes through remote and inaccessible country in this section, including the beautiful but unforgiving Presque Isle Gorge. Finally, it roars over several big waterfalls in its final reaches before finally emptying into Lake Superior. This potent combination of hazards makes these last 10 miles of the river unsuitable for all but the most advanced whitewater paddlers.

Access: The **M–64 Bridge** and **U.S. Highway 2 Bridge** are both located in Marenisco. **Yondota Falls Bridge** lies 3 miles north of Marenisco on County Road 523 (Copps Mine Road). **Mine Road Bridge** is another mile north on the same road. The **M–28 Bridge** lies 8 miles northeast of Wakefield. To reach **Steiger's Bridge**, take CR–519 north out of Wakefield for about 4.5 miles, then travel east on Old Camp Four Grade (an unmarked dirt logging road) for approximately 6 miles.

Additional Help

MA & G grid: 96, A2–A3; 108, B2–D2.

Camping: The Presque Isle River Unit of Porcupine Mountains State Park overlooks Lake Superior and includes trails that provide great views of the Presque Isle's lower rapids and falls. It contains eighty-nine sites and shower/bathroom facilities, but no electricity. The Presque Isle campground is located at the northern end of CR–519. In addition, the state park maintains a modern ninety-nine-site campground (Union Bay Campground) at its eastern end, on M–107. Paddlers looking to camp farther upstream should check out two Ottawa National Forest campgrounds: Bobcat Lake (twelve sites) is located 3 miles south-

One of the many waterfalls in the final few miles of the wild Presque Isle River.

east of Marenisco on Forest Road 8500; Henry Lake (eleven sites) is 10 miles southwest of Marenisco on FR–8100.

Food, gas, and lodging: Marenisco, Wakefield, Bergland.

For more information: Ottawa National Forest, Porcupine Mountains Wilderness State Park.

Canoe liveries: None.

Guided trips: Arctic Divide Expeditions.

Access Point	Float Distance To Next Access Point
M–64 Bridge	1 mile
U.S. 2 Bridge	3 miles
Yondota Falls Bridge	1 mile
Mine Road Bridge	9 miles
M–28 Bridge	8 miles
Steiger's Bridge	Take Out

65 Pretty Lakes Quiet Area

Character: This remote weekend getaway destination features five small and undeveloped lakes protected by no-motor regulations.

Location: Northwestern Luce County in Lake Superior State Forest.

Skill level: Beginner.

Hazards: Deep water.

Fishing: The Pretty Lakes group is stocked with a variety of fish species, including brook and rainbow trout, largemouth bass, and walleye.

Maps: USGS 1:25,000 Muskallonge Lake SW-MI; 1:100,000 Two Hearted River-MI; 1:250,000 Sault Ste. Marie-MI.

The paddling: Pretty Lakes Quiet Area is an unassuming little paddling sanctuary that is ideal for overnight and weekend camping excursions. The five lakes that form the heart of this recreation area are small and can easily be explored during the course of a day. Connected by short portages, they offer clear, cold water and unspoiled sandy shorelines of white pine, spruce, cedar, and poplar. Regulations forbidding the use of motors on the lakes add to the sense of tranquility and solitude that prevails on these waters. Overall, these attributes may not be sufficient to attract canoeists who prefer extended wilderness expeditions. But if you are a paddler who is simply looking for a peaceful spot to paddle, fish, hike, and camp for a day or two, then this is a destination well worth checking out.

Pretty Lake is the gateway to the rest of the recreation area. Its northeast side includes a wide, sandy beach, a day-use area, and eighteen rustic and shady campsites (no water or electricity) that are accessible by car (a campground host occupies one of these sites during the summer months). These sites are very popular on summer weekends and are often utilized by vacationers using nearby off-road vehicle trails. Vacancies are more likely during the middle of the week and during the fall, when usage drops off considerably. The finest camping areas lie elsewhere, however, at three canoe-accessible campsites scattered throughout the Quiet Area. These sites—on the east side of Camp Eight Lake, the north end of Long Lake, and the northeast end of Beaver House Lake—are easily accessible via short paddles and portages. Once ensconced in one of these remote and woodsy sites, you may not see another soul for the rest of the day.

Access: The Pretty Lakes Quiet Area is located about 23 miles northwest of Newberry and 5 miles south of Dee Park. From either town, take H–37 (County Road 407) to CR–416. Turn west on CR–416 and continue for about 3 miles, go turn left on CR–439 for less than a mile.

Pretty Lakes Quiet Area

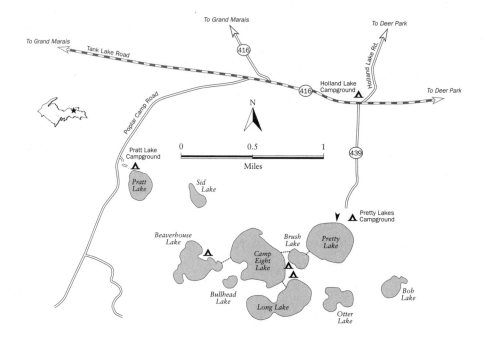

Additional Help

MA & G grid: 116, D3.

Camping: Pretty Lakes includes eighteen rustic campsites on three loops on the northern shore of Pretty Lake. Three rustic canoe campsites are also maintained in the quiet area. These can be found on Camp Eight Lake, Long Lake, and Beaverhouse Lake. Another area camping option is Holland Lake Campground (fifteen sites), located on CR–416 near its juncture with CR–439. Other state forest campgrounds in the area include High Bridge Campground (seven sites, on the Two Hearted River) and Headquarters Campground (eight sites), both of which lie directly off H–37 (CR–407) about half a dozen miles south of Deer Park. Muskallonge Lake State Park (179 modern sites) is another option, but the campground area is exceedingly claustrophic, with closely-spaced sites and little in the way of privacy. The park sits 23 miles north of Newberry on CR–407.

Food, gas, and lodging: Deer Park, Newberry.

For more information: Lake Superior State Forest.

Rentals/guided trips: None.

Portage Distances

Pretty to Brush Lake	75 feet
Brush to Camp Eight Lake	150 feet
Camp Eight to Long Lake	200 feet
Camp Eight to Beaverhouse Lake	250 feet

66 Sturgeon River

Character: An exciting whitewater run through the rugged and beautiful Sturgeon River Gorge.
Location: Baraga and Houghton Counties, near the base of the Keweenaw Peninsula.
Length: 115 miles.
Run: 27 miles, from Baraga Plains Road to Forest Highway 2270.
Average run time: 12–16 hours.
Class: I–III (class IV at Tibbets Falls).
Skill level: Advanced.
Optimal flow: April–May.
Average gradient: 27 feet per mile (much higher through Sturgeon River Gorge).
Hazards: Extremely dangerous, unrunnable waterfall (Sturgeon Falls); highly technical class IV run (Tibbets Falls); numerous unnamed class II–III rapids in a remote, inaccessible wilderness area.
Fishing: Walleye, smallmouth bass, brook and brown trout.
Maps: USGS 1:25,000 - Covington-MI, Sidnaw-MI, Prickett Lake-MI; 1:100,000 - L'Anse-MI; 1:250,000 - Iron River-MI.

The paddling: Not to be confused with the two other major rivers in the state bearing the same name, this northernmost Sturgeon provides a challenging whitewater experience for advanced paddlers through some of the most remote and scenic wilderness in Michigan. Designated a National Wild and Scenic River, it runs through the 14,000-acre Sturgeon River Gorge Wilderness Area, where it has carved a canyon out of red sandstone that is 13 miles long and up to 300 feet deep. The surrounding wilderness—reportedly home to the elusive Sidnaw North wolfpack—contains sections of old-growth red and white pine and hemlock, as well as northern hardwoods such as sugar maple and birch.

The Sturgeon is a seasonal river, with water levels normally high enough for good whitewater canoeing and kayaking only from mid-April through late May. In fact, Memorial Day often marks the end of paddling through the gorge for the year. But on occasion, heavy autumn rains will raise the water level enough for a trip during peak fall colors.

From the put-in at Baraga Plains Road, paddlers will encounter immediate fast water and some class I rapids. The river generally ranges from 50 to 80 feet wide and from 2 to 4 feet deep over sand and rocks. About a mile downstream from the put-in is the first class III run known as Right Elbow Ledgedrop, followed a few hundred yards later by Tibbets Falls. Tibbets is a highly technical class IV run with several consecutive drops of 2 to 4 feet through a jumble of large boulders. You can scout both of these runs from the North Country Trail, which runs along the right bank of the river. If you have any doubts about your ability to handle either run, use the NCT as a portage trail. Another option, often utilized by veteran Sturgeon River paddlers, is to use a logging road just north of the Baraga Plains Road Bridge as a put-in. This rough road leads to the top of a hill that overlooks Tibbets. From there, you can portage past Tibbets using the NCT.

Sturgeon River

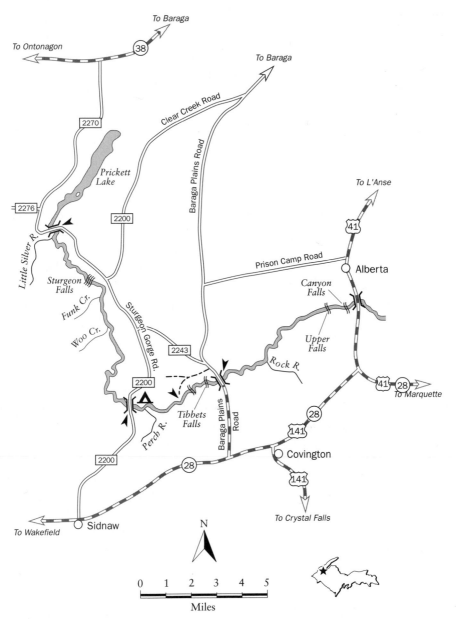

To Baraga

To Ontonagon

38

To Baraga

Clear Creek Road

Baraga Plains Road

To L'Anse

41

2270

Prickett Lake

2276

2200

Prison Camp Road

Alberta

Little Silver R.

Sturgeon Falls

Canyon Falls

Funk Cr.

Sturgeon Gorge Rd.

Upper Falls

Woo Cr.

2243

Rock R.

2200

41

28

To Marquette

Tibbets Falls

Baraga Plains Road

28

Perch R.

141

2200

Covington

28

141

Sidnaw

141

To Wakefield

To Crystal Falls

N

0 1 2 3 4 5

Miles

The Sturgeon throws its next challenge into paddlers' paths just a few hundred yards downstream from Tibbets—a triple whammy of class III drops in quick succession. Again, it is important to choose a route ahead of time and keep your boat straight. One member of our party learned the hard way that the river will reward the slightest sideways drift of your bow by unceremoniously dumping you on your head.

But paddlers who emerge from this section a little worse for wear soon get a chance to recover. For the next 4 to 5 miles, the Sturgeon offers up a mixture of flatwater, light riffles, and class I rapids. Then comes an exhilarating run of about 4 miles of continuous class II rapids, perhaps with isolated pockets of class III, depending on the water level. The bridge for Forest Highway 2200 and the Sturgeon River Campground appear about two-thirds of the way through this class II stretch. You may encounter a light sprinkling of anglers along the shore through here, especially near the campground.

The Sturgeon returns to its mild manner for the next 7 to 8 miles, with easy flatwater punctuated by occasional riffles and patches of class I rapids. We spotted a number of fine campsites along this stretch. You then begin to enter the gorge. At this point, bluffs begin to appear along the shoreline, pushing the mixed pine and hardwood forests higher above the river. But the gorge does not begin in earnest until after Sturgeon Falls. This spectacular 30-foot waterfall is the heart of the Sturgeon River Gorge Wilderness, and it should be treated with respect and caution. Guarded on its upstream side by challenging rapids that can wreak havoc with unwary canoeists and kayakers, this powerful, unrunnable cataract has claimed the lives of a number of paddlers over the years.

The appearance of class II rapids at the end of the aforementioned calm stretch marks the approach to Sturgeon Falls. The rapids churn for about 200 yards before subsiding into a brief stretch of flatwater. At this point, the river makes a 90-degree bend to the left. **Take out on the right at this bend,** which can also be identified by the presence of a small creek that runs into the Sturgeon on river right. From this bend, the portage to the base of the falls is a 0.25-mile hike through woods and over a rocky hill. As you lug your boat and gear along here, you may encounter a day-hiker or two (0.75 mile hiking trail located off Forest Highway 2270 provides hikers with easy access to Sturgeon Falls).

Directly downstream from this take-out site is a 0.25 mile stretch of class II rapids that sits directly above Sturgeon Falls. At higher water levels, these rapids reach class III levels or higher, with standing waves that can easily swamp an open canoe. Some expert paddlers run these rapids at lower water levels and begin their portage just above Sturgeon Falls proper, but all other canoeists and kayakers should take out at the aforementioned 90-degree bend. After all, a mistake in these rapids can have grave consequences due to the fast current and the proximity of the falls.

These class II–III rapids subside briefly before culminating in a 2-foot ledge drop that spans the width of the river (about 100 feet at this point) just above the waterfall. As the river flows over this ledge, it recirculates left and kicks out directly over the falls. If you get caught in the Sturgeon's grip at this point, only a very swift rescue will prevent you from going over. At the top of the falls, the river funnels into a narrow rock channel, bashing back and forth between the walls to create a washing-machine effect. It then bursts out the other side and pounds onto the rocks below. We cannot emphasize enough how important it is for paddlers to exercise caution on the approach to these beautiful but deadly falls.

The excitement continues immediately below Sturgeon Falls with a 0.5-mile stretch of class II–III rapids. When you pull out of the eddy below the falls, stay to the left of the island. As you maneuver through a flurry of class II stuff, look for a tall, sandstone cliff on the left. This landmark signals the approach to a class III ledge drop, located just around the corner as the river bends to the left. The best spot to hit the 4-foot drop is about 20 feet left of the big rock on the right bank. If all goes well, you should come over the lip and then plow straight into a 3-foot standing wave. It is possible to scout the ledge drop from the top of the gorge by continuing along the right bank from the portage trail around the falls.

From here, paddlers will encounter another 3.5 miles of class II and III rapids as the Sturgeon threads its way through the high, sandstone cliffs and forested hillsides of the gorge. Then the river slows and deepens as it winds gently through lowland woods. The last couple of miles above the bridge at Forest Highway 2270 is flatwater. The take-out is on the left bank.

Overall, paddling through the Sturgeon River Gorge is an experience that will thrill advanced whitewater paddlers. As if the many challenging class II and III runs weren't enough, the red sandstone walls, intense green forest, and tumbling, molasses-colored water provide a feast for the senses. But Sturgeon contains some serious hazards, and its location in the middle of a remote wilderness area means that outside help is not readily available. Exercise caution throughout, and line or portage any rapids that look too dicey for you or your paddling partners.

Access: To reach the **Baraga Plains Road** access site, take M–28 West to Covington, where it splits off from U.S. Highway 141 South. Continue on M–28 for 2.5 miles past the split, then turn right (north) on Baraga Plains Road and follow it 4 miles to the bridge. The logging road that leads to Tibbets Falls is located 1 mile northwest of the Baraga Plains Road bridge. To reach the **Sturgeon Gorge Road** access site, continue driving west on M–28 about 6 miles past Baraga Plains Road. Turn right (north) on Forest Highway 2200, just before you reach the town of Sidnaw. Follow FH–2200 northeast about 6 miles to the bridge at the Sturgeon Falls Campground. To reach the **Forest Highway 2270** access site, continue driving northeast on FH–2200 past the campground about 6 miles to FH–2270. Turn left (northwest) and follow 2270 about 4 miles to the bridge. Alternately, take M–38 west from Baraga about 10 miles and turn left (south) on Prickett Dam Road. Follow Prickett Dam Road 2.5 miles and turn right (west) on FH–2270. Proceed about 7 miles southwest to the bridge.

Class IV Tibbetts Falls on the Sturgeon River.

Additional Help

MA & G grid: 110, C3 and D4.

Camping: Backcountry camping is allowed along the river in Ottawa National Forest. Ottawa also maintains the Sturgeon River Campground (9 rustic sites), about 6 miles northeast of Sidnaw on FH–2200. Also nearby is Big Lake Campground (15 rustic sites) in the Copper Country State Forest, about 9 miles northwest of Covington off of Baraga Plains Road.

Food, gas, and lodging: L'Anse, Baraga.

For more information: Ottawa National Forest, Kenton Ranger District.

Canoe liveries: None.

Guided trips: Arctic Divide Expeditions.

Access Point	Float Distance To Next Access Point
Baraga Plains Road	8 miles
Sturgeon Gorge Road (FH–2200)	19 miles
Forest Highway 2270	Take Out

Sylvania Wilderness Area

Character: Michigan's pocket-sized version of Minnesota's famed Boundary Waters is a wonderful mecca for wilderness campers, canoeists, and anglers.

Location: Gogebic County in the western Upper Peninsula along the Michigan-Wisconsin border.

Size: Thirty-four lakes totaling more than 4,000 acres scattered across 18,327 acres in the Ottawa National Forest.

Skill level: Beginner/intermediate.

Hazards: General wilderness conditions. Visitors looking to explore Sylvania's outlying lakes and ponds should possess good orienteering skills.

Fishing: Lake trout, smallmouth and largemouth bass, walleye, and northern pike can be found in the Sylvania Wilderness Area, but many special angling regulations apply. For example, possession limits are enforced on most species (largemouth and smallmouth bass are strictly catch-and-release), and size limits are high. In addition, anglers are required to use barbless hooks, unscented bait, and artificial lures at all times. Contact Sylvania for complete fishing rules and regulations.

Maps: USGS 1:25,000 - Black Oak Lake-MI, Land of Lakes-MI; 1:100,000 - Wakefield-MI; 1:250,000 - Iron River-MI.

The paddling: Michigan's Sylvania Wilderness is a place where the mournful cries of loons and wolves still echo across crystal-clear lakes and green seas of ancient pine, hemlock, and hardwoods. A wild and unspoiled region, Sylvania is home to a grand array of wildlife, from the bald eagles that carve patterns in its skies to the black bears that lumber through its old-growth forests. This untamed character, combined with a management plan that places a premium on solitude and natural beauty, makes the Sylvania Wilderness a true paradise for wilderness canoeists.

The Sylvania area has been prized as an outdoor recreation destination since the late nineteenth century, when a Wisconsin lumberman named A. D. Johnson purchased 80 acres on the south end of Clark Lake. Visiting friends were so dazzled by the area's beauty and hunting and fishing possibilities that they bought large parcels of adjacent land and formed the Sylvania Club. Members of this private club roamed the region for years, hunting and fishing and erecting a number of lodges and boathouses. They also built several roads that now serve as the backbone of the area's hiking and ski trail system. Eventually, however, the land was put up for sale. Ownership of Sylvania changed several times until 1967, when it became the first purchase of the U.S. Forest Service's Land and Water Conservation Fund Act. The Forest Service promptly removed the lodges and boathouses and introduced measures designed to protect the area's natural charms.

Today, the Sylvania Wilderness includes thirty-four named lakes nestled in old-growth forests of red pine, white pine, and hemlock, some of which are 400 to 500 years old. Twenty-five miles of portage trails connect many of these lakes. The lengths of these portages vary considerably; the longest is about 0.75 mile in length. Paddling and hiking are the sole means of getting around in Sylvania, since motorized and mechanized equip-

Sylvania Wilderness Area

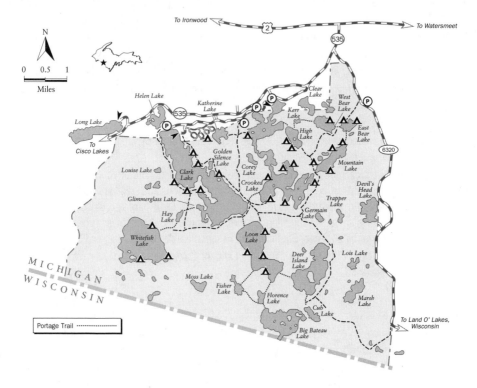

ment is prohibited within its borders. The only exception to this rule is on Crooked Lake, where electric boat motors with a maximum thrust of 48 pounds (four-horsepower equivalent) are permitted. These restrictions do much to preserve the area's tranquil and wild character.

Of the lakes within the Sylvania Wilderness, Clark and Crooked Lakes receive the most paddling traffic. These lakes hold the wilderness area's two main launch sites, the lone developed campground facility (on the northern end of Clark Lake), and a dozen of the area's fifty campsites. They also serve as the gateway to Loon Lake, Whitefish Lake, and other waters located deep in the heart of Sylvania's wilderness. But even if you spend most of your time on Clark or Crooked Lake, encounters with fellow paddlers are infrequent. And if you decide to spend your day paddling the remote waters of Deer Island Lake, Big Bateau Lake, or the Bear Lakes, the only human voices you're likely to hear are the ones in your own party. This variety of exploration options is one reason why many paddlers who visit Sylvania linger for a week or more.

All visitors are required to register for campsite permits from May 15 to September 30 annually. Many permits can be secured in advance by using Sylvania's reservation system, which operates from January 15 to May 15. Approximately one-fourth of all sites are held for walk-in campers, however, and after May 15, unreserved campsites are available on a first come, first served basis.

A number of special regulations are enforced within Sylvania's boundaries to ensure that its beauty is preserved for future generations. Various fishing restrictions ensure the continued viability of the many game fish species that prowl Sylvania's lakes and ponds; contact Ottawa National Forest for detailed regulations. Other notable regulations include a ban on cans, bottles, and Styrofoam products in wilderness areas, leash rules for dogs (except during sanctioned state hunting seasons), limitations on island landings (prohibited until July 15 in order to protect nesting loons), and limitations on group size (no more than ten people in a travel party, no more than five people per campsite). A complete list of Sylvania Wilderness rules and regulations is available from the Ottawa National Forest offices.

Access: Sylvania Wilderness Area is located on County Road 535, 3 miles west of Watersmeet off U.S. Highway 2. The launch sites at Clark Lake and Crooked Lake are both accessible from CR–535.

Additional Help

MA & G grid: 97, B6 and C6.

Camping: Fifty backcountry campsites are maintained in the Sylvania Wilderness, but most are nicely spaced to ensure solitude and privacy. Each site includes a fire ring and a wilderness latrine (watch out for slugs!). In addition, a 48-site drive-in facility is maintained at the northeastern side of Clark Lake.

Food, gas, and lodging: Watersmeet, Land O' Lakes (Wisconsin).

For more information: Ottawa National Forest.

Canoe liveries: Sylvania Outfitters, Hawk's Nest Turtle-Flambeau Canoe Outfitters.

Portage Distances

Crooked to High Lake	350 feet
Crooked to Corey Lake	545 feet
Crooked to Clark Lake	1,790 feet
Crooked to Mountain Lake	210 feet
Mountain to East Bear Lake	1,540 feet
West Bear to Kerr Lake	1,550 feet

West Bear to East Bear Lake	640 feet
High to Kerr Lake	610 feet
Clark to Loon Lake	1,580 feet
Glimmerglass to Hay Lake	2,015 feet
Whitefish to Hay Lake	2,530 feet
Whitefish to Whitefish Parking	3,875 feet
Loon to Fisher Lake	2,240 feet
Loon to Florence Lake	1,250 feet
Loon to Deer Island Lake	1,475 feet
Deer Island to Cub Lake	1,265 feet
Cub to Big Bateau Lake	110 feet
Florence to Fisher Lake	2,130 feet
Florence to Big Bateau Lake	540 feet

Fishermen enjoying a misty morning in the remote Sylvania Wilderness Area.

68 Tahquamenon River

Character: A big, slow river offering pleasant day trips and multi-day paddles through remote wilderness.

Location: Luce and Chippewa Counties in the east-central Upper Peninsula.

Length: 95 miles.

Run: Approximately 65 miles, from Dollarville Dam east of Newberry to Whitefish Bay on Lake Superior.

Average run time: 4–6 days.

Class: I.

Skill level: Beginner/intermediate.

Optimal flow: June–September.

Average gradient: 2 feet per mile.

Hazards: Deep water, motorboat traffic, portages around Upper and Lower Tahquamenon Falls.

Fishing: Good fishing for pike, muskellunge, walleye, perch, and smallmouth bass.

Maps: USGS 1:25,000 - McMillan-MI, Newberry-MI, Roberts Corner-MI, Soo Junction-MI, Gimlet Creek-MI, Betsy Lake South-MI, Timberlost-MI, Emerson-MI; 1:100,000 - Manistique Lake-MI, Two Hearted River-MI; 1:250,000 - Sault Ste. Marie-MI.

The paddling: The legendary Tahquamenon—which is mentioned in Longfellow's famous poem "Song of Hiawatha"—flows wide and deep through nearly 100 miles of the east-central Upper Peninsula. But most tourists tend to be familiar with only the short stretch that tumbles over two popular waterfalls in Tahquamenon Falls State Park. At 200 feet across and nearly 50 feet high, Upper Tahquamenon Falls is the second-largest waterfall east of the Mississippi, after Niagara Falls. Four miles downstream, the river divides into two channels around an island and cascades another 23 feet over Lower Tahquamenon Falls.

But while the waterfalls attract the crowds, the remainder of the river offers paddlers several options for afternoon jaunts or multi-day trips through remote wilderness. The Tahquamenon originates from spring-fed lakes northwest of McMillan in Luce County. It acquires its deep red color from the tannin of hemlock swamps in its upper drainage area. The river gradually increases in size as it intersects with smaller streams on its way to Whitefish Bay in Lake Superior. With the exception of the areas near the waterfalls, the Tahquamenon has a mild current that makes it suitable for beginning paddlers.

A day-trip option on the Upper Tahquamenon begins at the Dollarville Dam, just west of Newberry. At this point the river is 40 to 50 feet wide and moves fairly quickly, with occasional tight bends. Over the next 3 miles, paddlers will pass through a marshy area known as Spider Bay and cross under M–123. About 6 miles later, the Sixteen Creek State Forest Campground appears on the left bank. The river slows and widens over the next 2 miles before reaching McPhee's Landing, at the end of County Road 462. Day-trippers will want to take out here, as it is the last developed access site for over 30 miles, until the river enters the state park.

Mighty Upper Tahquamenon Falls are the best-known feature of the Tahquamenon River.

Tahquamenon River

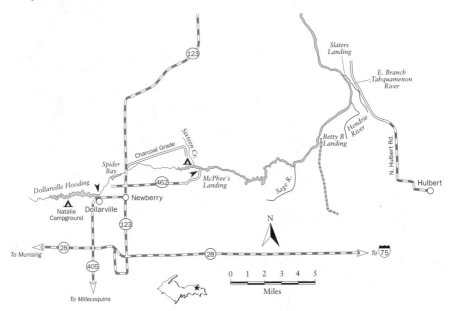

Beyond McPhee's Landing, the Tahquamenon meanders through low, swampy marshlands another 9 miles to its intersection with the Sage River. Although the shoreline is mostly public land, there are few high-and-dry campsites available along this stretch. About 4 miles downstream from the intersection with the Sage is Betty B Landing, where the Toonerville Trolley narrow-gauge railroad drops off passengers for a riverboat trip to the Upper Falls. From this point on, the river channel straightens and the banks become steeper. Camping options remain limited in this middle section of the river because of private property, but intrepid anglers nonetheless seek this water out because of the big walleye and muskie that roam through here.

By the time the Tahquamenon intersects with the Hendrie River 4 miles downstream from Betty B Landing, it has increased in size to 100 feet wide. The river is also very deep where the Tahquamenon intersects with the Sage, Hendrie, and East Branch, as well as in the vicinity of Joy Island. Paddlers are likely to see anglers in motorboats between here and the Upper Falls. It is another 2 miles to the intersection with the East Branch Tahquamenon River and Slater's Landing, the launching point for the Tom Sawyer Riverboat tour. Over the next 15 miles, paddlers will pass Baird Creek, Popps Creek, and Linton Creek before entering Tahquamenon Falls State Park.

At nearly 40,000 acres—or about 60 square miles—Tahquamenon Falls is the second-largest of Michigan's state parks. The area away from the falls is mostly undeveloped woodlands and peat bogs. The park contains one of the state's largest stands of virgin hardwoods,

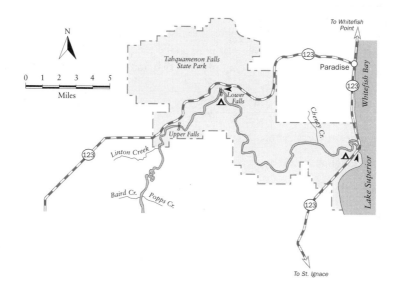

as well as a variety of wildlife that includes moose, black bears, coyotes, occasional wolves, otters, deer, foxes, porcupines, beavers, minks, eagles, and sandhill cranes. Other than hiking the park's 25 miles of maintained trails, one of the best ways to experience the remote areas and view the wildlife is by paddling quietly past in a canoe.

Shortly after entering the state park, paddlers will see signs warning them to take out and portage around the Upper Falls. The joy of portaging occurs again 4 miles downstream at the Lower Falls. There is access at the state park campgrounds below the Lower Falls. This is the starting point for another pleasant day trip on the Tahquamenon. Beginning below the Lower Falls, the river ranges from 100 to 150 feet wide and flows slow and deep between high banks. The terrain gradually changes to low, wooded banks and finally to sandy marshland as the Tahquamenon meanders 15 miles through remote wilderness to its mouth at Whitefish Bay. The take-out is at the state park boat launch, a short distance below the Rivermouth Campground.

Access: To reach the **Dollarville Dam** access site, take CR–405 west 2 miles from Newberry, and follow the signs to the dam on the north side of Dollarville. To reach **McPhee's Landing**, take M–123 north 0.5 mile from Newberry, turn east on CR–462, and proceed about 5 miles to the river. The **Lower Falls** access in Tahquamenon Falls State Park is located 10 miles east of Paradise on M–123. The State Park's **Rivermouth access** is located 5 miles south of Paradise on M–123.

Additional Help

MA & G grid: 104, B3–B4; 105, B5, B6, and A6; 117, D6–D8.

Camping: Limited camping is available along the river on public land. In addition, Lake Superior State Forest maintains two campgrounds on the Tahquamenon: Natalie State Forest Campground, on Dollarville Flooding off CR–434; and Sixteen Creek State Forest Campground, 5 miles northeast of Newberry off Charcoal Grade. Tahquamenon Falls State Park offers four developed campgrounds, two modern campgrounds totaling 177 sites near the Upper Falls, and a seventy-six-site modern campground and fifty-five-site rustic campground at the Rivermouth Unit.

Food, gas, and lodging: Newberry, Paradise.

For more information: Tahquamenon Falls State Park.

Canoe liveries: Mark's Rod and Reel.

Access Point	Float Distance To Next Access Point
Dollarville Dam	11 miles
McPhee's Landing (CR–462)	34 miles
Lower Tahquamenon Falls	20 miles
Rivermouth Boat Launch	Take Out

69 Two Hearted River

Character: Forever linked to favorite son Ernest Hemingway, this scenic river provides some of the best paddling in the eastern Upper Peninsula.

Location: Northern Luce County.

Length: 35 miles.

Run: 22 miles.

Average run time: 10–12 hours.

Class: I (except during high-water periods).

Skill level: Intermediate (beginner below Reed and Green Bridge).

Optimal flow: June–October.

Average gradient: 4 feet per mile.

Hazards: Fallen trees, logjams, submerged logs, especially above Reed and Green Bridge.

Fishing: Menominee whitefish, brook trout, and steelhead (especially in the river's lower reaches during spring and fall).

Maps: USGS 1:25,000 - Muskallonge Lake SE-MI, Muskallonge Lake East-MI, Betsy Lake NW-MI; 1:100,000 - Two Hearted River-MI; 1:250,000 - Sault Ste. Marie-MI.

The paddling: The Two Hearted River is one of Michigan's legendary streams. Its stature is due in no small measure to Ernest Hemingway, who immortalized the river when he appropriated its evocative name for a short story ("The Big Two Hearted River") based on his fishing experiences on the nearby Fox River. But the Two Hearted River's continued popularity as a destination for anglers and paddlers alike is due more to its wild and remote surroundings and trout-filled waters than to any story. With this stream, reality matches the northwoods imagery conjured up by its name.

The Two Hearted River is the only stream in Michigan that has been designated a Wilderness River. It flows through state forest for much of its length, winding past woodlands of northern hemlock, aspen, birch, and pine before emptying into Lake Superior. In addition to its mainstream, the Two Hearted includes five major tributaries (Dawson Creek and the north, south, east, and west branches) that offer prime trout fishing opportunities. The allure of these waters leads many paddlers who also fish to put in at High Bridge, which is the practical upstream limit for decent paddling. From High Bridge to Reed and Green Bridge you can count on 10 miles or so of quiet and solitude, though a dozen or so portages over logjams and fallen trees may prompt you to punctuate the silence with a muttered curse or two. In fact, this narrow (25 to 40 feet) and obstacle-strewn segment of the waterway is really not suitable for inexperienced paddlers. Seasoned wilderness canoeists, though, should have no difficulty handling this upper section, which is pool-and-riffle with a generally modest current. The prime camping spot through here is the Two Hearted River Canoe Campground, about 6 miles downstream from High Bridge. This campground is technically closed and is no longer maintained, but the area remains available to overnight visitors.

Two Hearted River

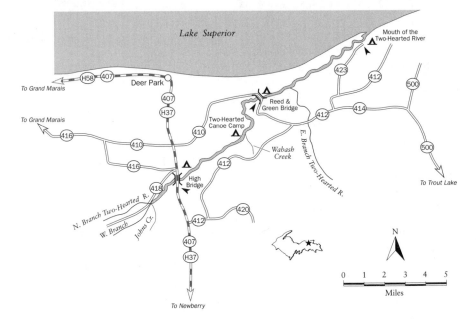

Day trips on the Two Hearted River begin at Reed and Green Bridge, which also includes a small but attractive rustic campground. The 12-mile stretch from the bridge to the rivermouth is a four- to five-hour paddle through a beautiful valley that alternates between grassy lowlands bursting with ferns and wildflowers and towering, sandy bluffs topped with forest. The river remains moderately narrow (40 to 60 feet) in this lower section, which continues to include tight bends and submerged logs. But the big logjams and fallen trees that dot the river's upper reaches are largely absent, making this stretch far more suitable for family outings. Numerous sandy landing sites, meanwhile, provide potential camping and picnicking spots. As with the entire river, the water through here is clear with a reddish tint, offering good views of its river bottom of mixed gravel and sand. Water depth is mostly shallow (1 to 4 feet) with occasional deeper holes.

Paddling trips on the Two Hearted conclude at the rivermouth. Facilities here include a large and well-maintained rustic state forest campground and a pedestrian suspension bridge that provides access to an attractive cobble beach backed by sandy dunes. This campground is a popular one and attracts visitors not only during the summer, but also during the spring and fall steelhead runs.

All in all, the Two Hearted River offers good paddling opportunities for a variety of experience levels, from veteran wilderness-trippers to beginners. But no matter what your paddling capabilities are, you should keep two things in mind before planning any trip on this stream. First, passage down the river can be quite perilous during the spring, when snowmelt and seasonal rains can raise water levels by 5 feet or more. Second, blackfly numbers often reach epic proportions during early and midsummer, so either arm yourself with the appropriate defenses or plan for August or later.

Access: High Bridge is located on County Road 407, 24 miles northwest of Newberry and 5 miles south of Deer Park. **Reed and Green Bridge** is on CR–410. It can be reached from Deer Park by taking CR–407 south for 3 miles, then taking CR–410 east for about 6 miles. To reach the bridge from Newberry, take CR–407 north for 25 miles, then follow CR–410 east for 6 miles. The **Mouth of the Two Hearted River Campground** is located at the northern terminus of CR–423. To reach it, take CR–407 to CR–412. Follow CR–412 for approximately 14 miles to CR–423; the campground lies 3 miles north on the southern shore of Lake Superior.

Additional Help

MA & G grid: 116, C4; 117, C5.

Camping: Options range from primitive shoreline camping along the river to the four state forest campgrounds located on the banks of the Two Hearted River. High Bridge Campground (7 rustic sites), Reed and Green Bridge Campground (4 rustic sites), and Mouth of Two Hearted River Campground (45 rustic sites) all offer pleasant and scenic camping accessible by car. The old Two Hearted River Canoe Campground is accessible only by canoe or kayak.

Food, gas, and lodging: Newberry, Deer Park.

For more information: Lake Superior State Forest.

Canoe liveries: Two Hearted Canoe Trips, Mark's Rod & Reel.

Access Point	Float Distance To Next Access Point
High Bridge	10 miles
Reed and Green Bridge	12 miles
Mouth of the Two Hearted River	Take Out

The scenic Two Hearted River was immortalized by Ernest Hemingway.

70 Whitefish River

Character: This attractive river mixes light rapids and slow water as it winds through unspoiled countryside teeming with wildlife.

Location: Southern Delta County.

Length: 50 miles.

Run: 16 miles.

Average run time: 4–6 hours.

Class: Flatwater/class I.

Skill level: Intermediate.

Optimal flow: April–June.

Average gradient: 7 feet per mile.

Hazards: Boulders and stone shelfs in upper reaches; deeper holes in lower sections.

Fishing: Rainbow and brook trout, smallmouth bass.

Maps: USGS 1:25,000 - Baker Creek-MI, Poplar Lake-MI, Rapid River-MI; 1:100,000 - Manistique-MI, Munising-MI; 1:250,000 - Escanaba-MI, Marquette-MI.

The paddling: The Whitefish River is a great destination for springtime canoeists looking to shake the rust off after a long winter of paddling inactivity, for it features both a nice variety of water and the sort of scenery (a pretty mix of marshland and low-lying cedar, pine, and hardwood forest) that is guaranteed to bring smiles of satisfaction. The Whitefish's upper reaches are characterized by quick water that produces significant riffles and standing waves as it races over the rocks and stone shelves that predominate throughout the river, while its downstream sections mellow into an extended float that will give you plenty of time to practice your J-stroke and watch resident bald eagles wheel and soar overhead. The presence of numerous good camping spots along the low-lying shoreline further add to the river's allure. But perhaps the best reason to explore the Whitefish's cool waters and handsome shoreline during the spring is that the stream punishes summertime paddlers with clouds of insects and low water volume that makes canoeing all but impossible. So check out the Whitefish in late April or May (June at the latest), before the river's mood turns sour.

The Whitefish River is a designated Wild and Scenic River. Both the mainstream and its tributaries wander through long stretches of Hiawatha National Forest before eventually uniting and emptying into northern Lake Michigan's Little Bay de Noc. National Forest literature cites both East and West Branches of the Whitefish as canoeable—and a handful of whitewater enthusiasts reportedly run sections of both branches during the height of spring runoff—but both of these streams are narrow and choked with fallen trees and other obstructions at various points. These factors, coupled with beaver activity, can make for pretty frustrating conditions. You should instead put in on the East Branch at Forest Road 2236, about 3 miles upstream from its confluence with the West Branch. From FR–2236 to the junction of the two branches, you can expect a quick pool-and-

Whitefish River

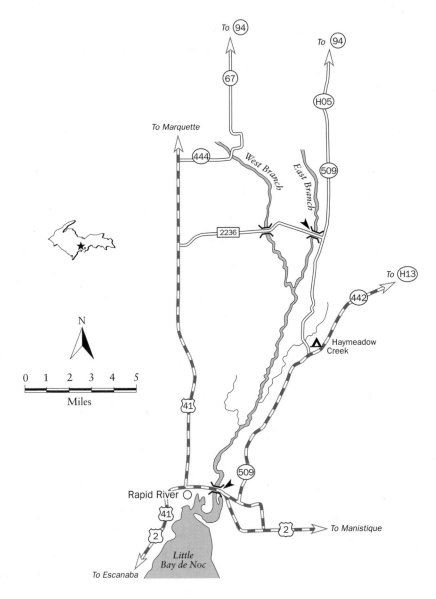

The mellow Whitefish meanders through Hiawatha National Forest.

riffle river of moderate width (30 to 50 feet). Light rapids capable of producing standing waves pop up on a regular basis throughout the first 5 miles or so below FR–2236, then gradually taper off in frequency and intensity. This is the most enjoyable section of the Whitefish, but even in May you will likely run into occasional bump-and-scrape conditions as you progress down the rocky riverbed.

Water depth increases noticeably as the Big West Branch and Little West Branch join the mainstream. As you continue downstream, occasional shoreline cottages and other indications of private landholdings increase and wilderness camping options undergo a corresponding decrease. The river corridor remains woodsy and attractive, however, and continues to hold large populations of eagle, great blue heron, and a wide range of other waterfowl. During the last 3 to 4 miles of the Whitefish River Canoe Trail (as it is known in USFS circles), the river widens, the current diminishes, and an estuary-like setting of deep pools and open marshlands prevails. Stiff southerly winds in this latter segment will prod canoeists into periods of sustained paddling, but otherwise these last miles offer a pleasant float. You can take out at the U.S. Highway 2 Bridge on the left.

Access: To reach the launch at the **Forest Road 2236 Bridge**, take County Road 509 north from U.S. 2 for 16 miles, then turn west on FR–2236 for about 0.5 mile. The take-out at the **U.S. 2 Bridge** is located approximately 1 mile east of Rapid River.

Additional Help

MA & G grid: 90, A1; 102, D1.

Camping: Camping is permitted along the shoreline on National Forest land. An established rustic campground is also maintained on a tributary of the Whitefish known as Haymeadow Creek. This Hiawatha National Forest campground—called Haymeadow Creek—includes 9 large campsites. It is located approximately 11 miles from Rapid River. Take U.S. 2 east from the town for 1.6 miles, then turn left on CR–509 and go north 9.4 miles to the entrance.

Food, gas, and lodging: Rapid River.

For more information: Hiawatha National Forest.

Canoe liveries: None.

Access Point	Float Distance To Next Access Point
FR–2236	16 miles
U.S. 2 Bridge	Take Out

Appendix of Contact Information

Lower Peninsula

Government Agencies (National Forests, State Forests, State Parks)

Au Sable State Forest, Box 939, Mio, MI 48647, (517) 826–3211.

Flat River State Game Area, 6640 Long Lake Road, Belding, MI 48809, (616) 794–2658.

Harrisville State Park, P. O. Box 326, Harrisville, MI 48740, (517) 724–5126.

Huron-Clinton Metroparks, 13000 High Ridge Drive, P. O. Box 2001, Brighton, MI 48116-8001, (800) 47–PARKS.

Huron-Manistee National Forest, 1755 South Mitchell Street, Cadillac, MI 49601, (800) 821–6263 or (231) 775–2421; Baldwin/White Cloud Ranger District, 650 North Michigan Avenue, Baldwin, MI 49304, (231) 745–4631; Manistee Ranger Station, 412 Red Apple Road, Manistee, MI 49660, (231) 723–2211; Mio Ranger District, 401 Court Street, Mio, MI 48647, (517) 826–3252; Huron Shores Ranger Station, 5761 North Skeel Road, Oscoda, MI 48750, (517) 739–0728.

Ludington State Park, P. O. Box 709, Ludington, MI 49431, (616) 843–8671.

Mackinaw State Forest, P. O. Box 667, Gaylord, MI 49735, (517) 732–3541.

Pere Marquette State Forest, 8015 Mackinaw Trail, Cadillac, MI 49601, (231) 775–9727.

Pigeon River Country State Forest, 9966 Twin Lakes Road, Vanderbilt, MI 49795, (517) 983–4101.

Pinckney Recreation Area, 8555 Silver Hill Road, Pinckney, MI 48169, (734) 426–4913.

Port Crescent State Park, 1775 Port Austin Road, Port Austin, MI 48467, (517) 738–8663.

Rifle River Recreation Area, P. O. Box 98, Lupton, MI 48635, (517) 473–2258.

St. Clair Flats Wildlife Area, 1803 Krispin Road, Harsens Island, MI 48028, (810) 748–9504.

Sleeping Bear Dunes National Lakeshore, 9922 Front Street, Empire, MI 49630, (231) 326–5134.

Wilderness State Park, P. O. Box 380, Carp Lake, MI 49718, (231) 436–5381.

Canoe Liveries

A.A.A. Rogue River Canoe Rental, 12 East Bridge Street, Rockford, MI 49341, (616) 866–9264. Rogue River.

Alcona Canoe Rental, 6351 Bamfield Road, Glennie, MI 48737, (517) 735–2973 or (800) 526–7080. Au Sable River.

Alvina's Canoes, 6470 Betsie River Road, Interlochen, MI 49643, (231) 276–9514. Betsie River.

Argo Park, Ann Arbor, MI 48105 (734) 668–7411. Huron River.

Baldwin Canoe Rental, P. O. Box 269, Baldwin, MI 49304, (231) 745–4669 or (800) 272–3642. Pere Marquette River, Pine River.

Big Bear Adventures, 4271 South Straits Highway, Indian River, MI 49749, (616) 238–8181. Sturgeon River (Lower Peninsula).

Borchers Ausable Canoe Livery, 101 Maple Street, Grayling, MI 49738, (517) 348–4921 or (800) 762–8756. Au Sable River and South Branch.

Bosman's Canoe Rental, 131 Henderson Court, Cadillac, MI 49601, (231) 862–3601 or (877) 6–CANOES. Pine River.

Buckley's Mountainside Canoes, 4700 West Remus Road, Mount Pleasant, MI 48858, (517) 772–5437 or (877) 776–2800. Chippewa River.

Carlisle Canoes, 110 State Street, Grayling, MI 49738, (517) 348–2301. Au Sable River.

Chippewa Landing, (616) 824–3627. Manistee River.

Chippewa River Outfitters, 3763 Lincoln Road, Mount Pleasant, MI 48858, (517) 772–5474. Chippewa River.

Curler Canoe Rental, Fenwick, MI (517) 248–3466. Flat River.

Doe-Wah-Jack's Canoe Rental, P. O. Box 9063, Benton Harbor, MI 49023, (616) 782–7410 or (888) 782–7410. Dowagiac River.

Double R Ranch Campground, 4424 Whites Bridge Road, Smyrna, MI 48887, (616) 794–0520. Flat River.

Duggan's Canoe Livery and Campground, P. O. Box 29, Harrison, MI 48625, (517) 539–7149. Muskegon River.

Famous Jarolim Canoe Rental, 10647 South M–37, Wellston, MI 49689, (231) 862–3475. Pine River.

Gallup Park, Ann Arbor, MI 48105, (734) 662–9319. Huron River.

Gotts Landing, P. O. Box 441, Mio, MI 48647, (517) 826–3411 or (888) 226–8748. Au Sable River and South Branch.

Grand Rogue Campgrounds, 6400 West River Drive, Belmont, MI 49306, (616) 361–1053. Rogue River.

Great Lakes Docks and Decks, 7427 Dyke Road (M–29), Algonac, MI 48001, (810) 725–0009. Harsen's Island, St. John's Marsh.

Happy Mohawk Canoe Livery, 735 Fruitvale Road, Montague, MI 49437, (616) 894–4209. White River.

Heavner Canoe Rental, 2775 Garden Road, Milford, MI 48381, (248) 685–2379. Huron River.

Hell Creek Ranch, 10866 Cedar Lake Road, Pinckney, MI 48169, (734) 878–3632. Pinckney Recreation Area.

Hiawatha Canoe Livery, 1113 Lake Street, Roscommon, MI 48653, (517) 275–5213 or (800) 736–5213. Au Sable River and South Branch.

Hinchman Acres Canoe Rental, P. O. Box 220, Mio, MI 48647, (517) 826–3267. Au Sable River and South Branch.

Horina Canoe Rental, M–37 Route 1, Wellston, MI 49689, (231) 862–3470. Pine River.

Indian Valley, Middleville, MI 49333, (616) 683–5110. Thornapple River.

Ivan's Canoe Rental, P. O. Box 787, Baldwin, MI 49304, (231) 745–3361. Pere Marquette River.

Jim's Canoe Livery, 1706 Wakeley Bridge Road, Grayling, MI 49738. Au Sable River and South Branch.

Jordan Valley Outfitters, M–66, 311 North Lake Street, East Jordan, MI 49727, (616) 536–0006. Jordan River.

Kellogg's Canoes, P. O. Box 272, Hesperia, MI 49421, (616) 854–1415. White River.

Muskegon River Camp and Canoe, 6281 River Street, Evart, MI 49631, (231) 734–3808. Muskegon River.

Niles Canoe Rental, 1430 North Old U.S. 31, Niles, MI 49120, (616) 683–5110. Dowagiac River.

Old Log Resort, 12062 M–115, Marion, MI 49665, (231) 743–2775. Muskegon River.

Oscoda Canoes, 678 River Road, Oscoda, MI 48750, (517) 739–9040. Au Sable River.

Paddle Brave Canoe Livery, 10610 Steckert Bridge Road, Roscommon, MI 48653, (517) 275–5273 or (800) 681–7092. Au Sable River and South Branch.

Penrod's Paddlesports Center, P. O. Box 432, Grayling, MI 49738, (517) 348–2910 or (888) 467–4837. Au Sable River and South Branch.

Pine Creek Lodge, 13544 Caberfae Highway, Wellston, MI 49689, (616) 848–4431. Little Manistee River, Manistee River.

Pine River Paddlesports Center, 9590 South M–37, Wellston, MI 49689, (616) 862–3471 or (800) 71–RIVER. Manistee River, Pine River.

Rainbow Resort, 731 Camp Ten Road, Mio, MI 48647, (517) 826–3423 or (800) 737–4133. Au Sable River and South Branch.

Rifle River AAA, 2148 South School Road, Sterling, MI 48659, (517) 654–2333 or (517) 654–2556. Rifle River.

Riverbend Campground and Canoe, 864 Main Street, P. O. Box 6, Omer, MI 48749, (517) 653–2576. Rifle River.

Riverside Canoe Trips, 5042 Scenic Highway, Honor, MI 49640, (231) 325–5622. Platte River.

River View Canoe, P. O. Box 225, Sterling, MI 48659, (517) 654–2447. Rifle River.

Russell Canoes, 207 North Grove Road, Omer, MI 48749, (517) 653–2644. Rifle River.

Sawmill Tube and Canoe Livery, 230 Baldwin, Big Rapids, MI 49307, (231) 796–6408. Muskegon River.

Skip's Huron River Canoe Livery, 3780 Delhi Court, Ann Arbor, MI 48103, (734) 769–8686. Huron River.

Smithville Landing, P. O. Box 341, Lake City, MI 49651, (616) 839–4579. Manistee River.

Sportsman's Port, 10487 West M–55, Wellston, MI 49689, (231) 862–3571. Pine River.

Swiss Hideaway, 1953 Graves Crossing, Mancelona, MI 49659, (616) 536–2341. Jordan River.

Tall Pines Campground, 550 South Talcott, Morley, MI 49336, (616) 856–4556 or (800) 375–4672. Little Muskegon River.

Tomahawk Trails Canoe Trips, Box 814, Indian River, MI 49749, (616) 238–8703. Sturgeon River (Lower Peninsula).

Vic's Canoes, 8845 Felch Avenue, Grant, MI 49327, (231) 834–5494. Muskegon River.

Watters Edge Kayak and Canoe, P. O. Box 815, Roscommon, MI 48653, (517) 275–5568 or (800) 672–9968. Au Sable River and South Branch.

Whispering Waters Campground and Canoe, 1805 North Irving Road, Hastings, MI 49058, (616) 945–5166. Thornapple River.

White Birch Canoe Trips, 5569 Paradise Road, Falmouth, MI 49632, (231) 328–4547. Muskegon River.

White's Canoe Livery, 400 Old M–70, Sterling, MI 48659, (517) 654–2654. Rifle River.

Wilderness Canoe Trips, 6052 Riverview Road, Mesick, MI 49668, (616) 885–1485 or (800) 873–6379. Manistee River.

Wolynski Canoe Rental, 2300 Wixom Trail, Milford, MI 48381, (248) 685–1851. Huron River.

Outfitters/Guides

Northwest Outfitters Kayak Tours, Traverse City, MI 49684, (231) 946–4841. Provides guided trips in Grand Traverse Bay.

Associations and Chambers of Commerce

Traverse City Convention and Visitors Bureau, 101 West Grandview Parkway, Traverse City, MI 49684, (231) 947–1120 or (800) 872–8377.

Upper Peninsula

Government Agencies (National Forests, State Forests, State Parks)

Copper Country State Forest, U.S. Highway 41 North, P. O. Box 427, Baraga, MI 49908, (906) 353–6651.

Craig Lake State Park, c/o Van Riper State Park, P. O. Box 66, Champion, MI 49814, (906) 339–4461.

Escanaba River State Forest, 6833 U.S. Highway 2 and M–35, Gladstone, MI 49837, (906) 786–2351.

Hiawatha National Forest, 2727 North Lincoln Road, Escanaba, MI 49829, (906) 786–4062; Munising Ranger District, Route 2, Box 400, Munising, MI 49862, (906) 387–3700; Grand Island; Rapid River/Manistique Ranger District.

Isle Royale National Park, 800 East Lakeshore Drive, Houghton, MI 49931, (906) 482–0984.

Lake Superior State Forest, Route 4, Box 796, South M–123/M–28, Newberry, MI 49868, (906) 293–5131.

McLain State Park, Route 1, P. O. Box 82, M–203, Hancock, MI 49930, (906) 482–0278.

Michigan DNR—Gladstone; Norway; Sault Ste. Marie, 2001 Ashmun Box 798, Saulte Ste. Marie, MI 49783, (906) 635–5281.

Nicolet National Forest, 68 South Stevens Street, Rhinelander, WI 54501, (715) 362–1300.

Ottawa National Forest, E6248 U.S. Highway 2, Ironwood, MI 49938, (906) 932–1330.

Pictured Rocks National Lakeshore, P. O. Box 40, Munising, MI 49862, (906) 387–3700 or (906) 387–2607.

Seney National Wildlife Refuge, HCR #2, Box 1, Seney, MI 49883, (906) 586–9851.

Tahquamenon State Park, P. O. Box 225, Paradise, MI 49768, (906) 492–3415.

Canoe Liveries

Big Cedar Campground and Canoe Livery, Germfask, MI 49836, (906) 586–6684. Fox River, Manistique River.

Great Outdoors Sports Shop, 44 M–134, P. O. Box 546, Cedarville, MI 49719, (906) 484–2011. Les Cheneau Islands (kayaks).

Hiawatha Resort and Campground, Wetmore, MI 49895, (906) 573–2933. Indian River.

Mark's Rod & Reel and Canoe, Newberry, MI, (906) 293–5608. Tahquamenon River, Two Hearted River.

Northland Outfitters, P. O. Box 65, Germfask, MI 49836, (906) 586–9801. Fox River, Manistique River.

Northwoods Resort, HO3, Au Train, MI 49806, (906) 892–8114. Au Train River.

Northwoods Wilderness Outfitters, 4088 Pine Mountain Road, Iron Mountain, MI 49801, (906) 774–9009 or (800) 530–8859. Brule River.

Riverside Resort, Star Route Box 325, Au Train, MI 49806, (906) 892–8350. Au Train River.

Rohr's Wilderness Tours, 5230 Razorback Road, Conover, WI 54519, (715) 547–3639. Brule River.

Sylvania Outfitters, E23423 Highway 2 West, Watersmeet, MI 49969, (906) 358–4766. Ontonagon River System, Sylvania Wilderness Area.

Two Hearted Canoe Trips, P. O. Box 386, Newberry, MI 49868, (906) 658–3357. Two Hearted River.

Outfitters/Guides

Arctic Divide Expeditions, P. O. Box 753, Skanee, MI 49962, (906) 524–5962, www.eddycurrents.com. Leads guided multi-day trips on several whitewater rivers in the western Upper Peninsula, including the Presque Isle and Sturgeon Rivers. Also offers paddling trips in Ontario along Superior's north shore.

Argosy Adventures Rafting, Highway 8 East, P. O. Box 22, Niagara, WI 54151, (715) 251–3886. Rafting trips on the Menominee River.

Great Northern Adventures, P. O. Box 361, Marquette, MI 49855, (906) 225–TOUR, www.greatnorthernadventures.com. Provides guided trips to paddling destinations throughout the Upper Peninsula, including Pictured Rocks National Lakeshore, Grand Island, Les Cheneaux Islands, and the Garden Peninsula (Fayette State Park). Also offers a variety of mountain biking, backpacking, and women-only trips.

Keweenaw Adventure Company, Copper Harbor, MI 49918, (906) 289–4303. Offers day trips in Copper Harbor area at tip of Keweenaw Peninsula.

Kosir's Rapid Rafts, W1409 Highway C, Athelstane, WI 54104, (715) 757–3431, www.kosirs.com. Rafting excursions on the Menominee River.

Northern Waters Adventures, P. O. Box 314, Munising, MI 49862, (906) 387–2323. Offers single- and multi-day guided tours of the Pictured Rocks National Lakeshore and Grand Island.

Uncommon Adventures, P. O. Box 254, Beulah, MI 49617, (231) 882–5525, www.uncommonadv.com. Offers multi-day guided kayaking trips to Isle Royale National Park, the Straits of Mackinac, and Les Cheneaux Islands.

Upper Peninsula Adventure Travel, 816 Quincy Street, Hancock, MI 49930, (888) 937–2411. Offers guided trips in Bete Grise area on Keweenaw Peninsula.

Drummond Island Tourism Association, P. O. Box 200, Drummond Island, MI 49726, (906) 493–5245 or (800) 737–8666.

Hiawatha Water Trail Association, P. O. Box 7131, Marquette, MI 49855, (906) 226–7112.

Keweenaw Tourism Council, 326 Sheldon Avenue, Houghton, MI 49931, (906) 482–2388 or (800) 338–7982.

Les Cheneaux Island Area Tourist Association, P. O. Box 10, Cedarville, MI 49719, (906) 484–3935.

Marquette Convention and Visitors Bureau, 2552 West U.S. Highway 41, Suite 300, Marquette, MI 49855, (906) 228–7749.

Laurie and Kevin Hillstrom

About the Authors

Kevin Hillstrom and Laurie Collier Hillstrom are longtime Michigan residents who have paddled and backpacked throughout their home state. Their love of outdoor adventure has also taken them to some of the most spectacular wild places in North America, including Alaska's Brooks Range, the Canadian Rockies, Yosemite, and the Grand Canyon.

The Hillstroms are partners in Northern Lights Writers Group, a freelance writing and editorial services company. They are the authors of *Adventure Guide to Michigan* (Hunter Publishing, 1998), *Biography Today: Environmental Leaders* (Omnigraphics, 1997 and 2000), and *The Vietnam Experience: A Concise Encyclopedia of American Literature, Songs, and Films* (Greenwood Press, 1997), among many other books.